MOTHER SAID
Niina Lehtonen Braun

KERBER EDITION YOUNG ART

More often than not, it is those closest to us that we fight the most. Our conflicting memories of the woman who told us to don winter woolens when she herself felt the cold; that ubiquitous, comforting presence of our earliest fleeting childhood memories; that stern scowl of reproach when we broke the rules: all those expressions of (occasionally smothering) motherly love and lifetime expertise continue to exert a powerful influence over our own lives.

The statements assembled in MOTHER SAID have the power to trigger the magic moments or bristly reactions only a mother can inspire. Remember shirking away from those nimble fingers about to wipe your face with a spit-moistened tissue? Remember those repeated utterings of JUST GET TO MY AGE AND YOU WILL UNDERSTAND or AS LONG AS YOU LIVE UNDER MY ROOF YOU WILL DO AS I SAY that used to drive you up the wall?

With her incisive, insightful and delightful peek into the minds, methods and maternal instincts (or lack thereof) of mothers from across the globe, Finnish artist Niina Lehtonen Braun throws a touching and thoughtful spotlight on the sometimes treasured and always tricky relationship with those who raised us. At the same time, she also explores her own relationship with the woman who shaped her formative years. In 2008, one year after her mother's passing, the Berlin-based artist, a mother herself, found herself confronted with that confusing reversal of roles that coincides with the sudden fading of our parents, engendering us 'the responsible ones'.

In this context, Lehtonen Braun's temporary return to Finland sparked new insights and creative connections. She came across a stash of old diaries, sketchbooks, notes and photo albums, yet among the assembled recollections it was her mother's sayings that were most embedded in her memory. Pondering these time-tested words, invariably meant to give her guidance, Niina realised how much they continued to shape and support her. When she asked others about their own experiences, only a few of the contributed sayings turned out to be expressions of love and affection, with the rest more often thinly veiled fears, neuroses or prejudices passed on to the next generation.

Intrigued by this personal and psychological premise, the artist decided to gather more parental platitudes by asking friends, relatives and attendees of her exhibitions to submit their own family favourites. She then translated these unfiltered expressions from all continents and a variety of cultural and linguistic backgrounds into a series of pithy, playful collages.

As part of her hands-on research, Lehtonen Braun has captured plenty of charming regional or national idiosyncrasies {FANTASIES ARE THE STRAWBERRIES IN LIFE'S CREAM CAKE}, juxtaposed with refreshingly frank {RISE ABOVE THAT SHIT} or plainly surreal advice and admonishments {IF YOU SEE YOURSELF SLEEPING WHILE ASLEEP, DON'T WAKE YOURSELF UP}.

Encompassing the condensed and accumulated wisdom – or an approximation thereof – of five years of research, MOTHER SAID provides some excellent, tried-and-tested advice, but serves up even more splendid curiosities whose translation might have suffered a little between time zones, generations and translations to evolve into something that makes eminent sense, though ultimately only to the person who grew up with it {BE SURE TO STOP AT THE KAUHAJOKI INTERSECTION}.

With an open eye and ear for those who surround her, the artist has compiled a collaged collection and associative archive of juxtaposed hopes and fears, dusted off and recontextualised for a wider audience. In this spirit, MOTHER SAID offers a striking synergy of word and artwork, of familial insights and familiarity reassembled in visual form.

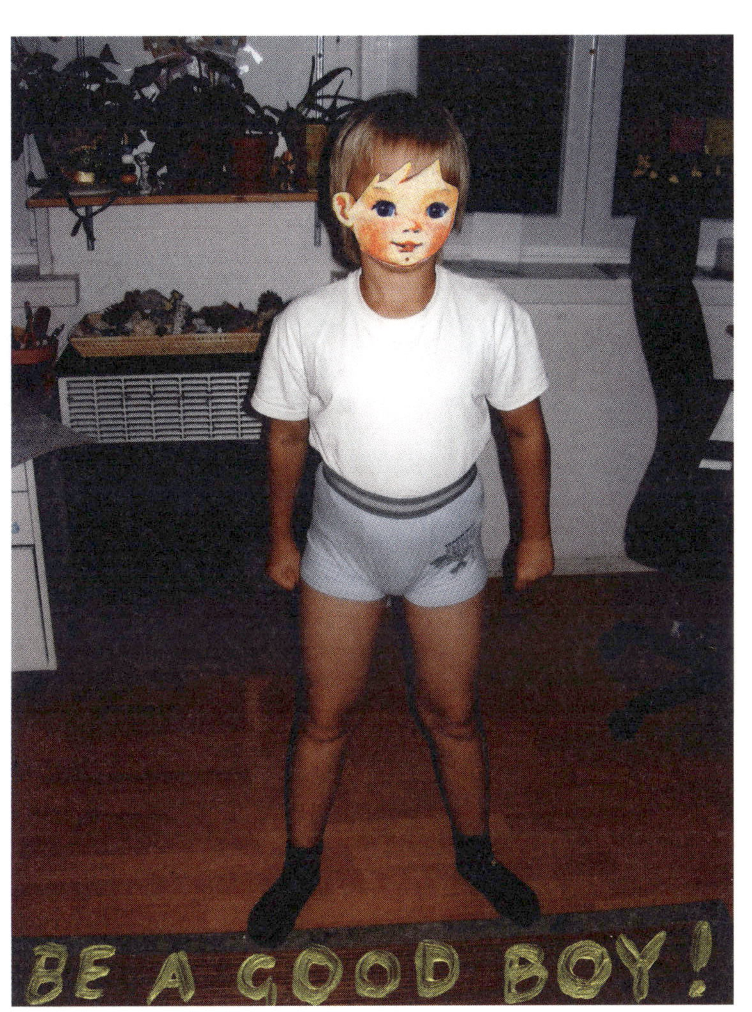
BE A GOOD BOY!

Couched in Niina's vivid imagination and collagist skills, the bright, bold and beautiful results distill these thoughts and sayings into a complex declaration of love for those who came before us and those about to follow in our footsteps.

Although intensely personal to the people who threw them into the mix, these expressions lend themselves equally well to artistic, even anthropological, study. Despite their idiosyncrasies, they are united in a universal sense of 'having to be the adult', of preparing the next generation for something they themselves might feel ill-prepared for.

About Niina Lehtonen Braun

RAISED IN HELSINKI, NOW BASED IN BERLIN, THE FINNISH ARTIST IS A GRADUATE OF PAINTING AND MULTIMEDIA AT THE ACADEMY OF FINE ARTS, HELSINKI AND ALSO DID A STINT AT THE ECOLE NATIONALE SUPERIEURE DES BEAUX-ARTS IN PARIS.

SWITCHING BETWEEN FINE ART, ILLUSTRATION, VIDEO AND PERFORMANCE NIINA LEHTONEN BRAUN DRAWS ON A RICH PALETTE OF MULTI-DISCIPLINARY INSPIRATION AND EXPERIENCE. SHE HAS SHARED IT WITH AUDIENCES THROUGH CLOSE TO 20 SOLO SHOWS AND MORE THAN TWICE THAT MANY GROUP EXHIBITIONS, PERFORMANCES AND FILM SCREENINGS TO DATE.

The future lies in the service sector. If I could choose again I'd go to a hotel school in Switzerland.

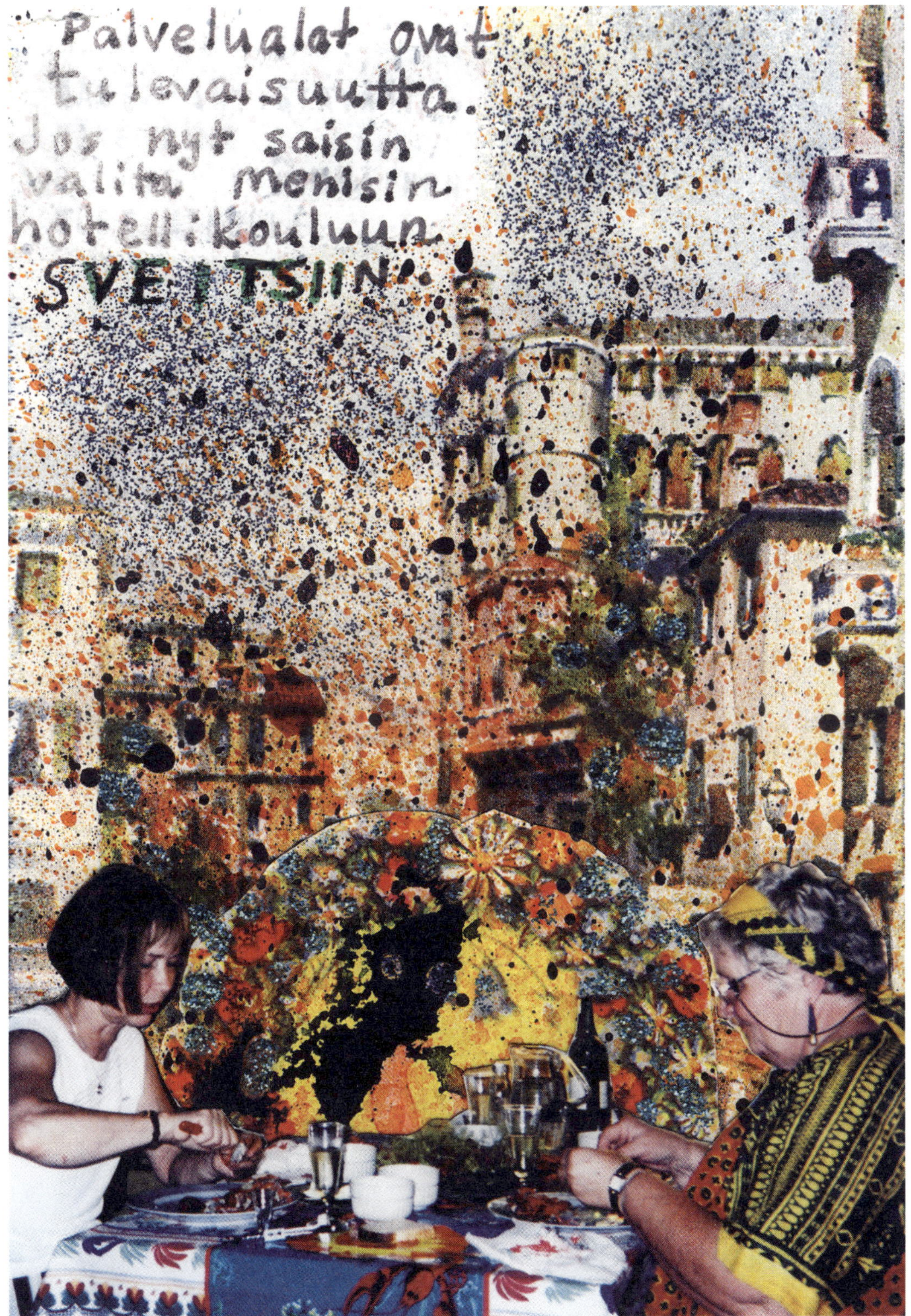

Palvelualat ovat
tulevaisuutta.
Jos nyt saisin
valita menisin
hotelli:kouluun
SVEITSIIN

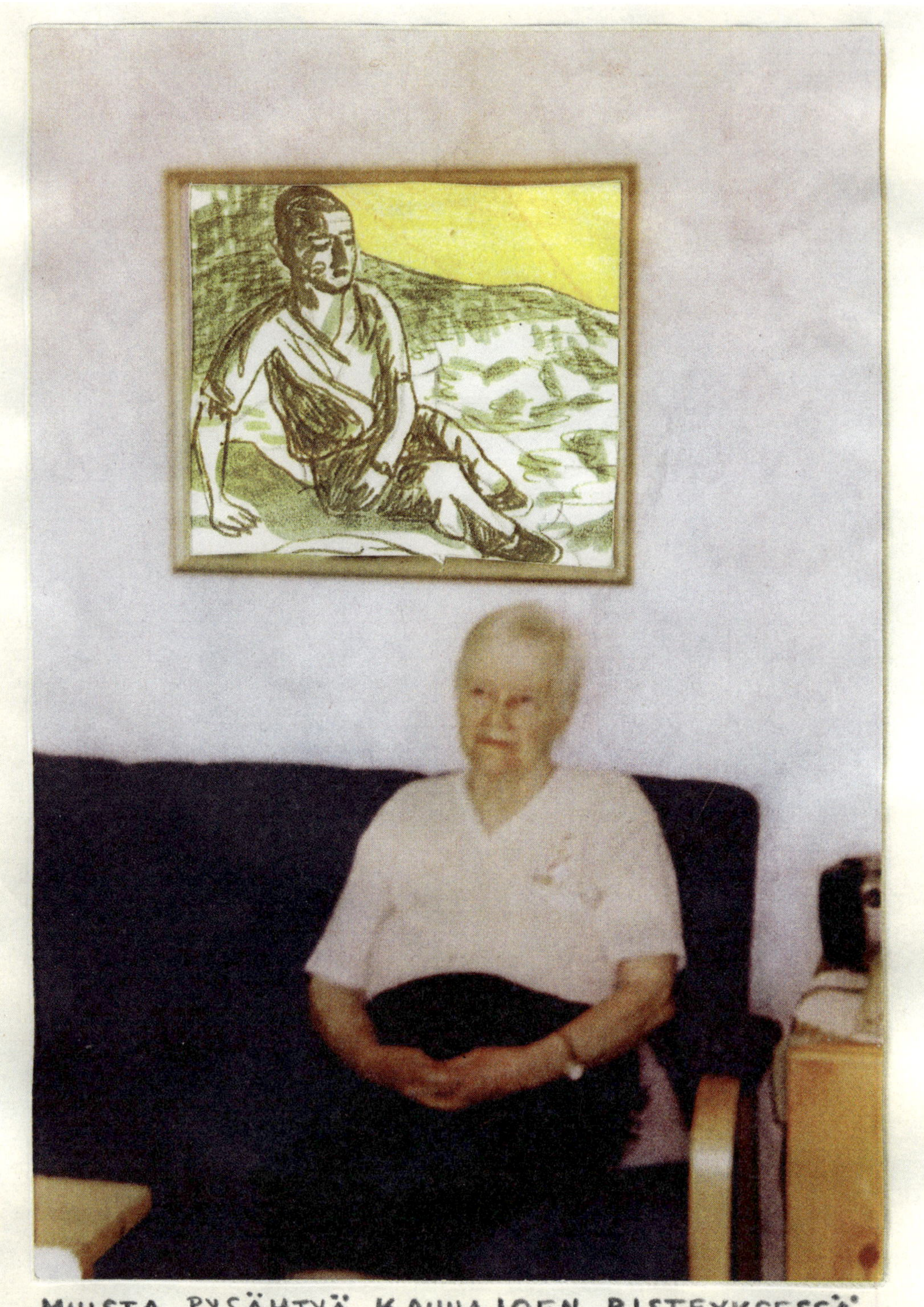

Be sure to stop at the Kauhajoki-intersection.

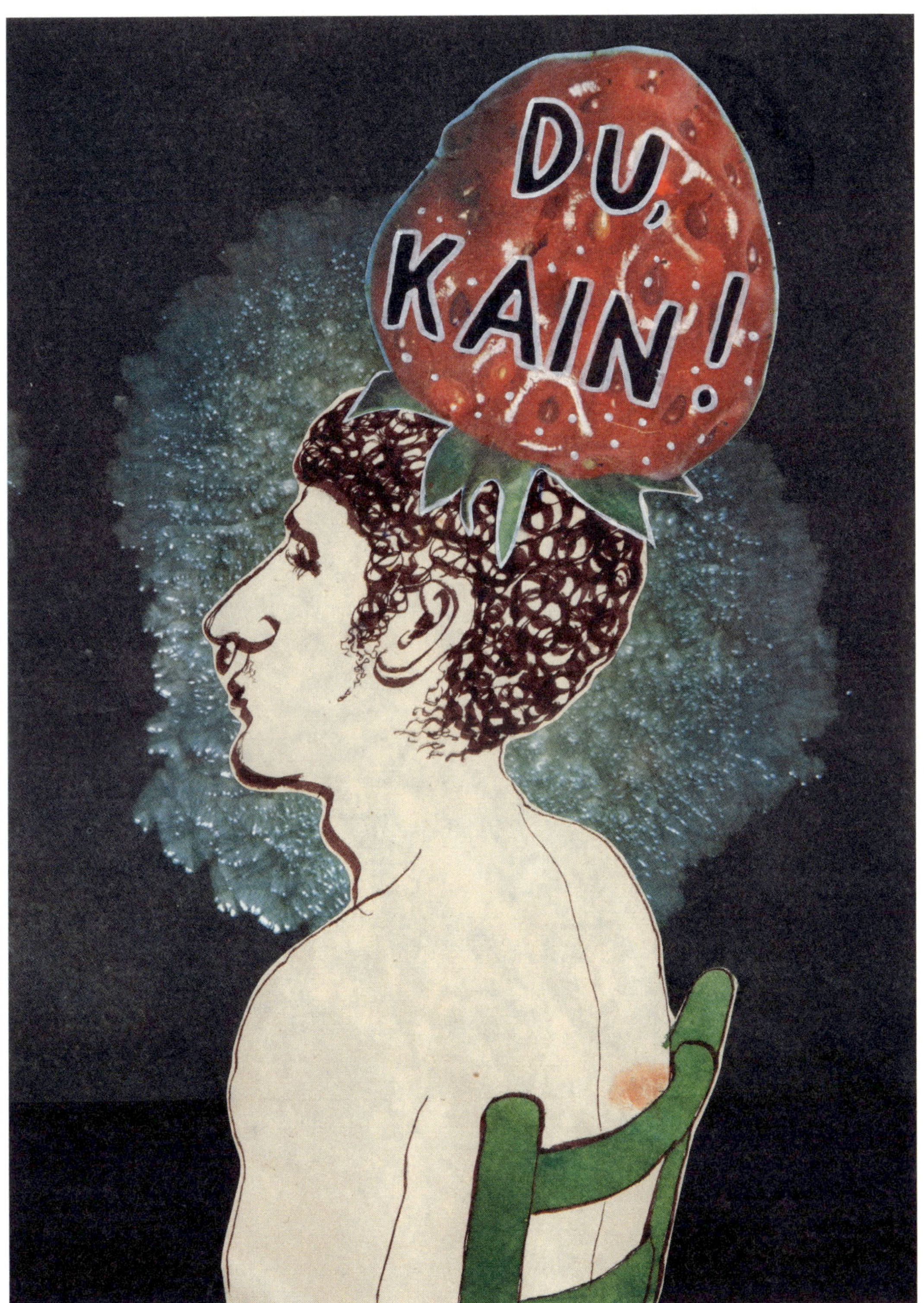

You, Cain!

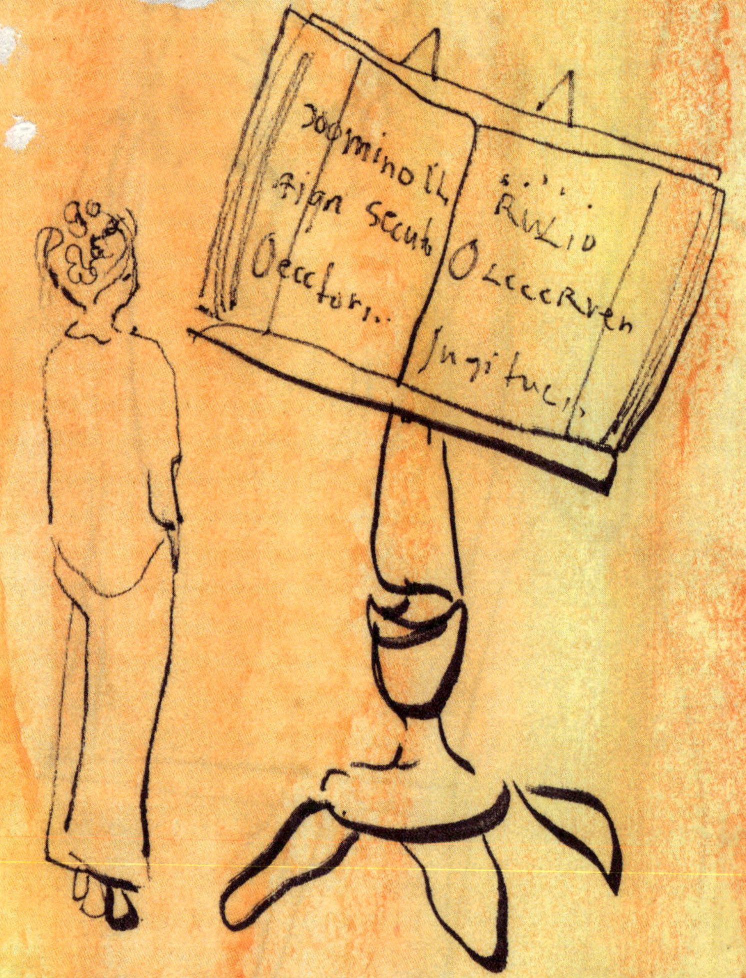

Ihr müsst nicht immer denken ihr wäret die götter.

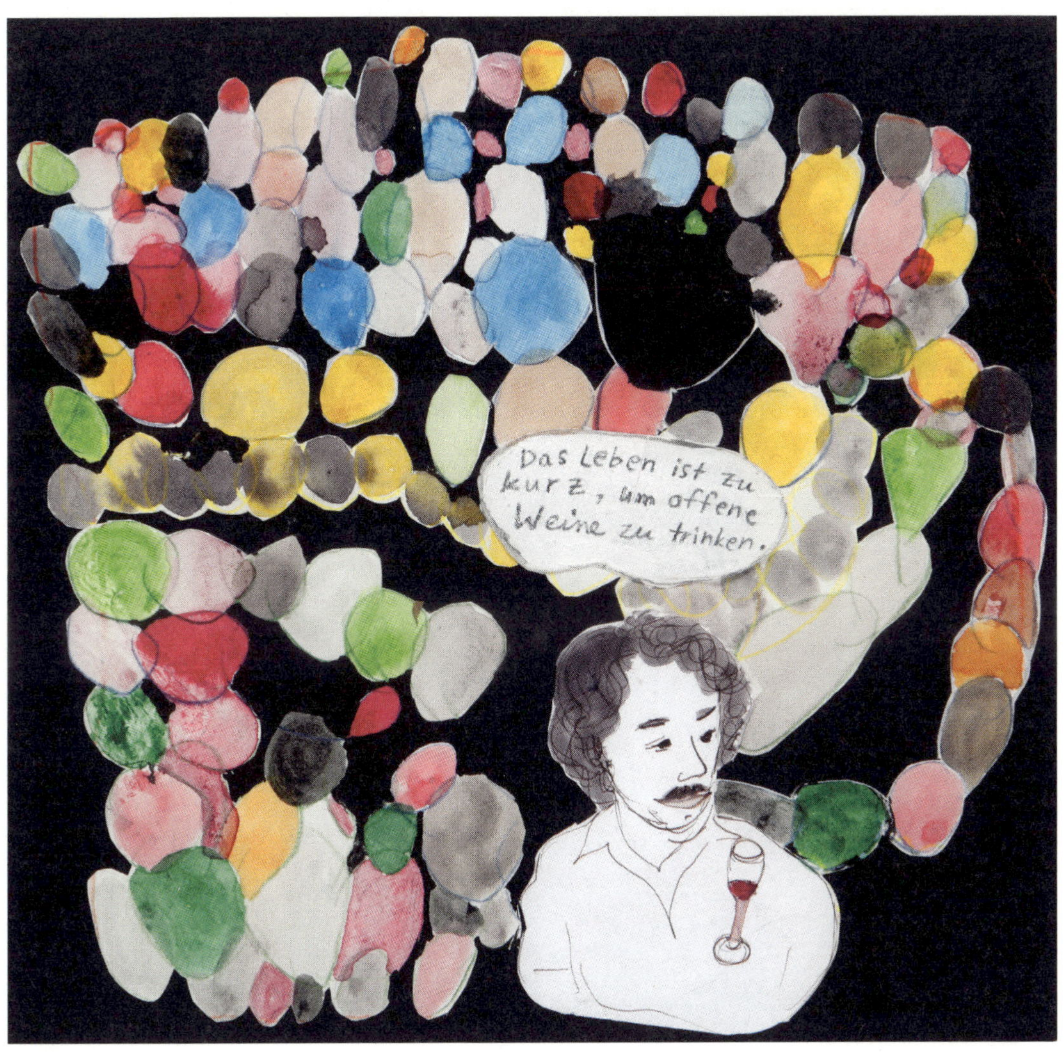

Life's too short
for drinking bad wine.

Stop always thinking that you are equal to the gods.

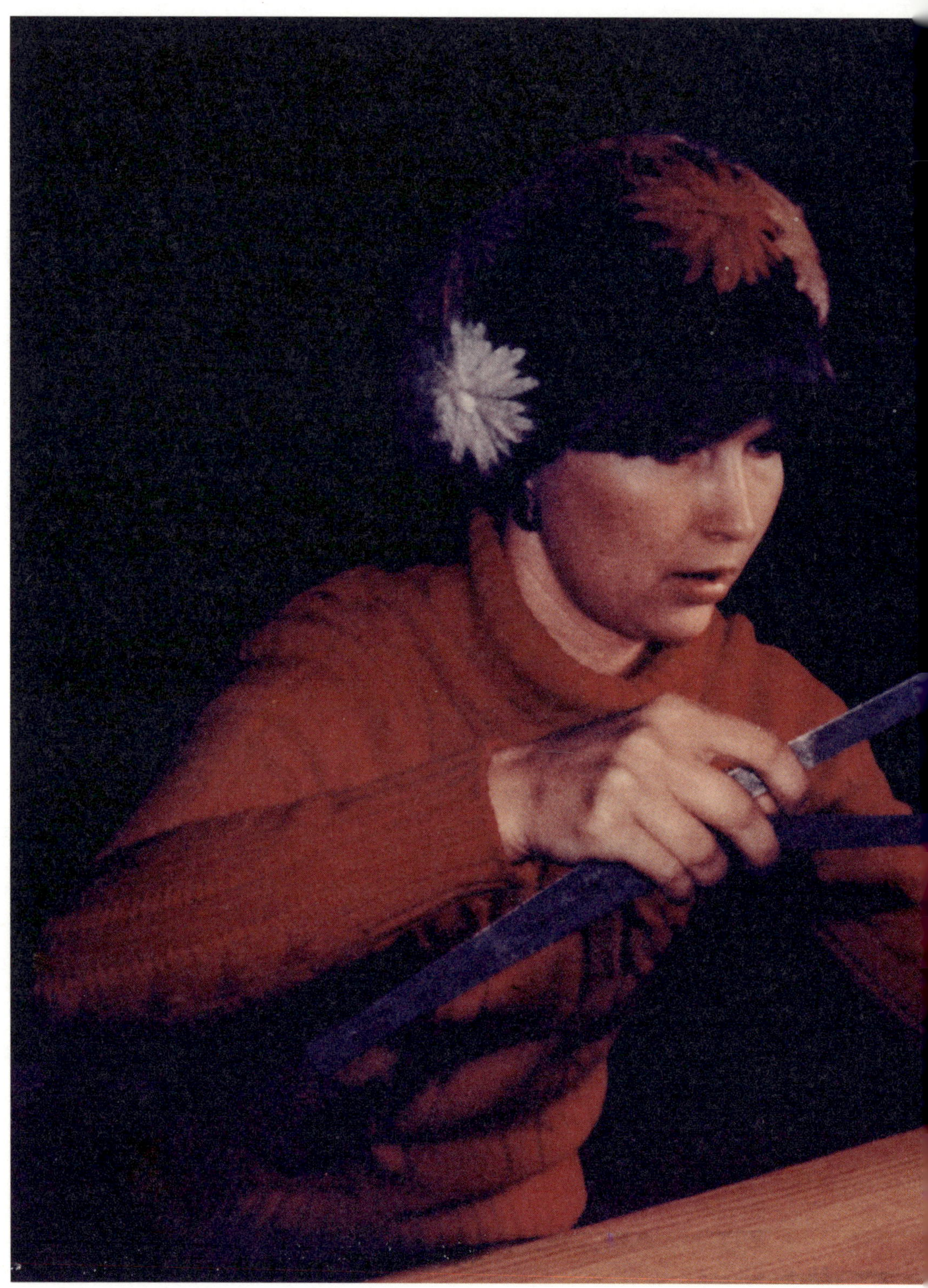

If you see yourself sleeping while asleep, don't wake yourself up!

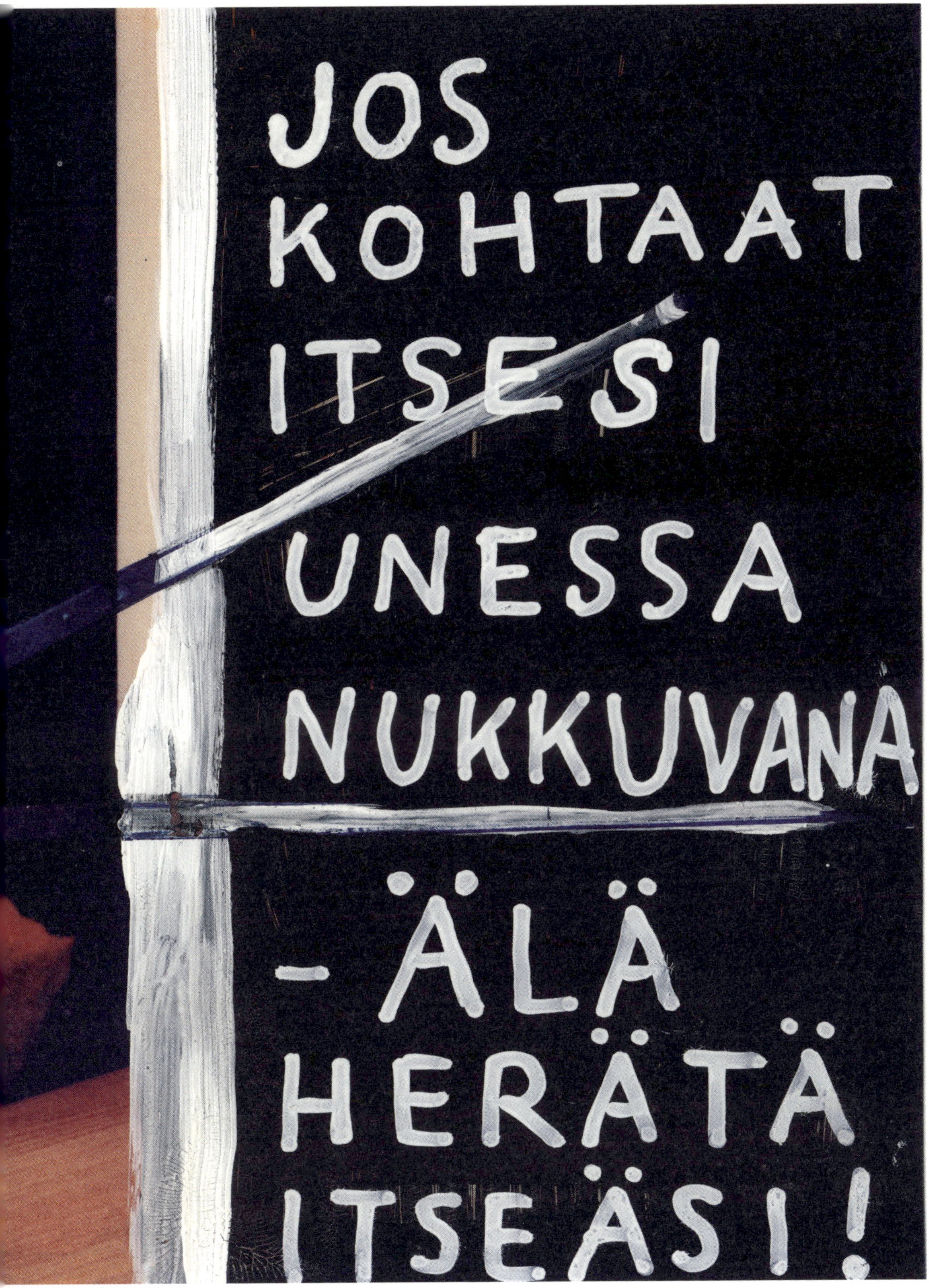

JOS
KOHTAAT
ITSESI
UNESSA
NUKKUVANA
-ÄLÄ
HERÄTÄ
ITSEÄSI!

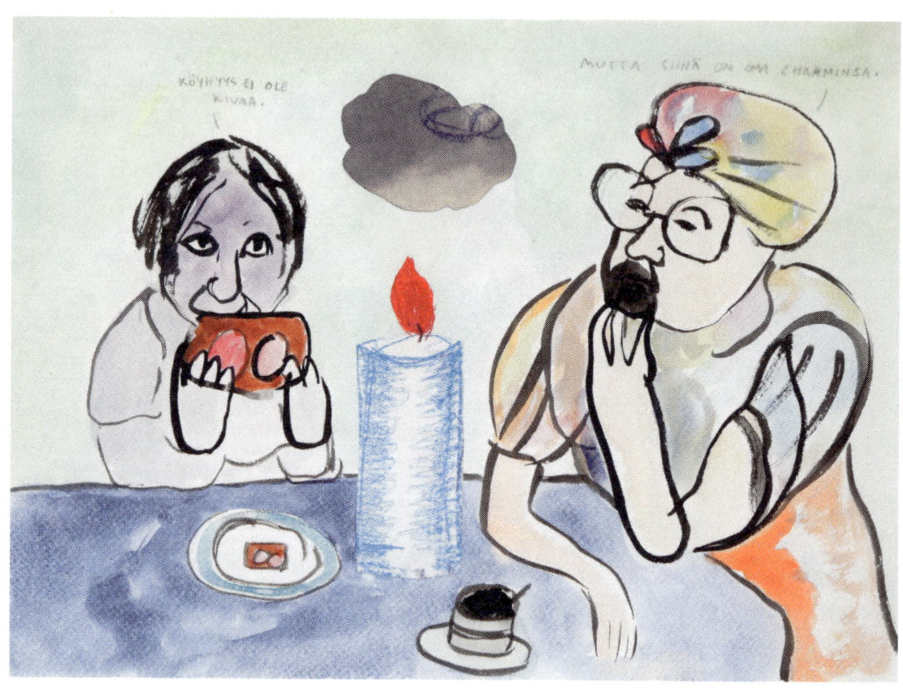

It's not nice being poor but there's a certain charm to it.

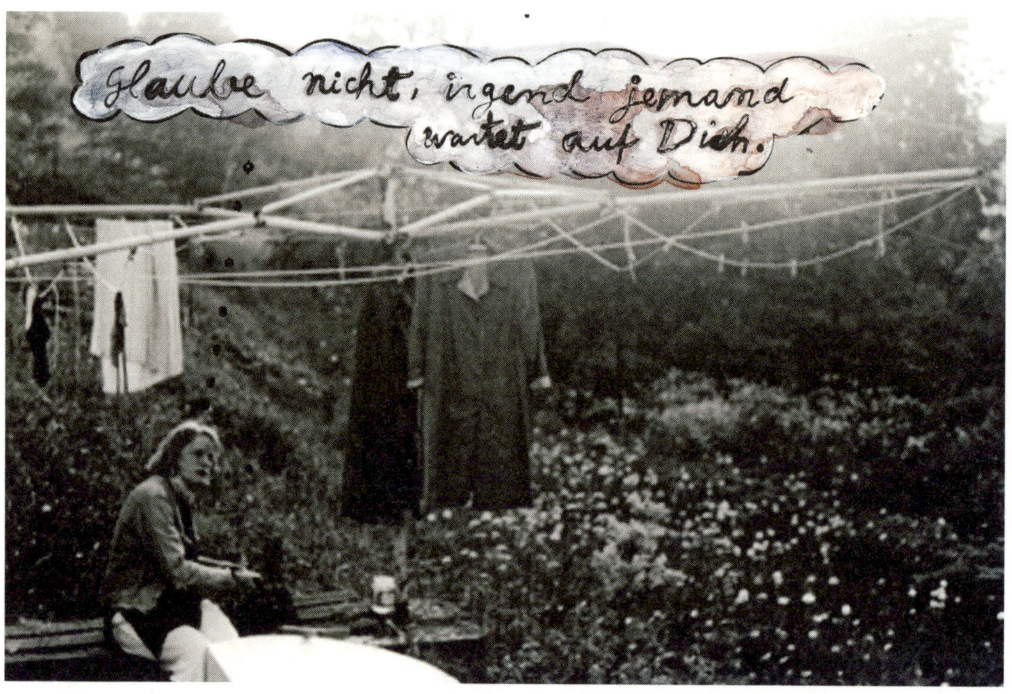

Don't start thinking there's anyone waiting for you.

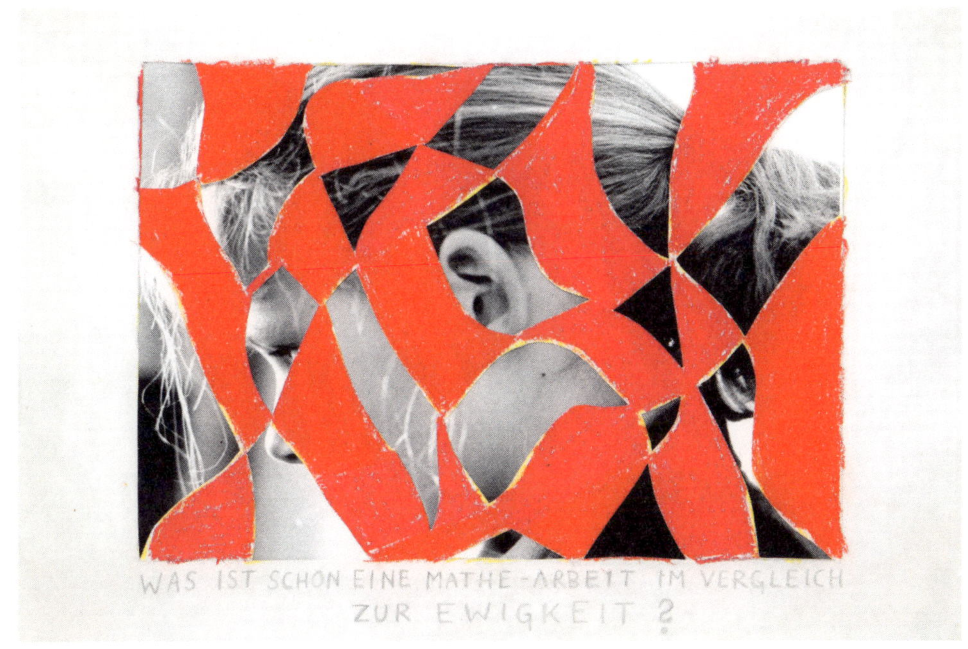

What is a single maths test compared with eternity?

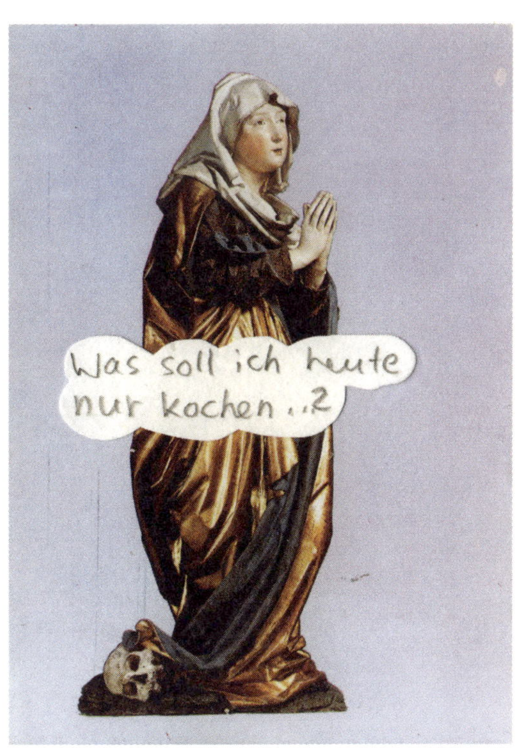

What should i cook today..?

Iß wenigstens das Fleisch

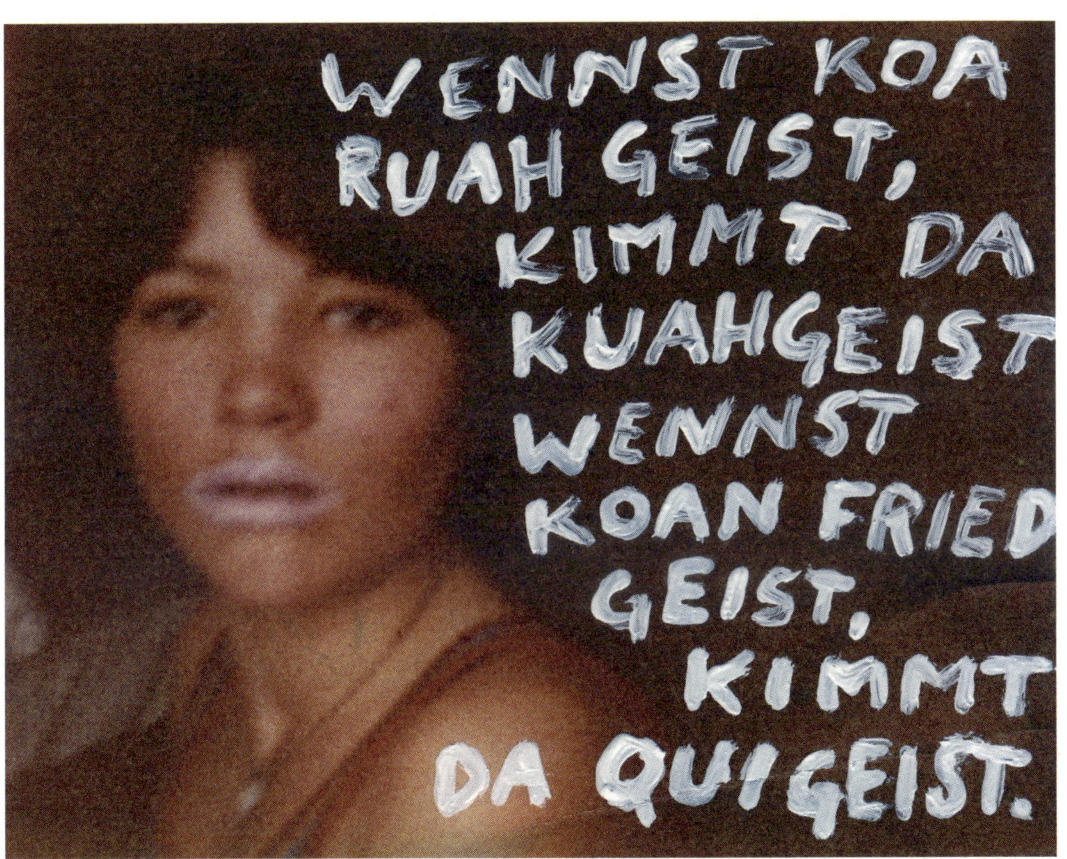

If you don't settle down,
the cow ghost will get you.

At least finish the meat.

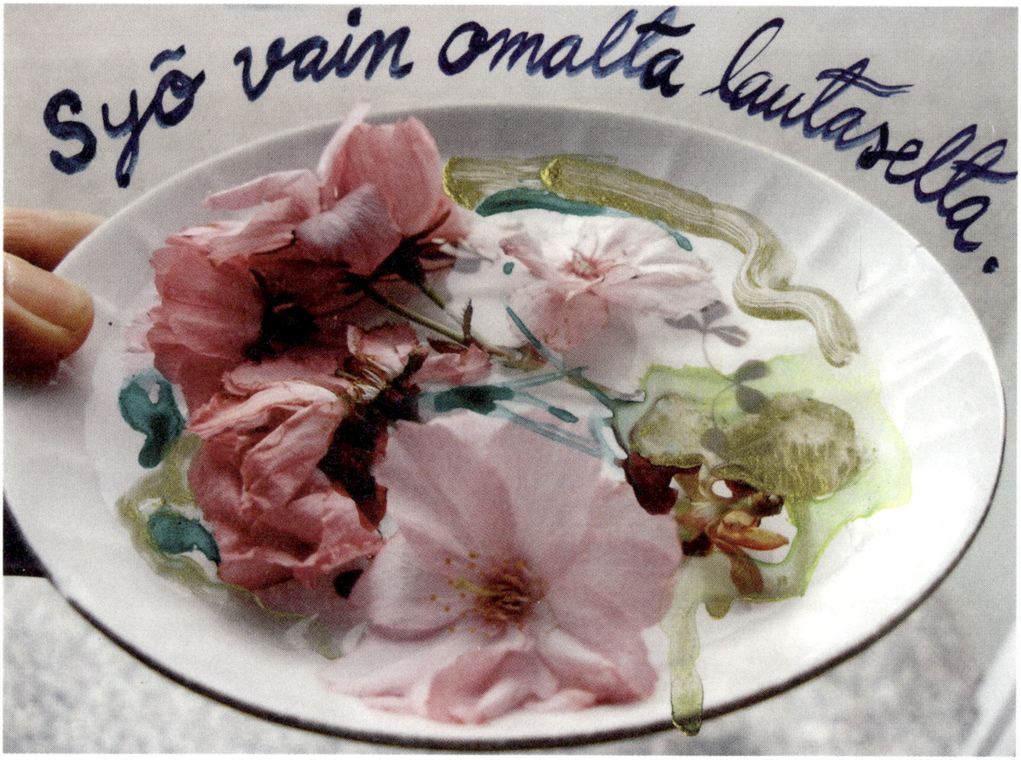

Eat only from your own plate.

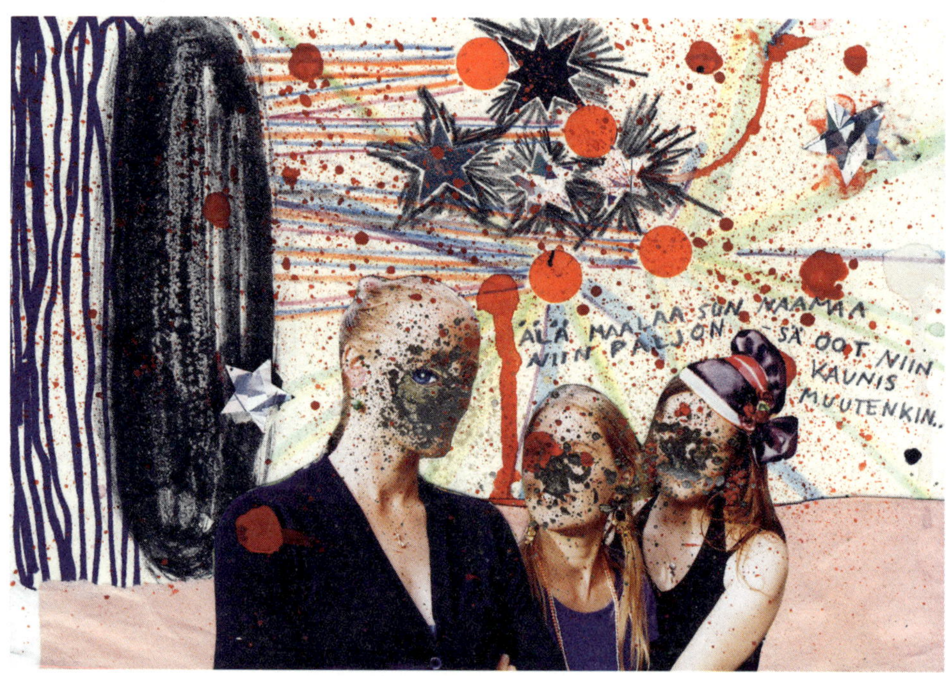

Don't paint your face so much. You're pretty as you are.

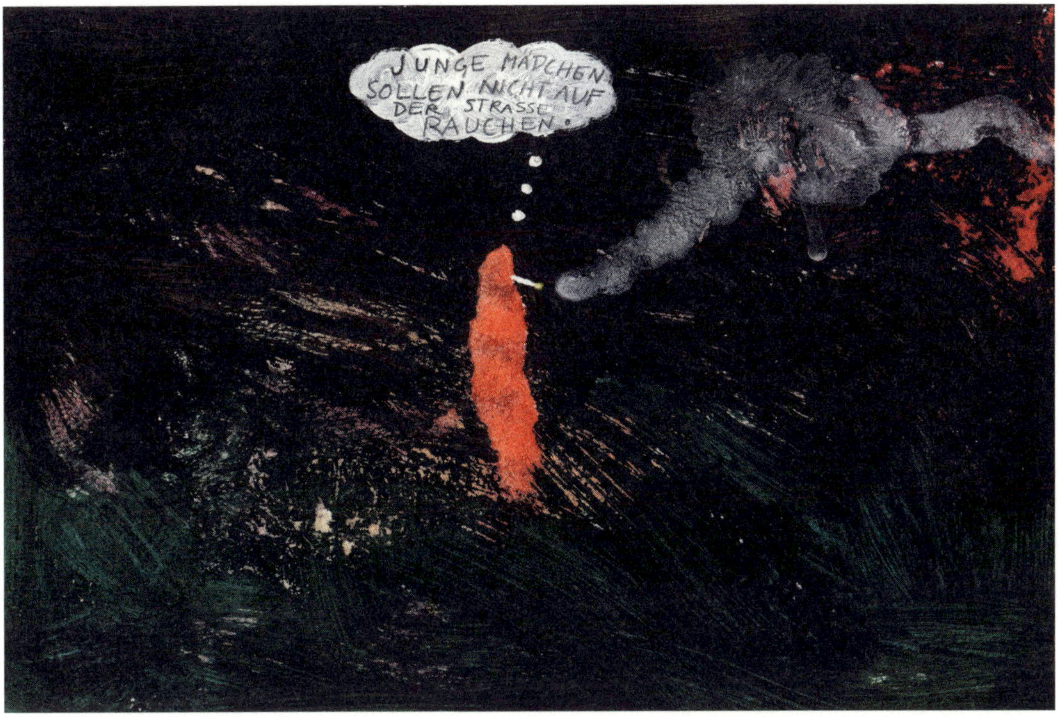

Young ladies should not be seen smoking in the street.

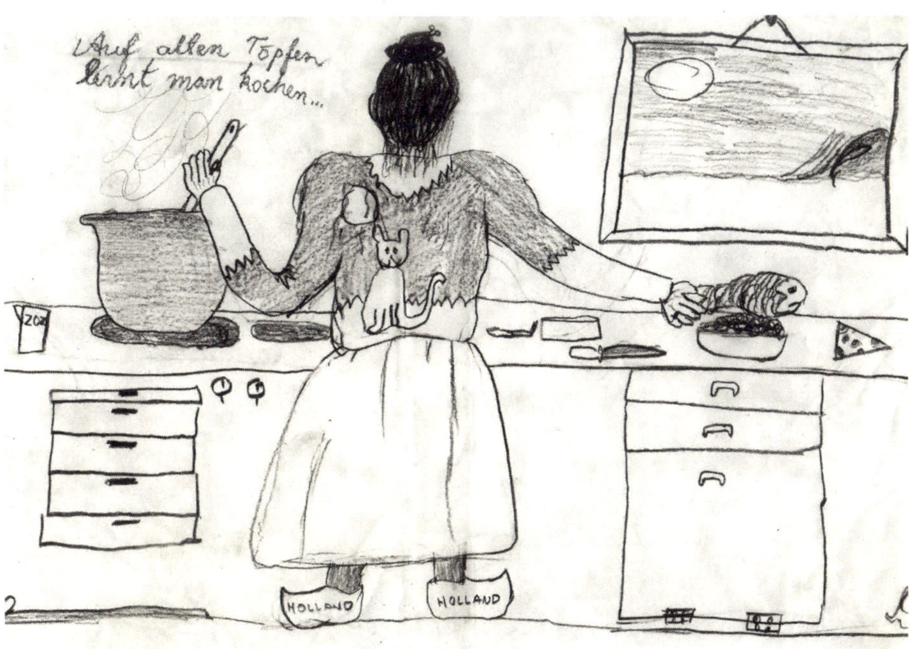

New brooms sweep well but the old ones know the corners better.

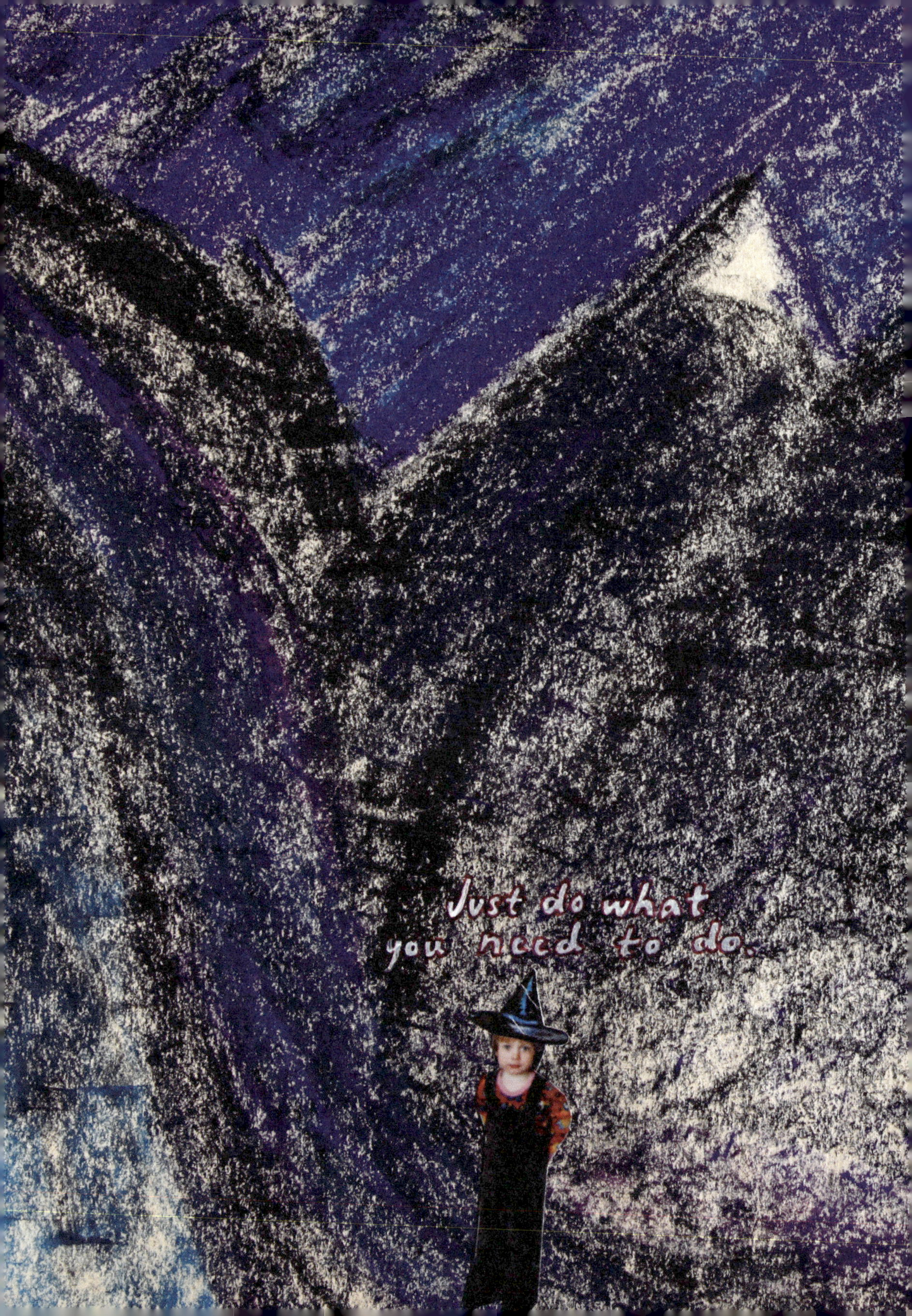

Just do what
you need to do.

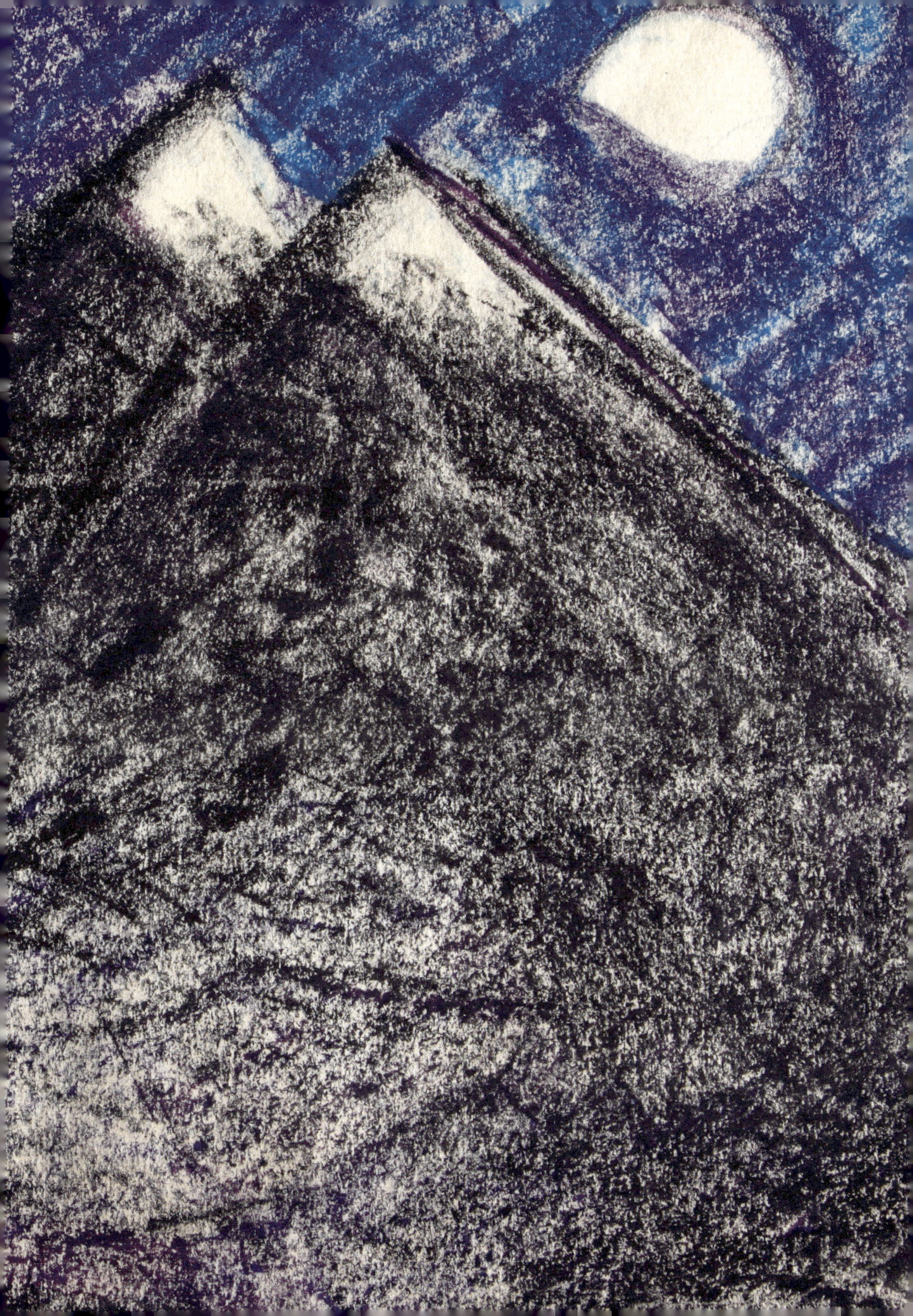

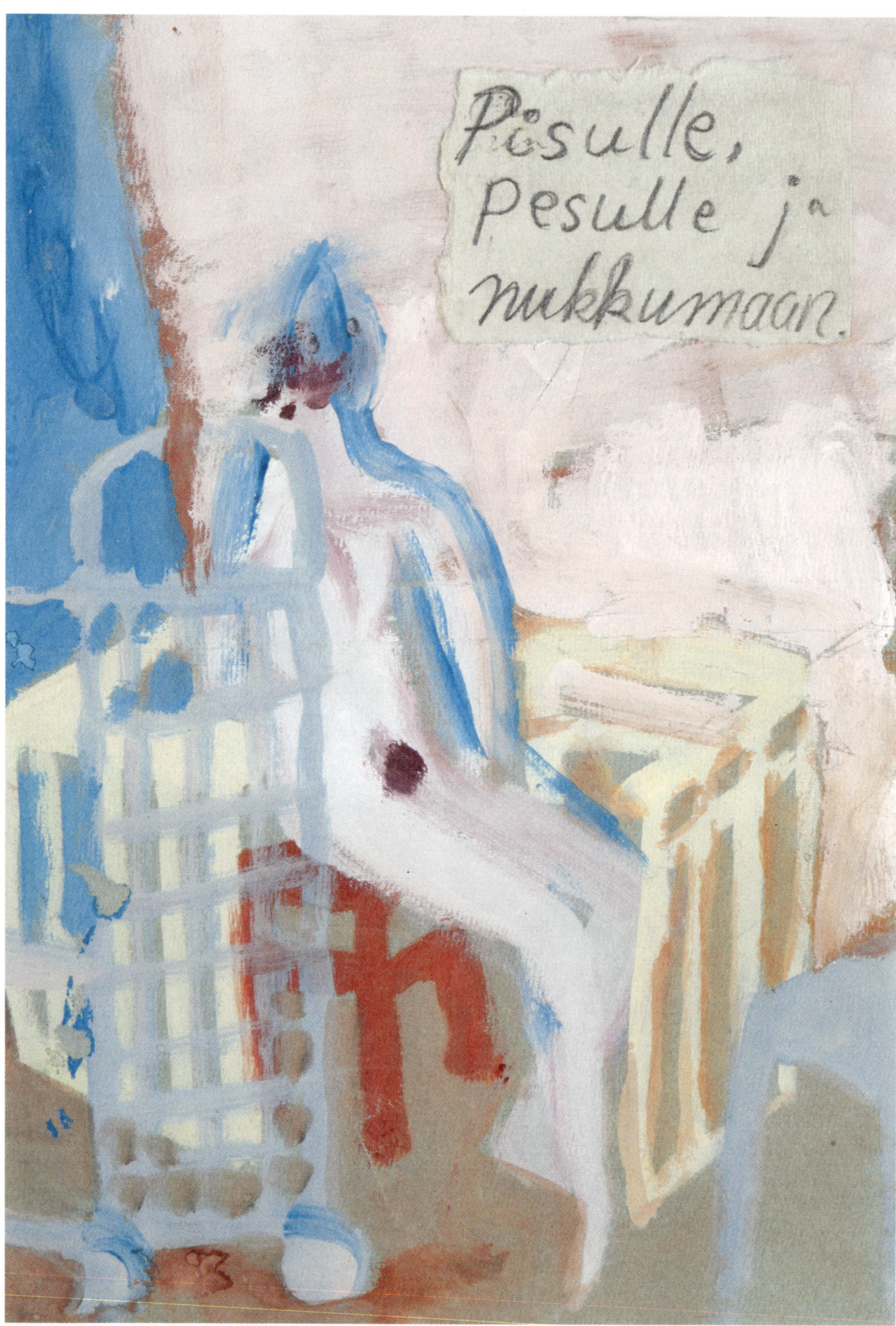

Pesulle,
Pesulle ja
nukkumaan.

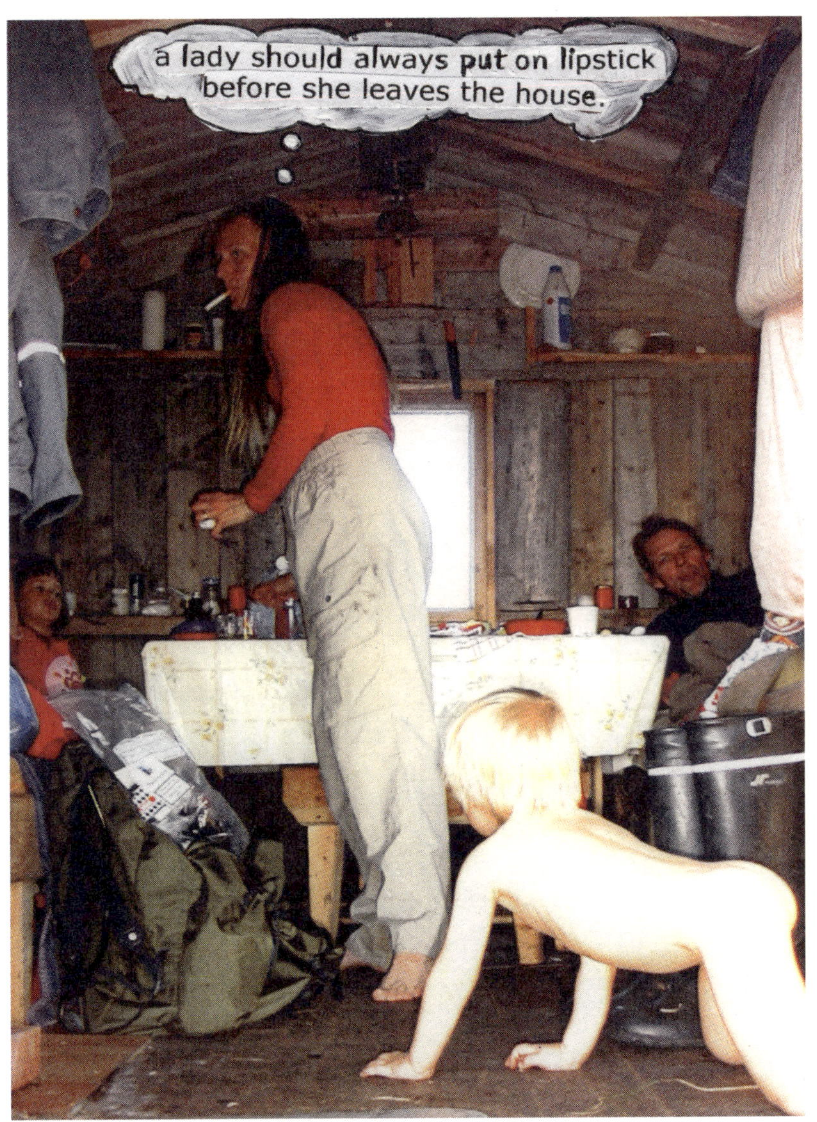

Pee, wash and off to bed.

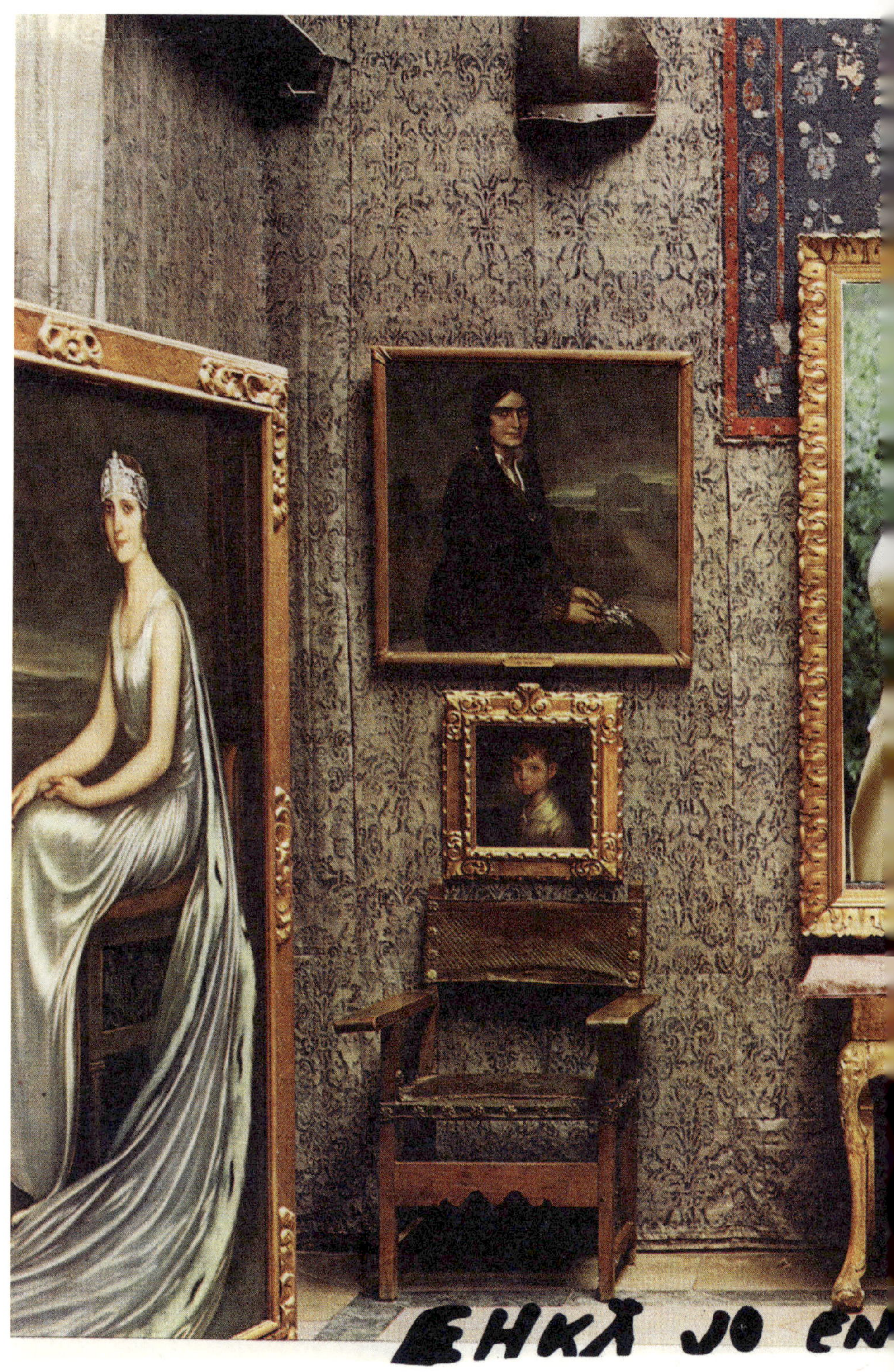

Maybe next year already.

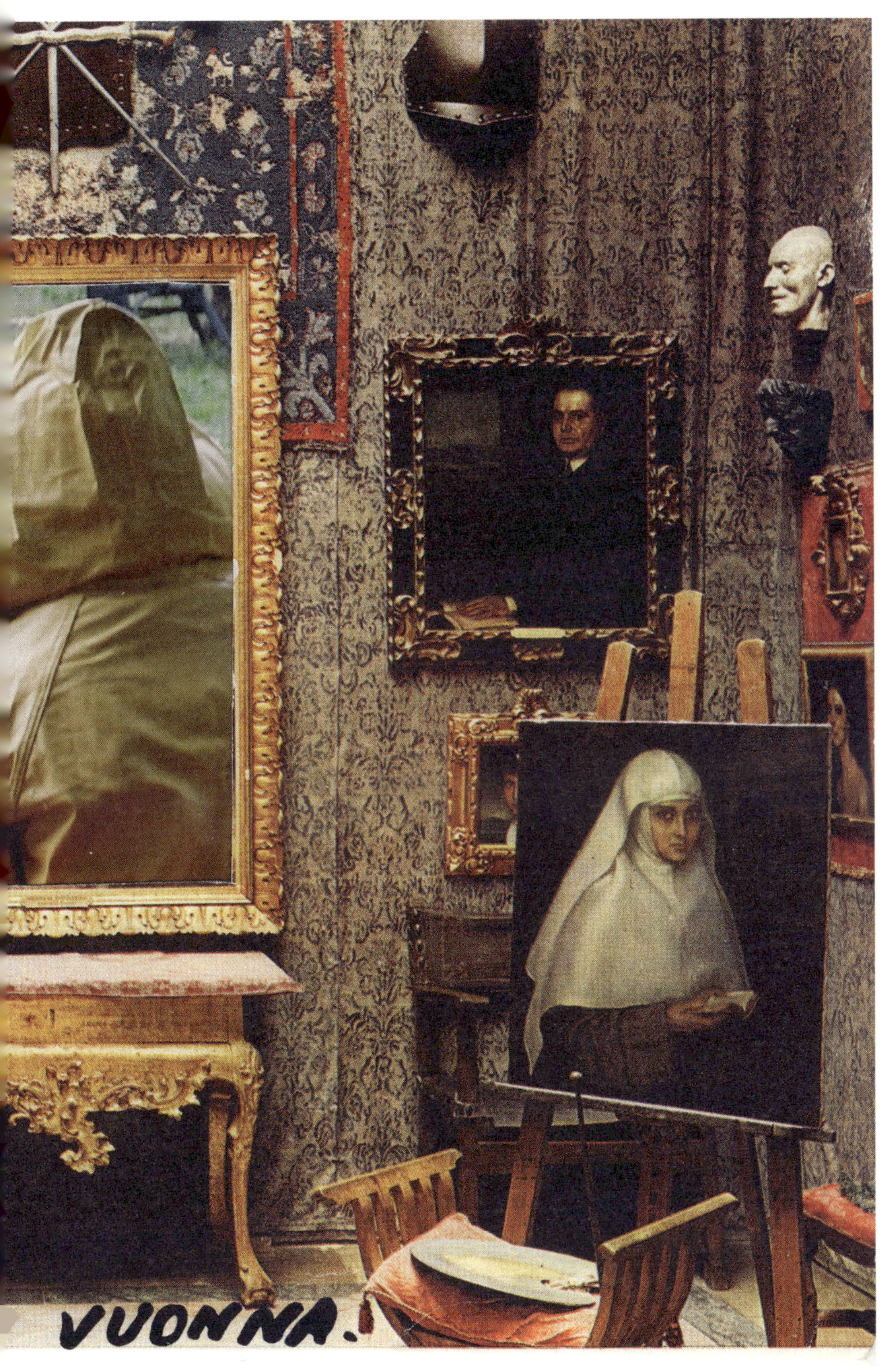
VUONNA.

MENSCH,
PASS BLOß AUF, DASS DIR KEINER
DIE IDEE KLAUT!

Alles hat seinen Platz und alles muss auf seinen Platz.

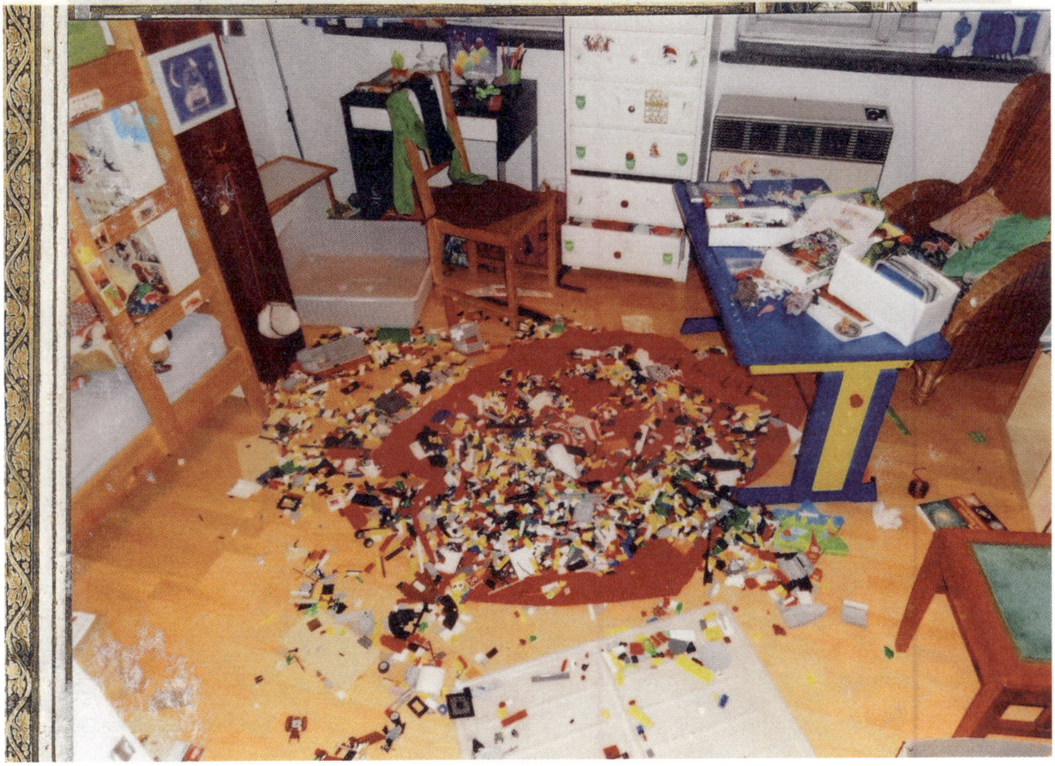

Put everything back where it belongs.

Remember, don't let anyone steal your ideas!

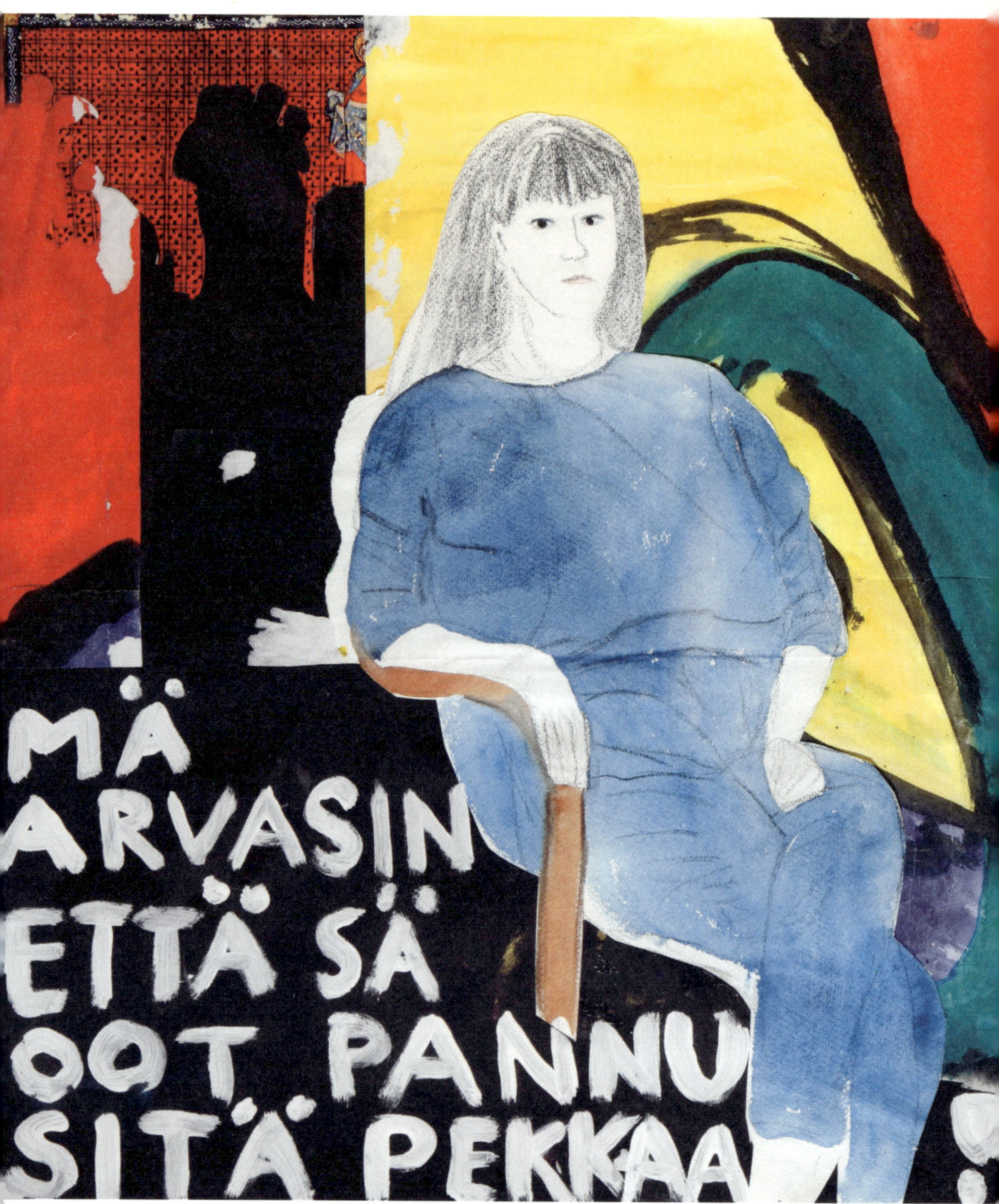

I knew you'd shagged that Pekka!

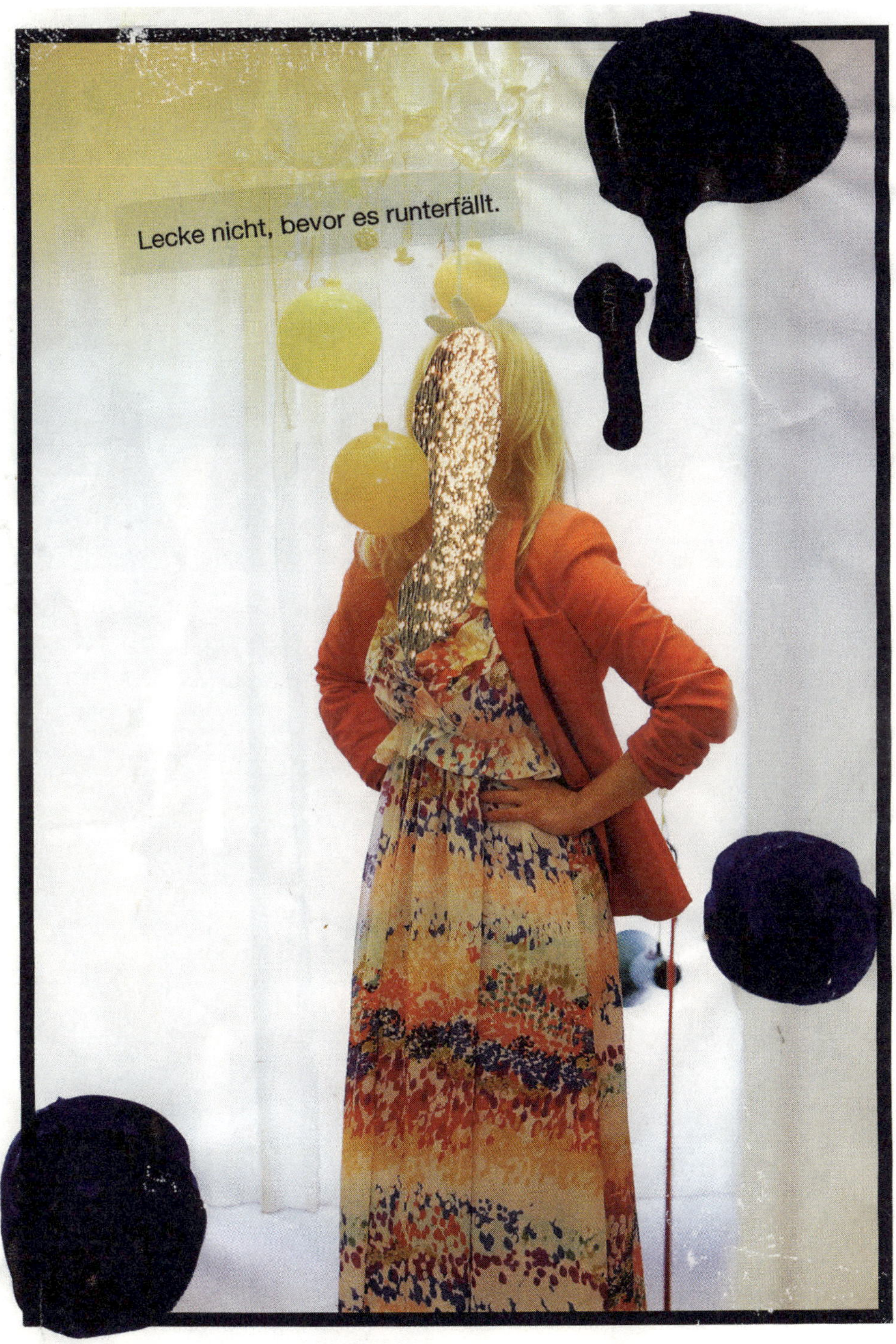

Don´t lick it before it falls.

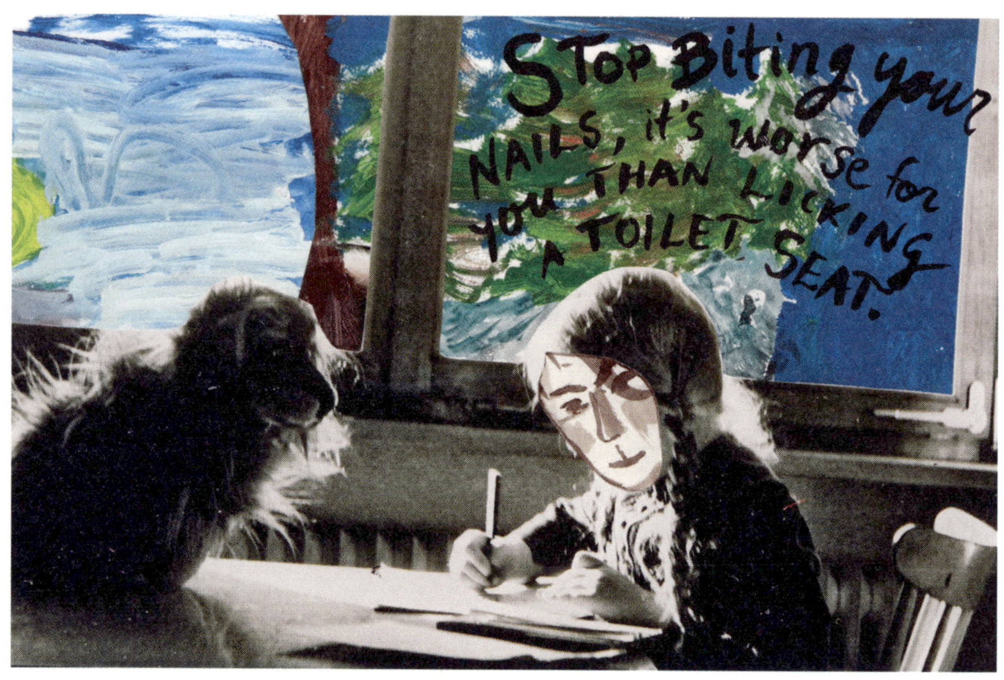

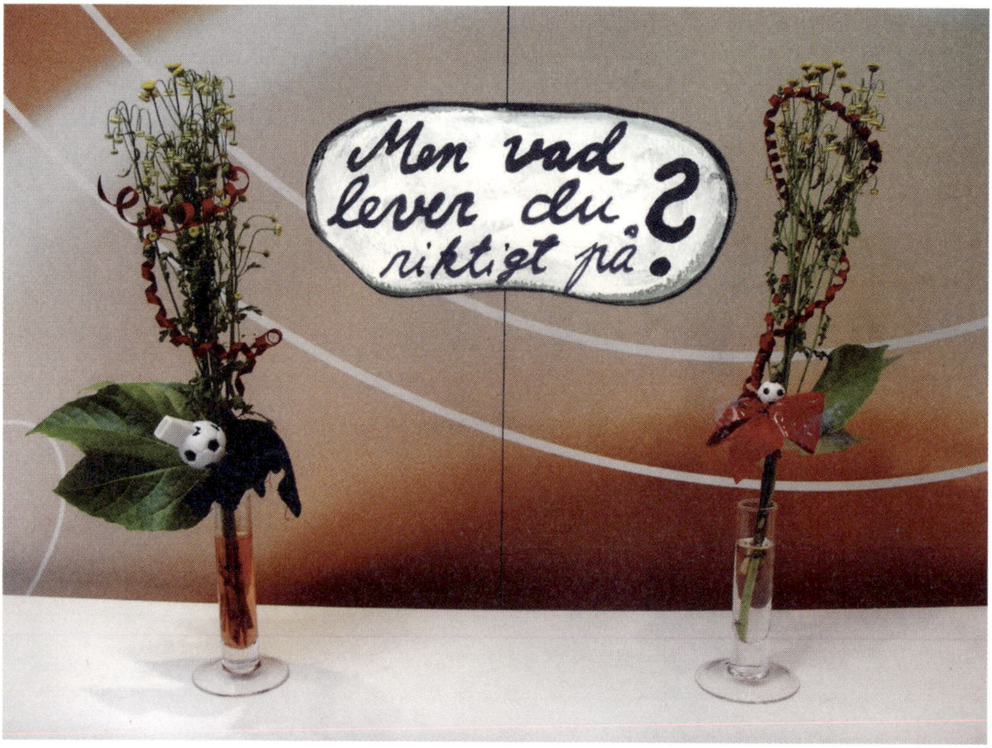

How do you actually make a living?

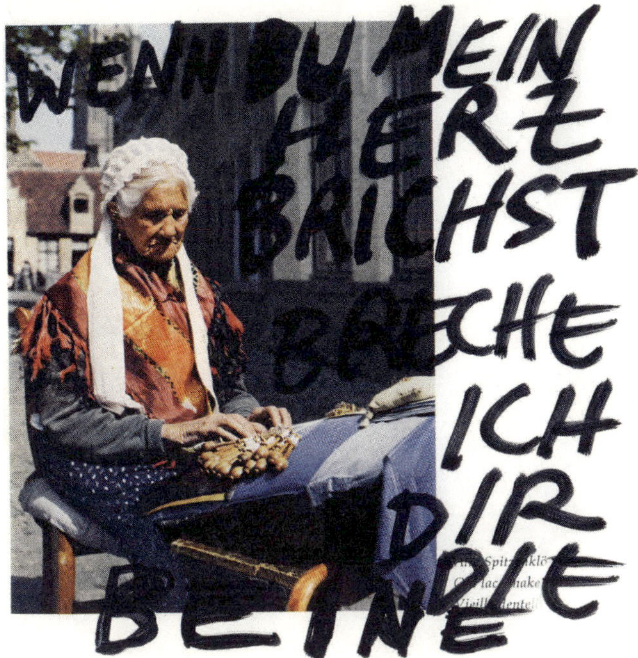

If you break my heart, I'll break your legs.

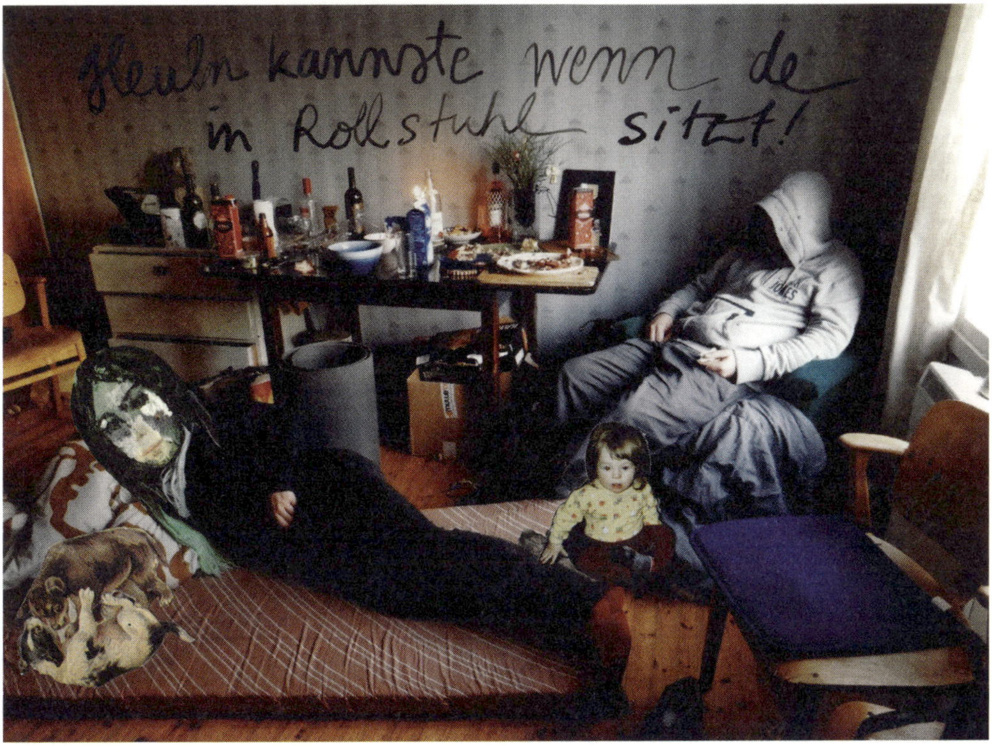

You can cry when you're in a wheelchair.

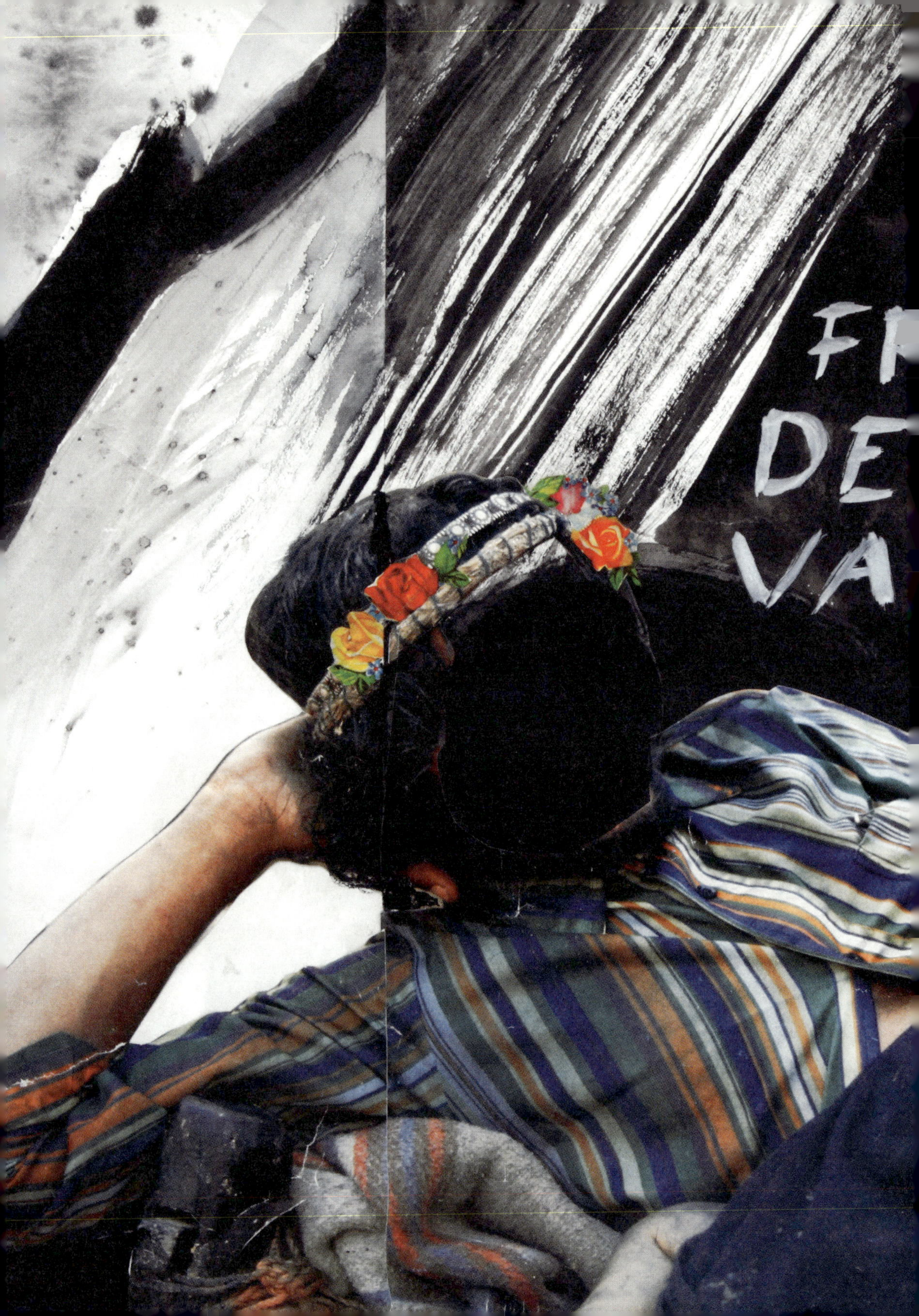
FI
DE
VA

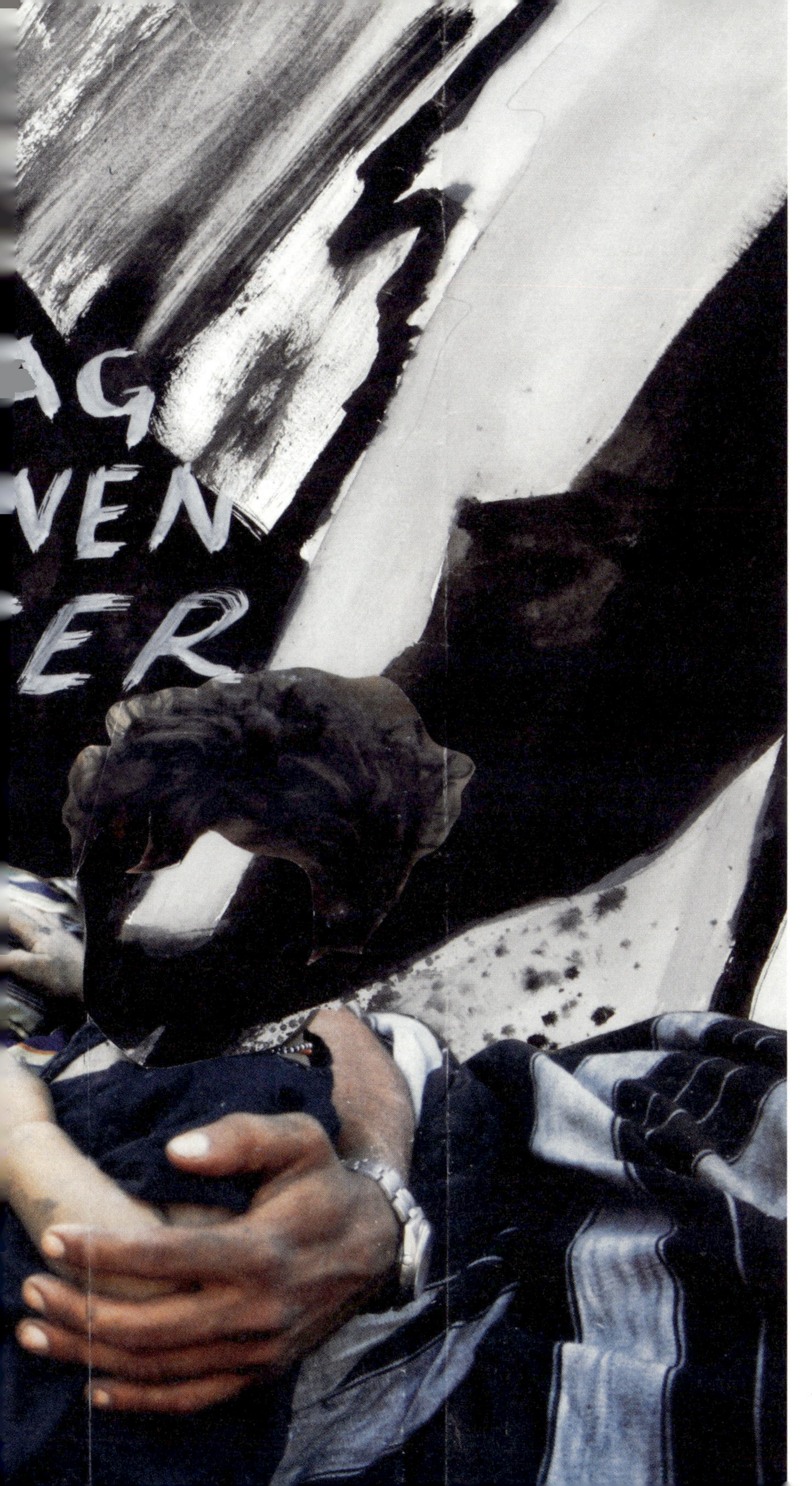

Ask your father.

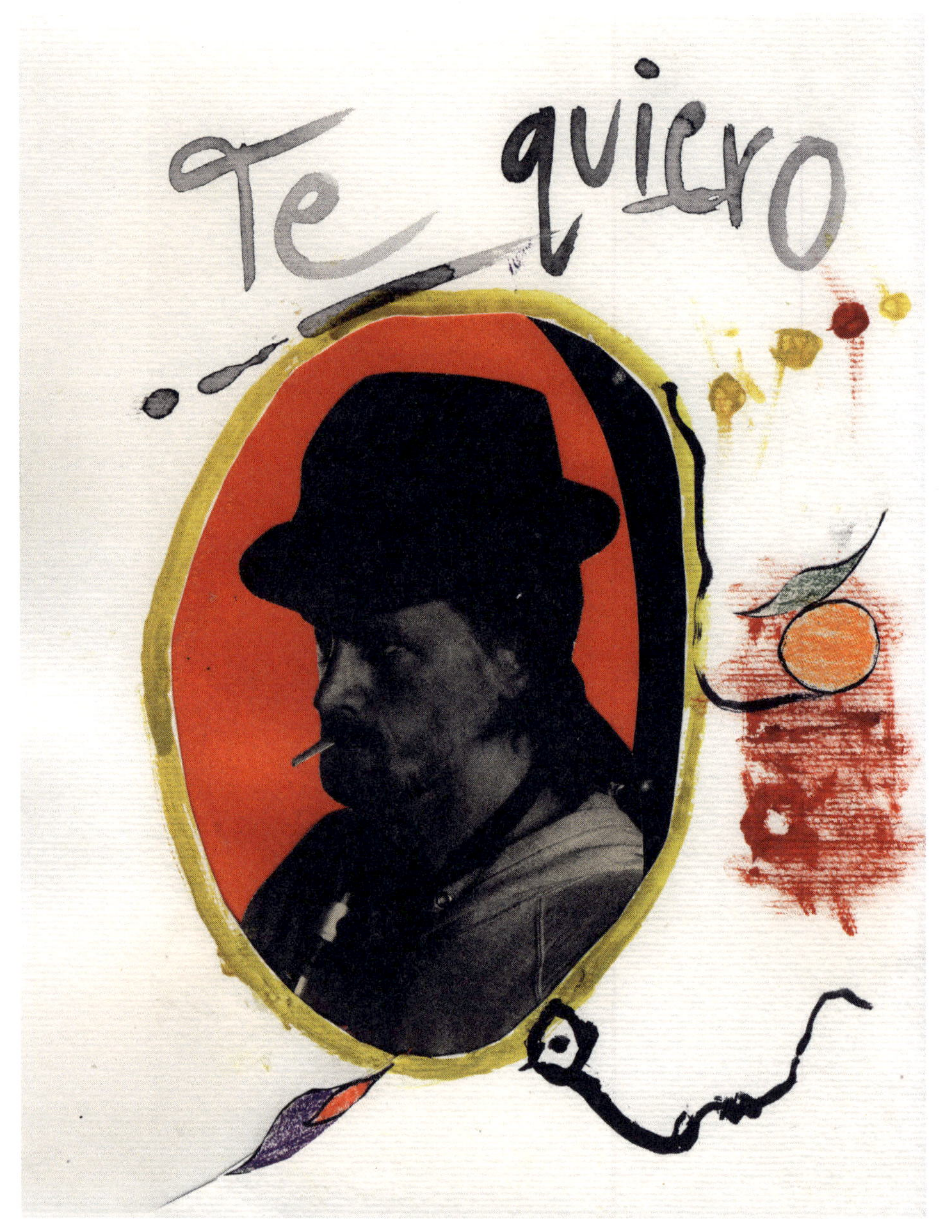

I love you.

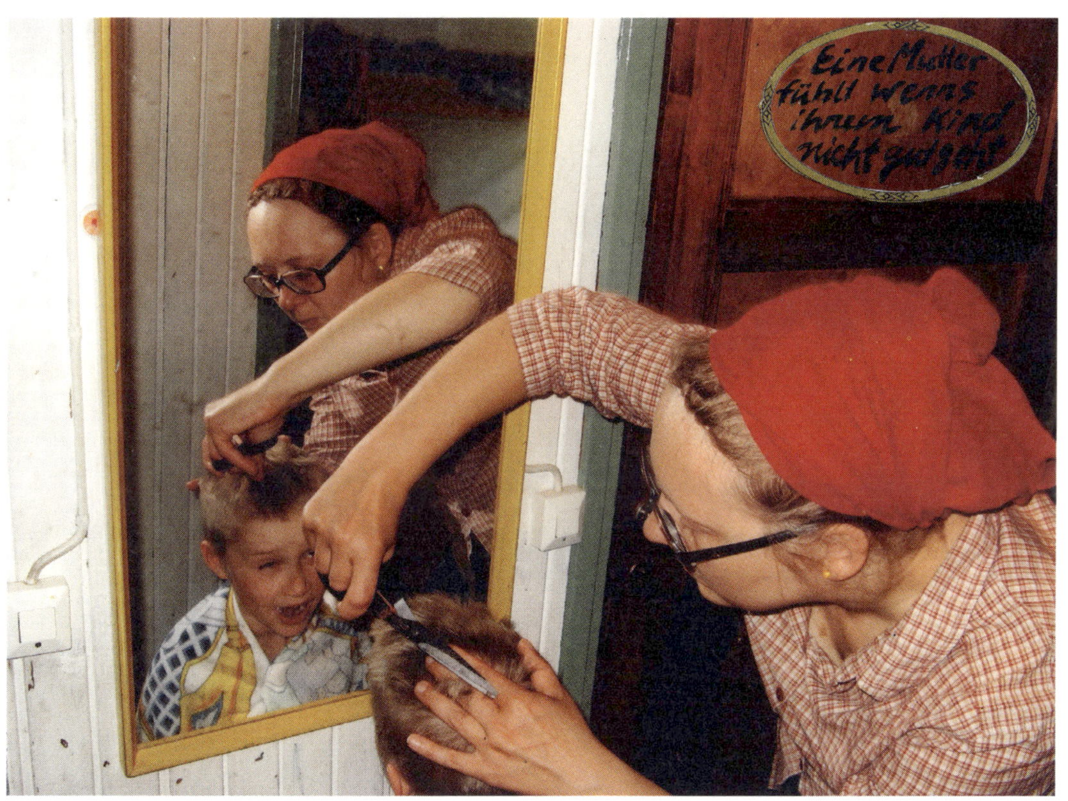

Every mother senses when her children are in peril.

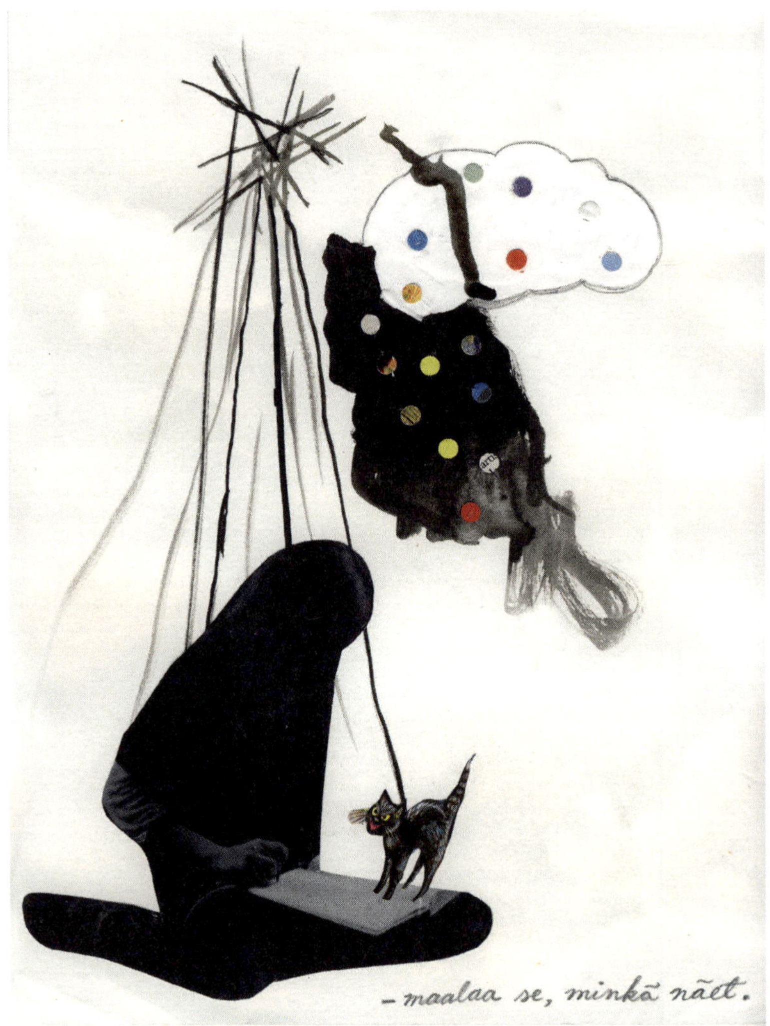

Paint what you see.

One talks about what one
does not have.

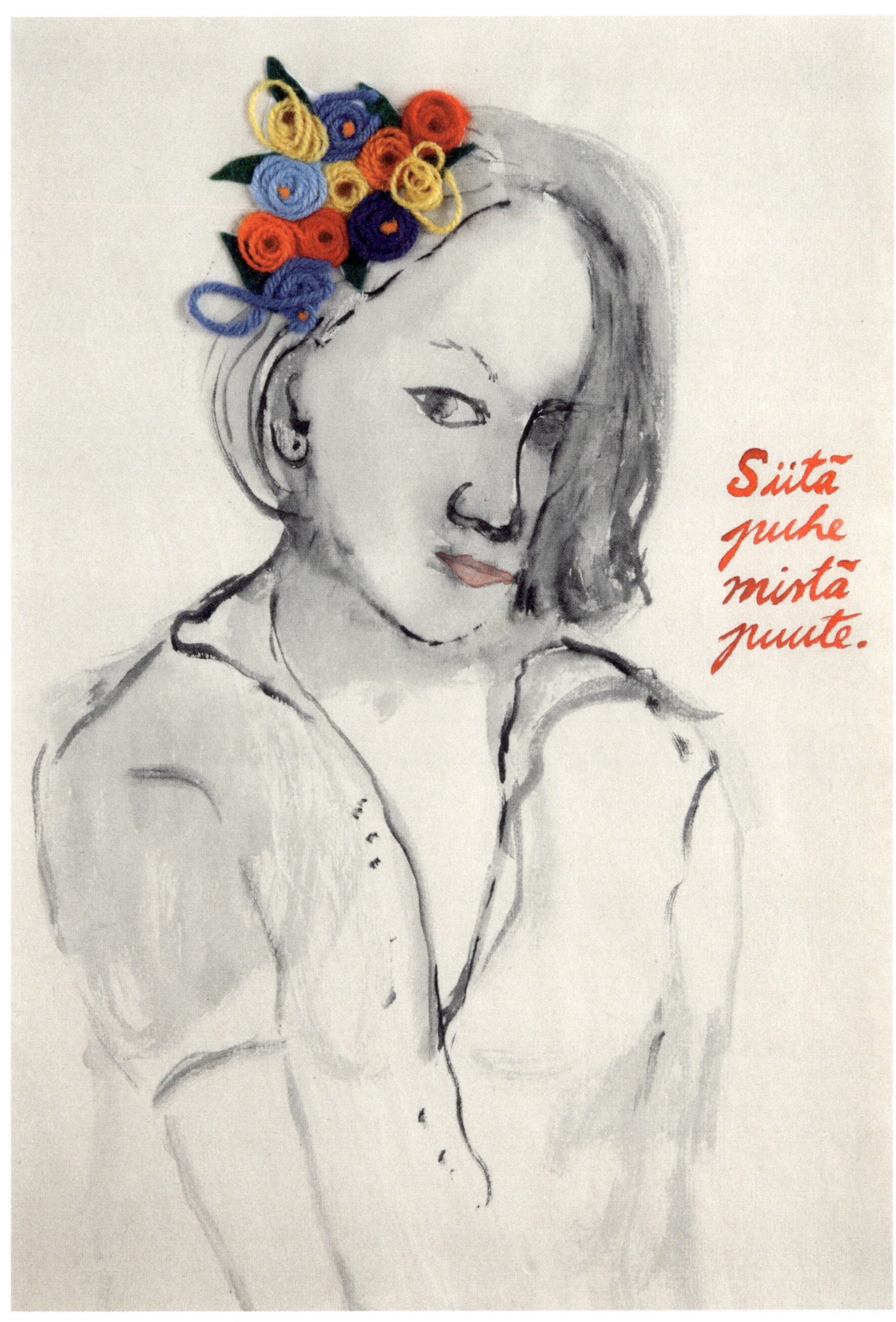

Siitä
puhe
mistä
puute.

One can be happy
with no-one.

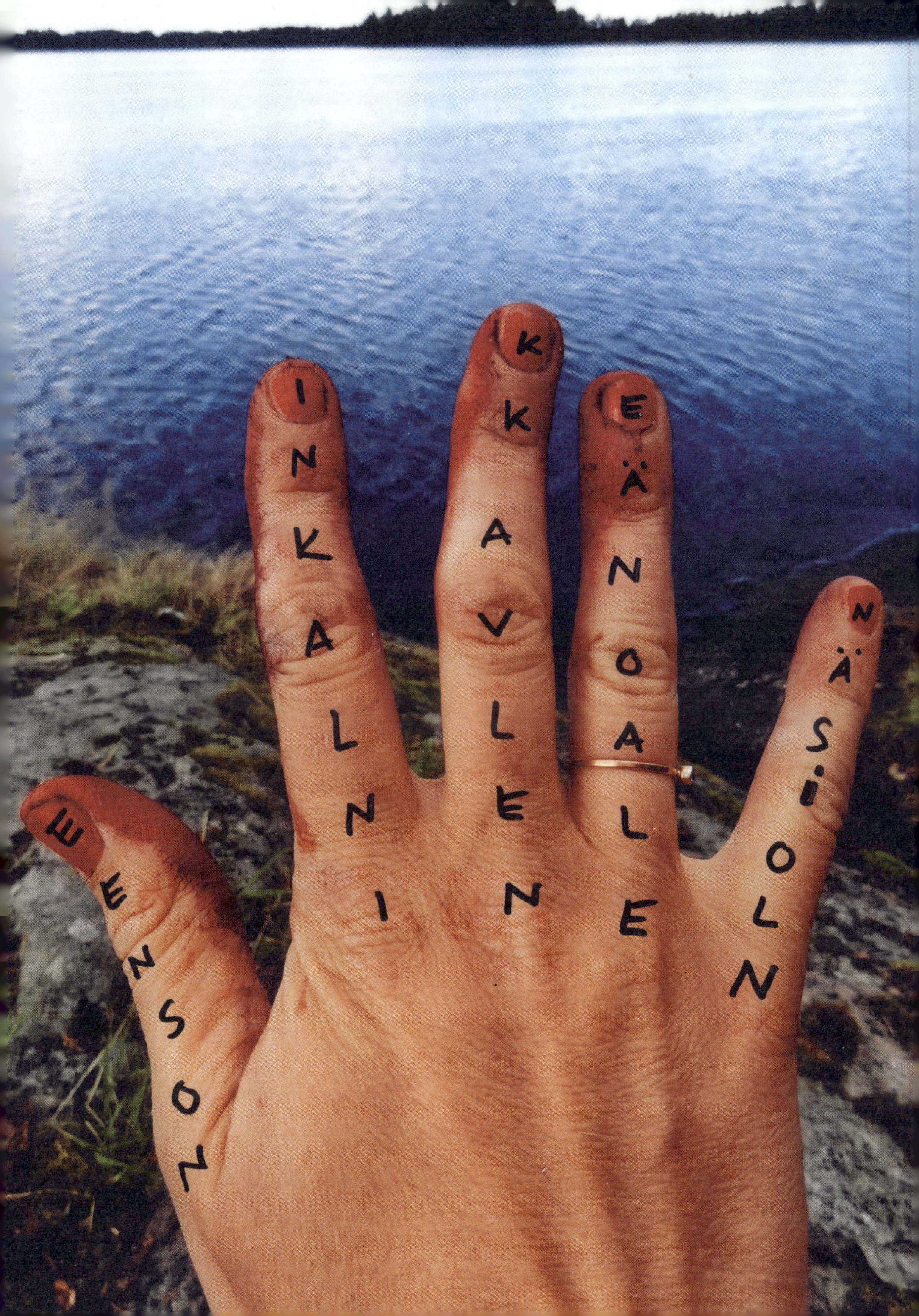

E
INKALNI
KAVLENE
KEÄNOALE
NÄSIOLN
ENSON

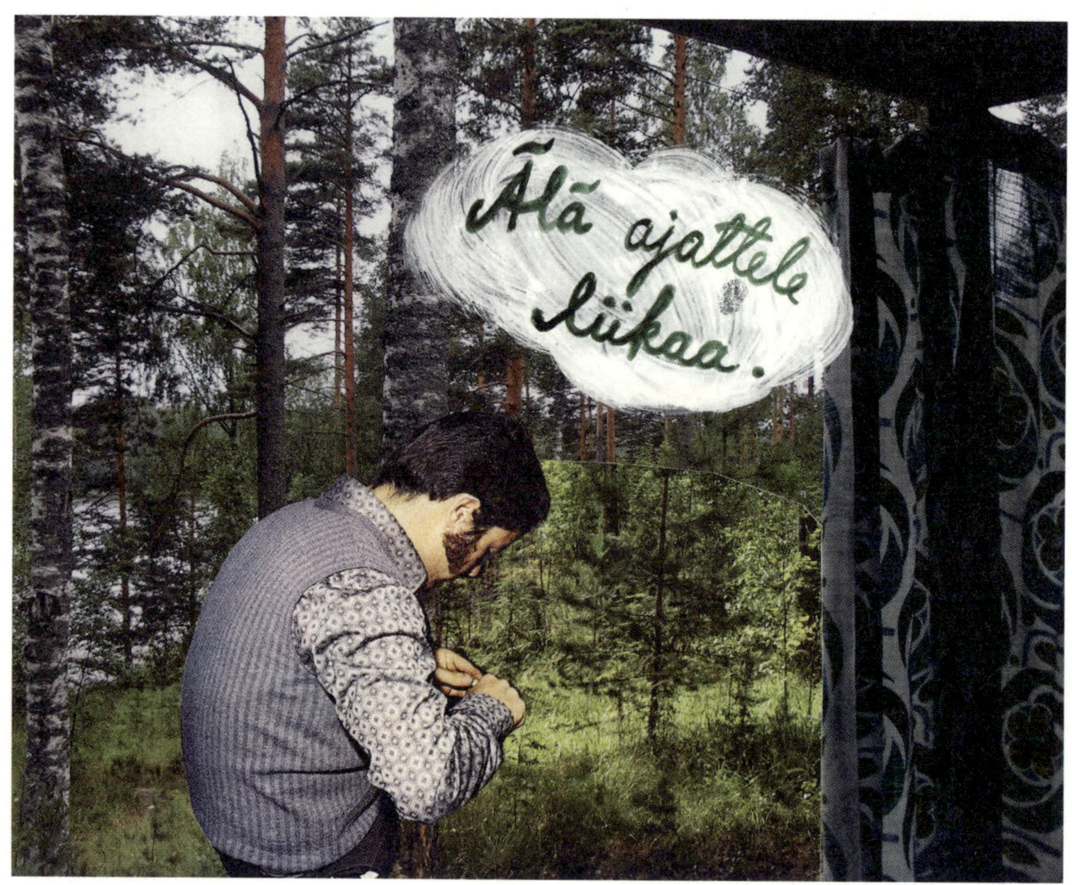

Don't think too much.

Why is everything
about sex?

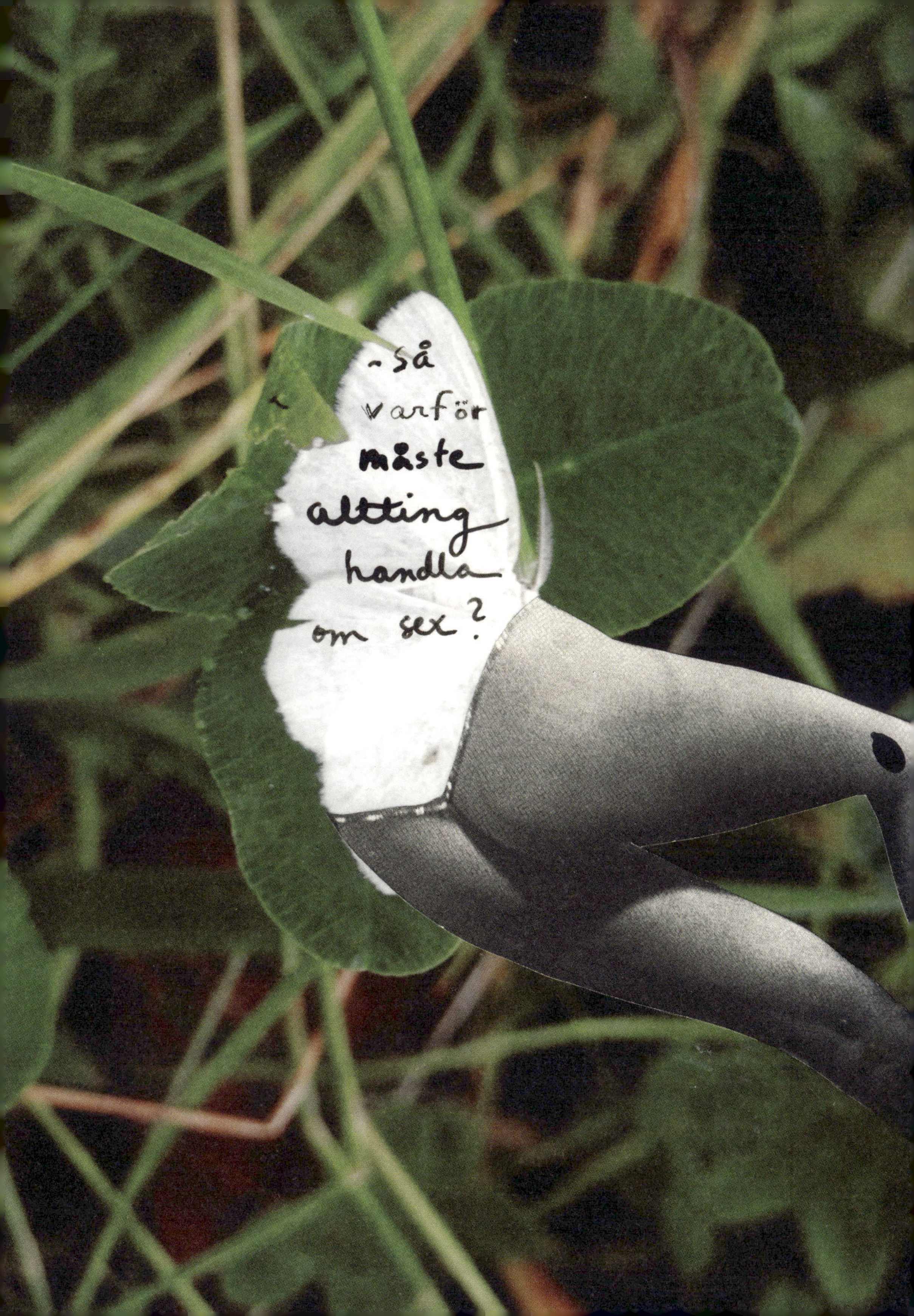
- så
varför
måste
altting
handla
om sex ?

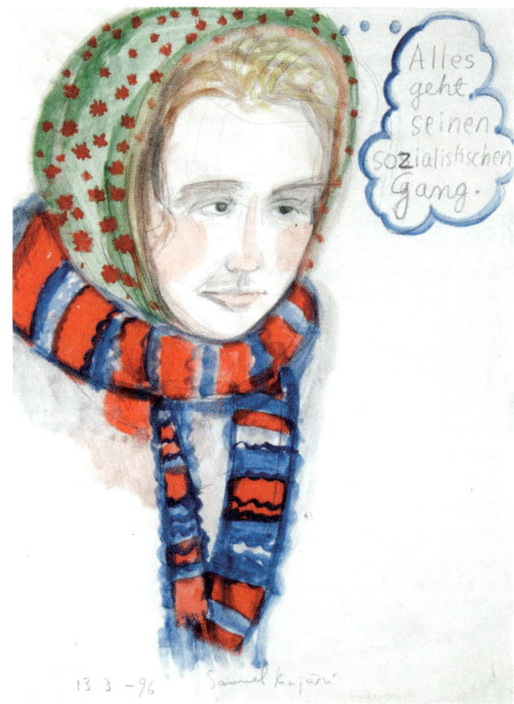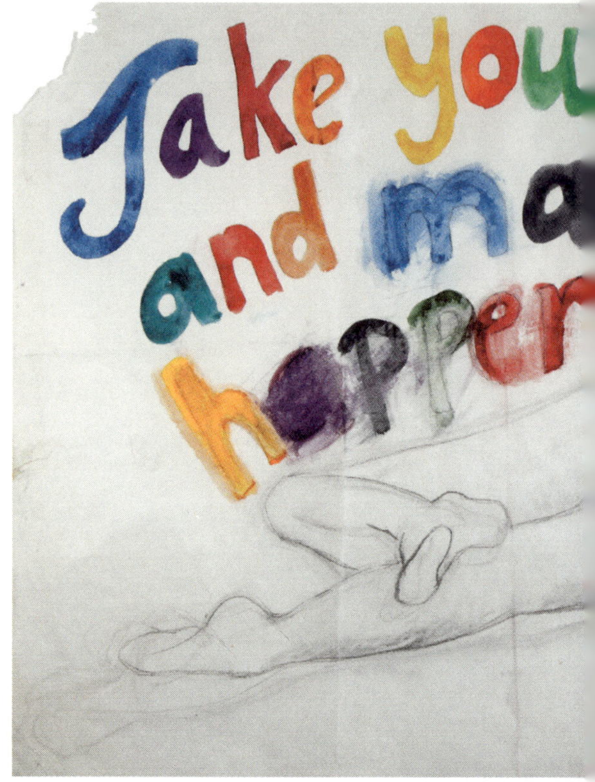

Everything will follow its natural
Socialist course.

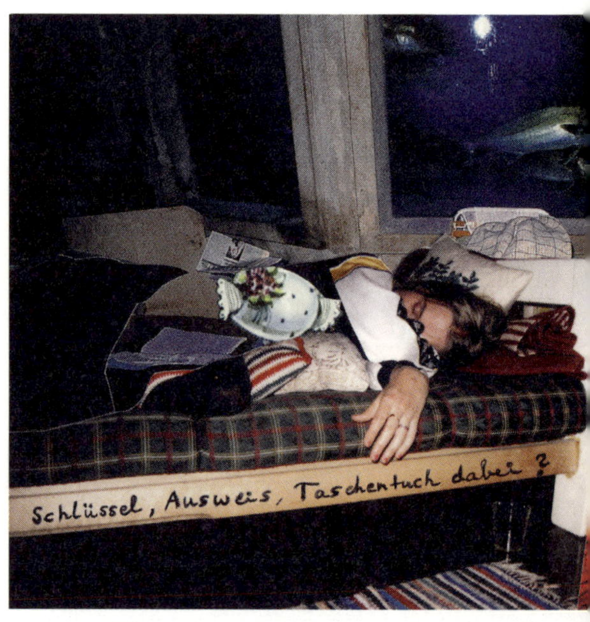

Checklist: Key, ID, hankies?

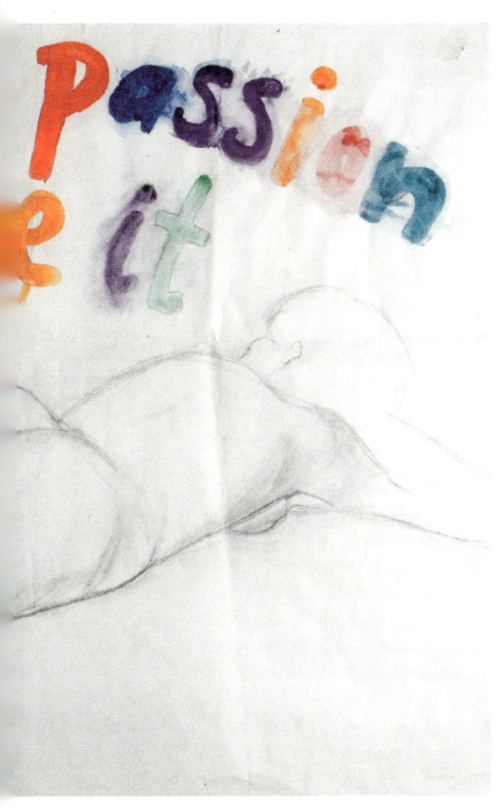

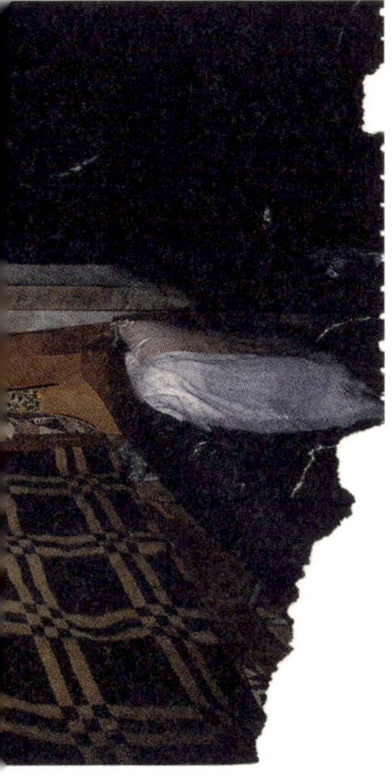

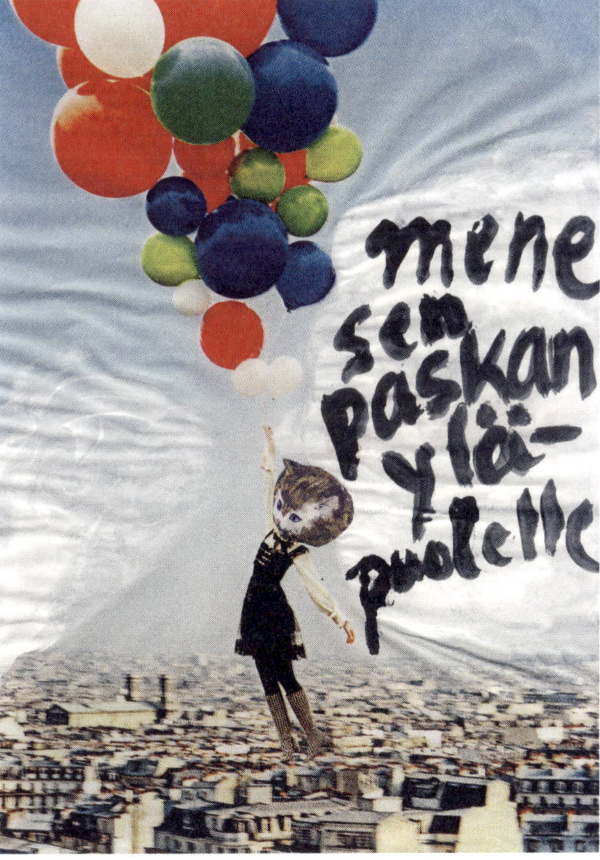

Rise above that shit.

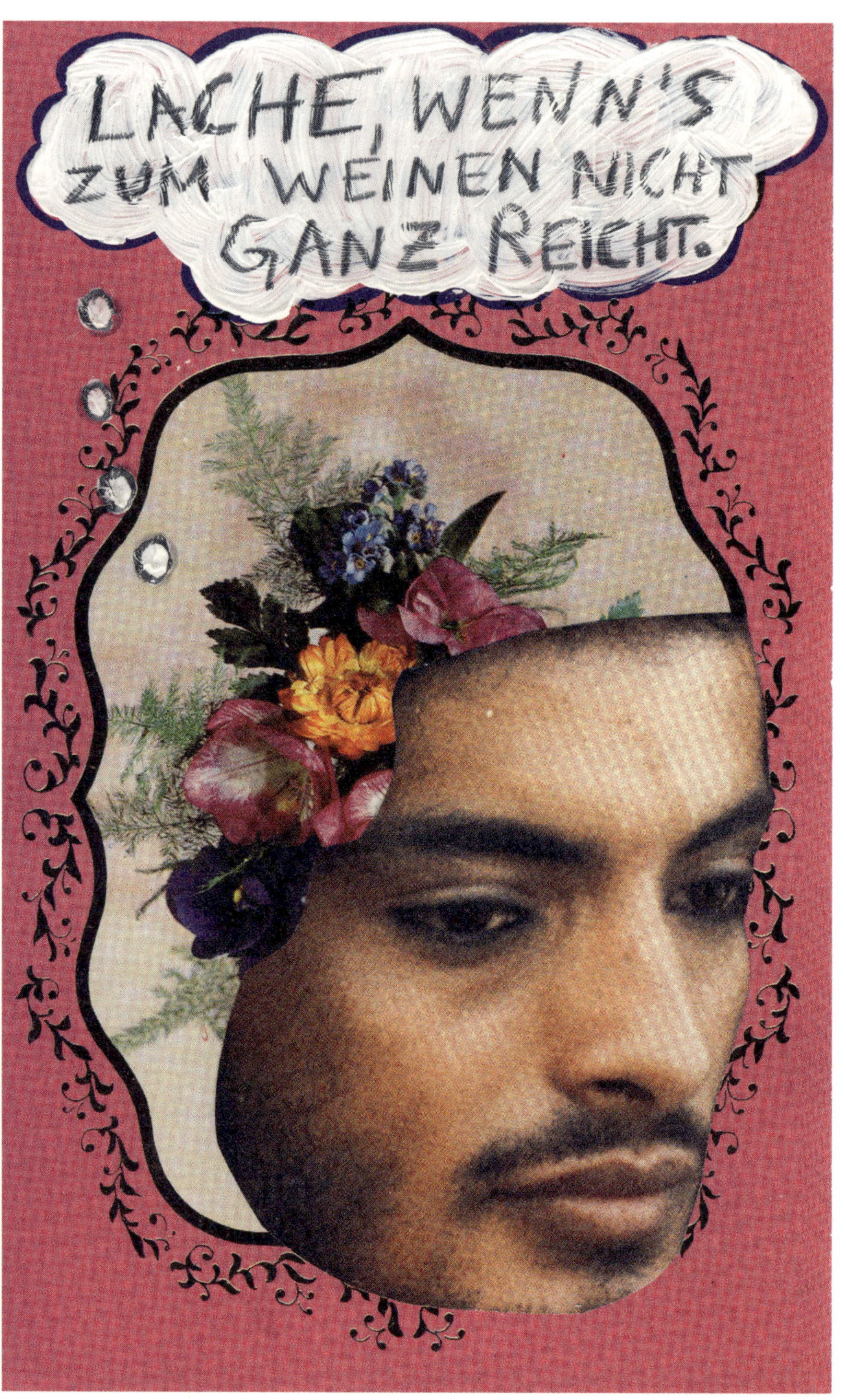

Laugh if it's not enough to make you cry.

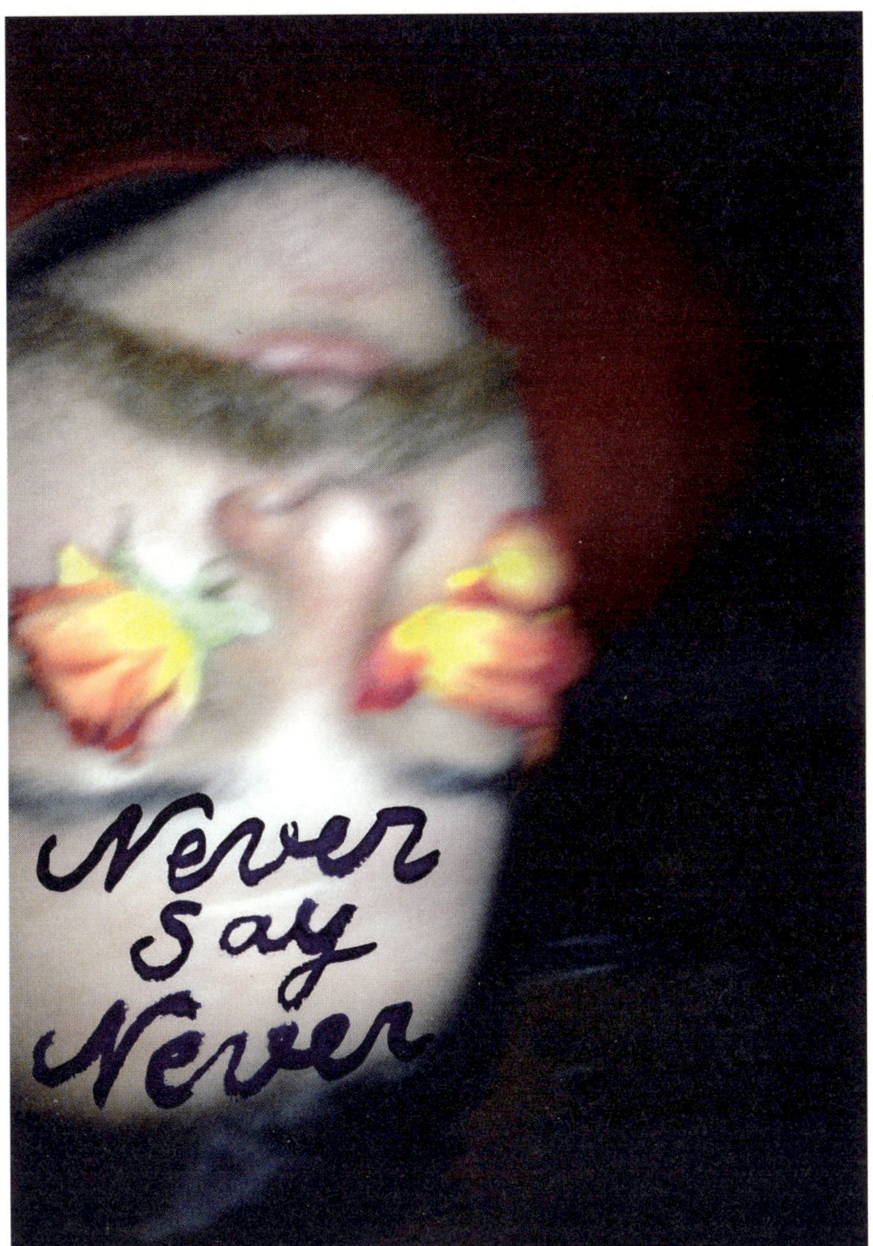
Never
Say
Never

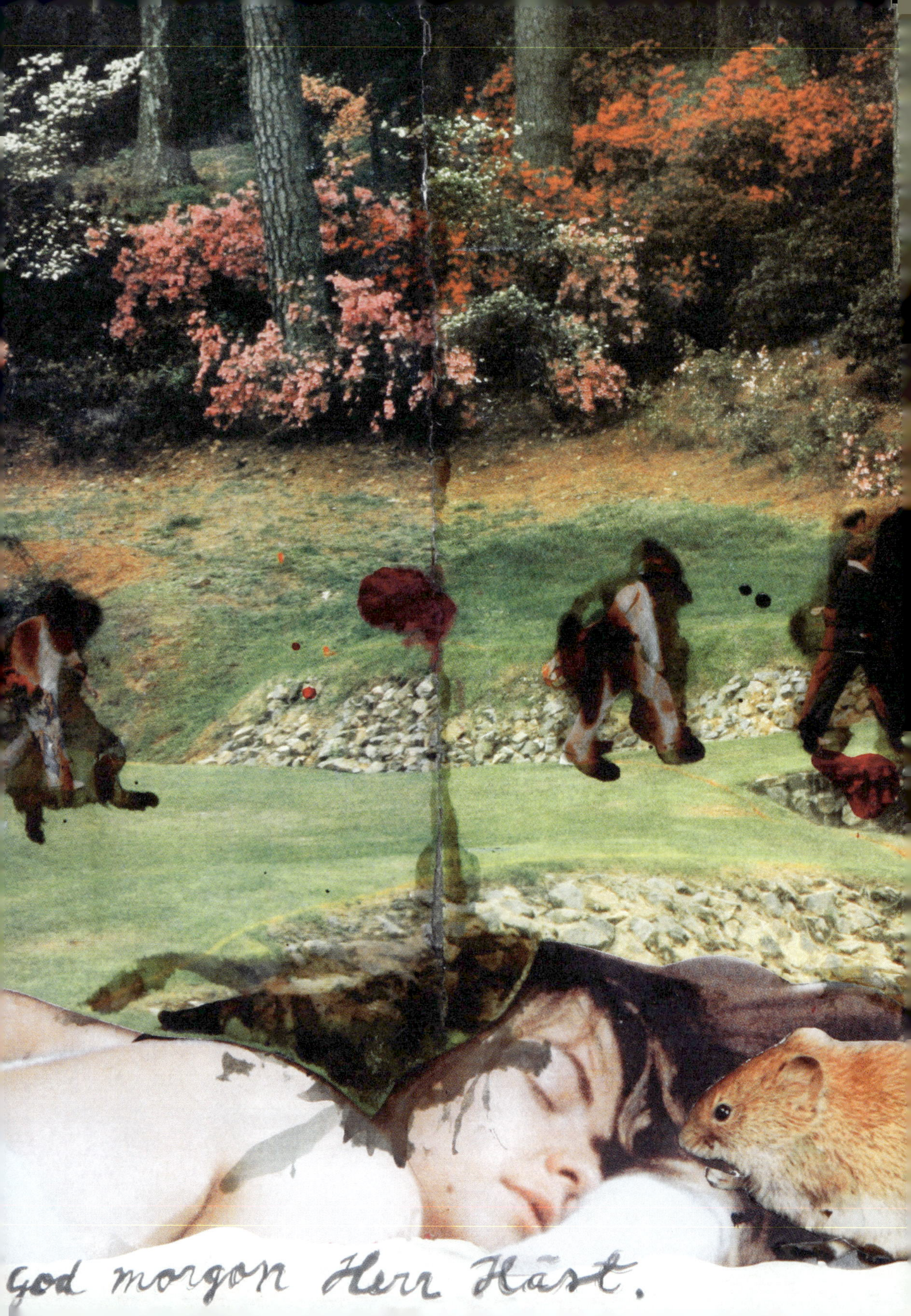
god morgon Herr Häst.

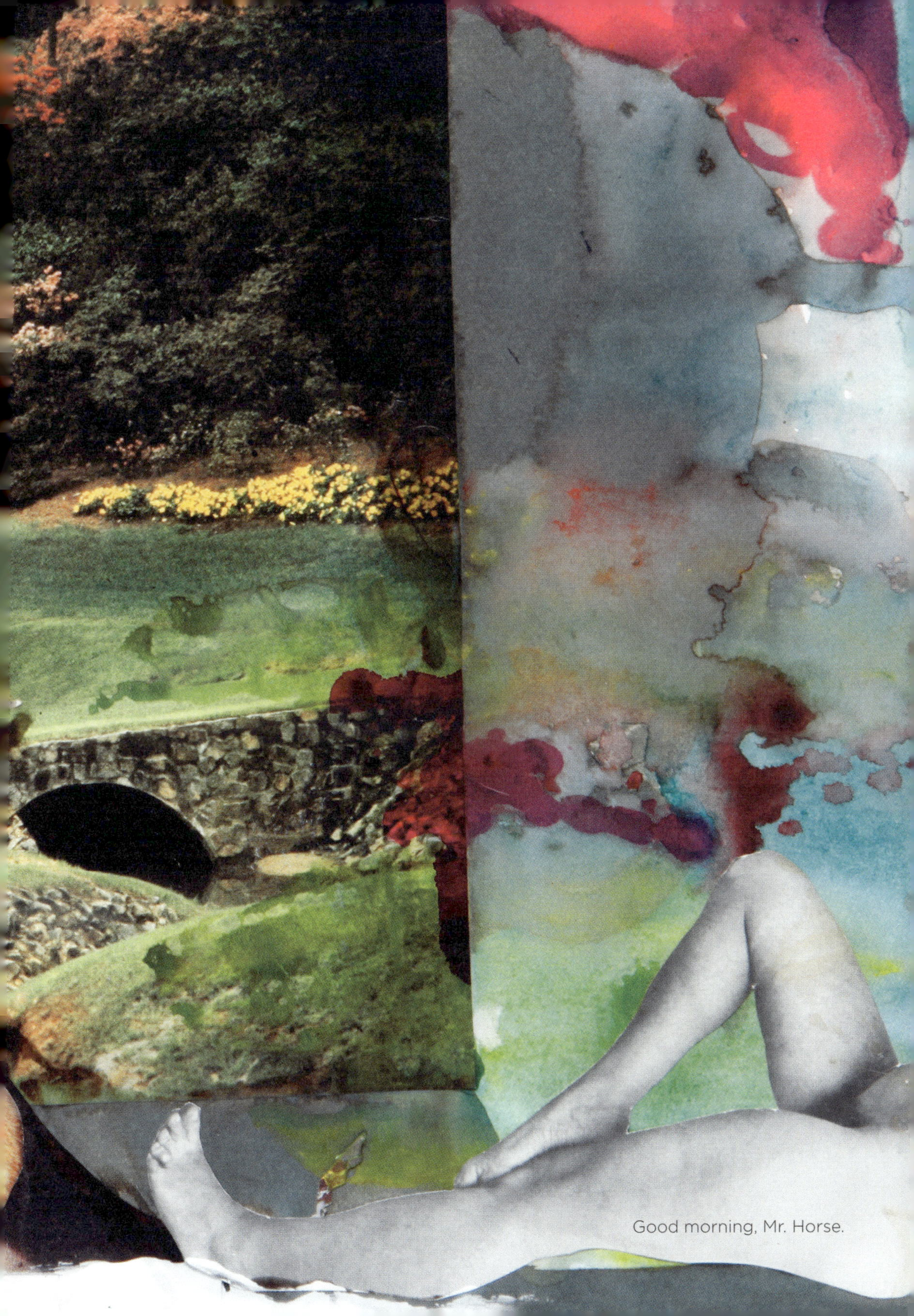
Good morning, Mr. Horse.

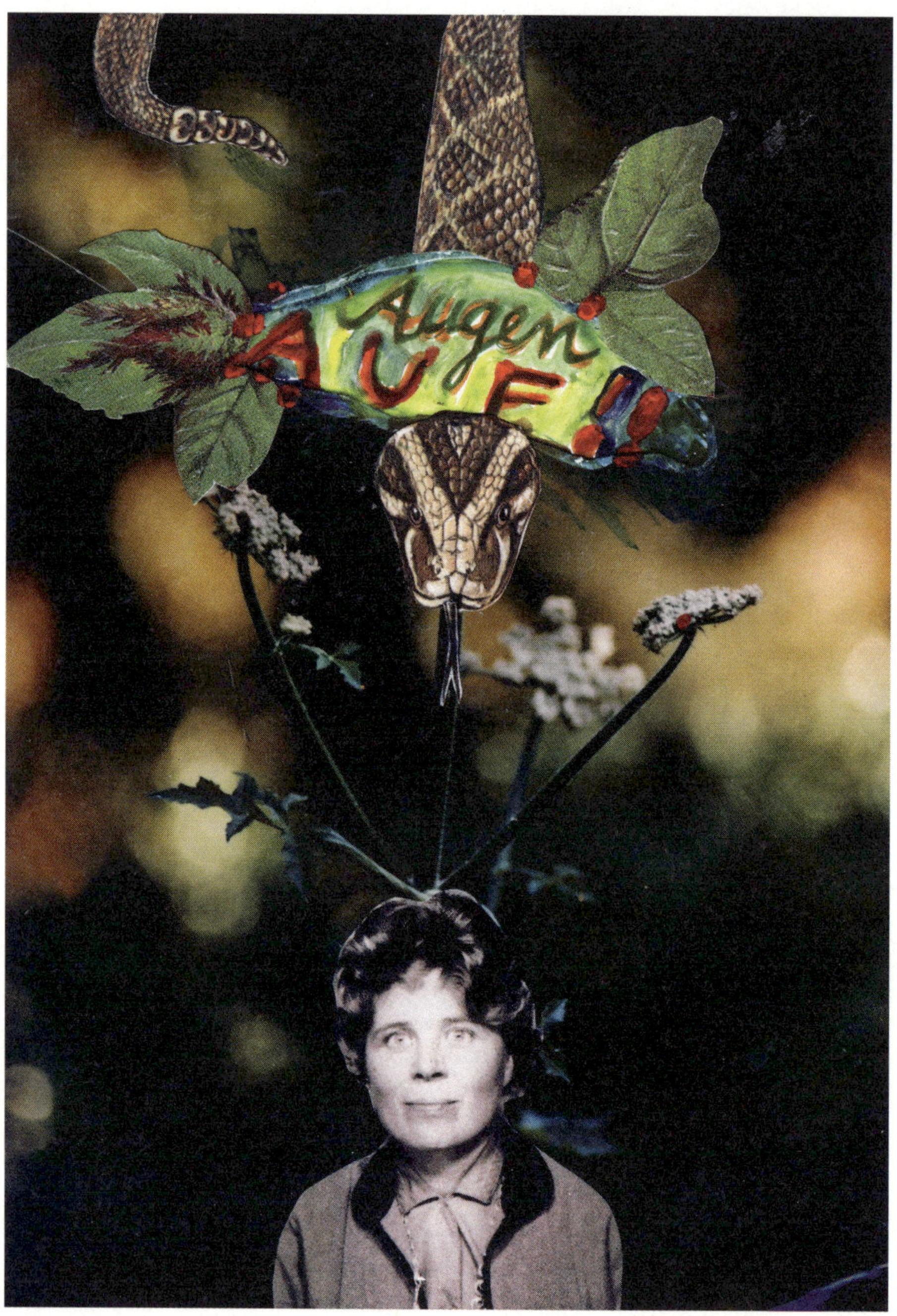

Eyes open!

The night is like the day,
just without the light.

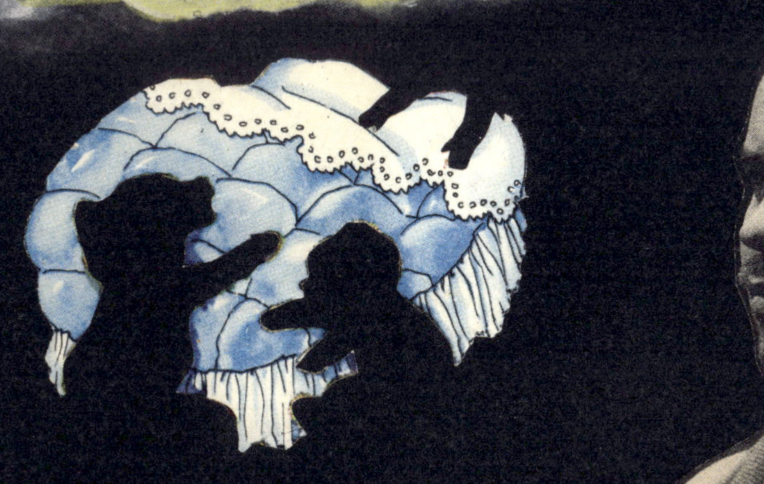

DIE NACHT
IST WIE DER TAG
NUR OHNE
LICHT.

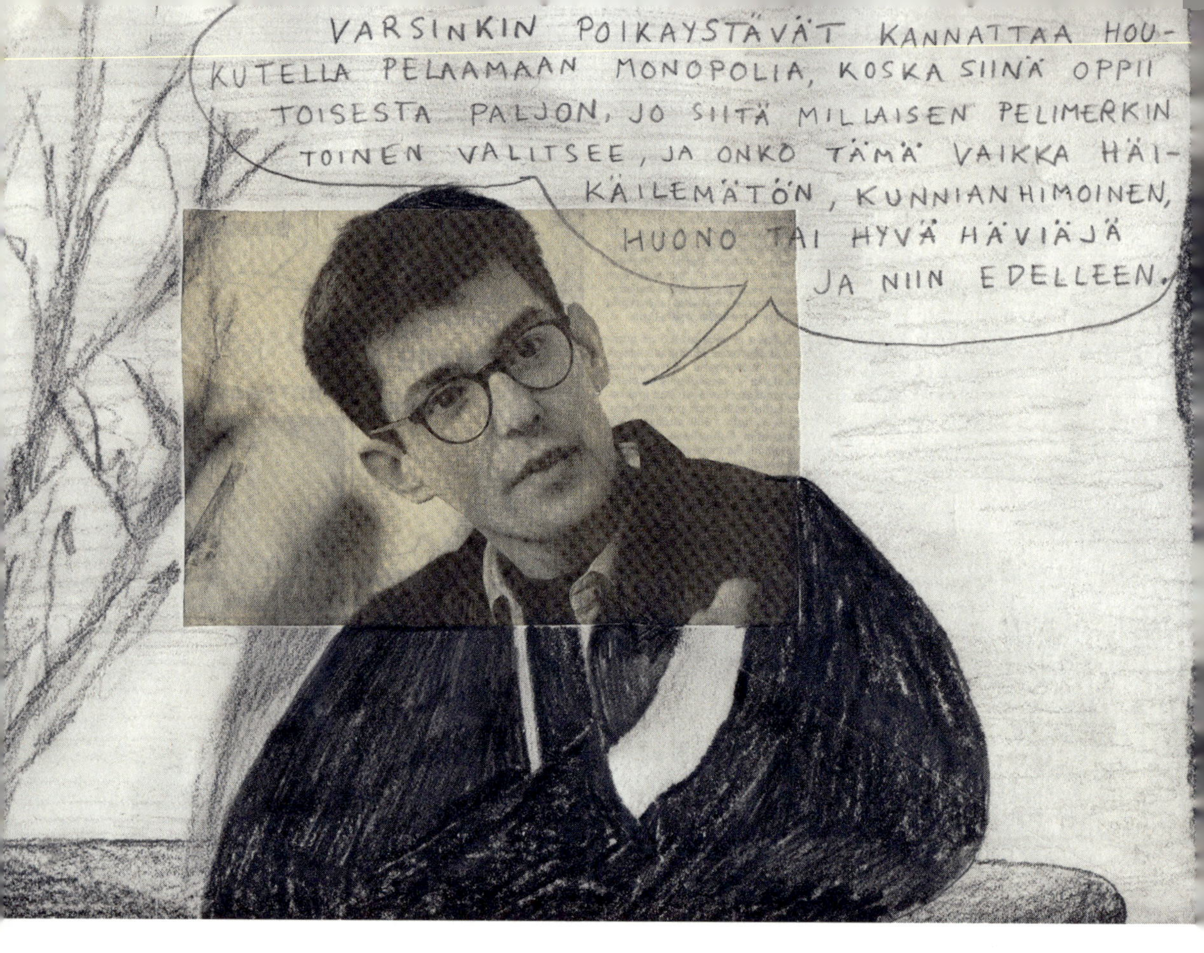

It is especially useful to encourage boyfriends to play
monopoly, as one can learn a lot about them, like the kind
of chip he likes to choose, or whether he's a ruthless or
ambitious player, a bad or a good loser, and so on.

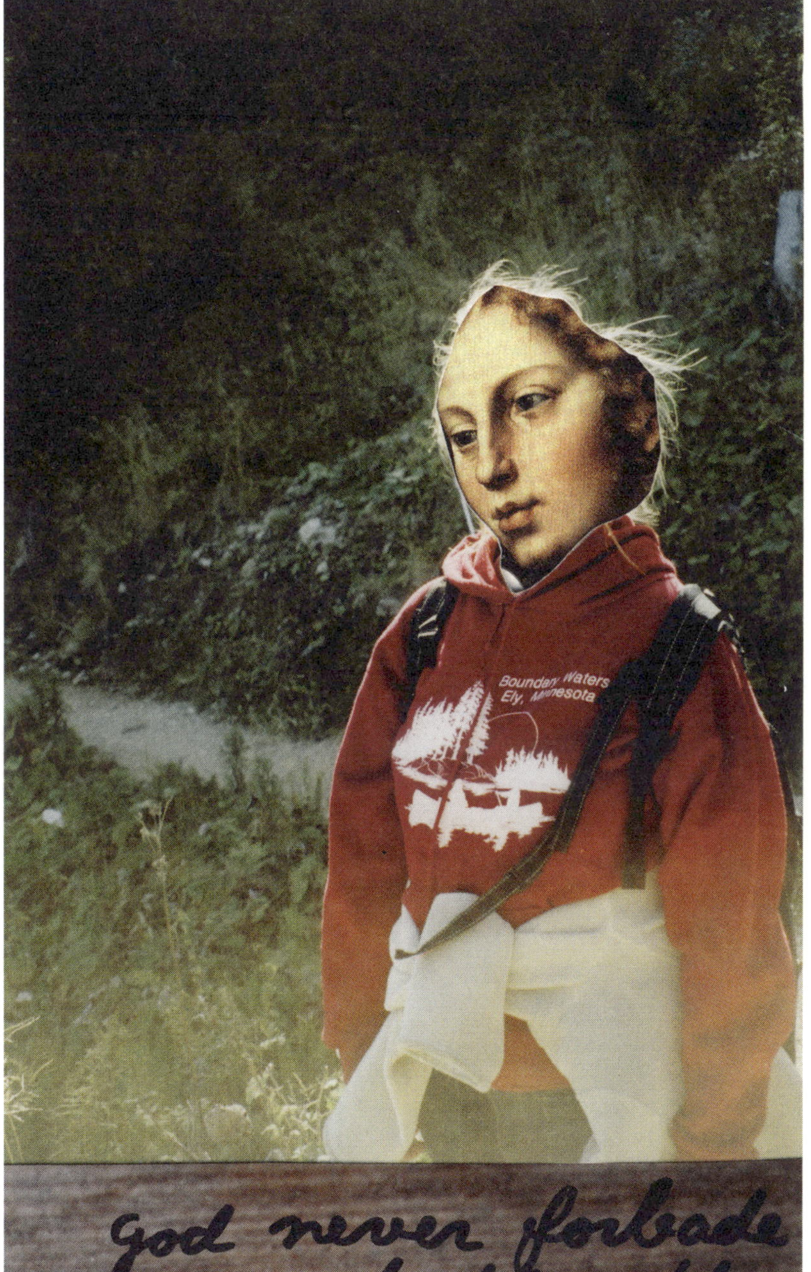

god never forbade
great thoughts.

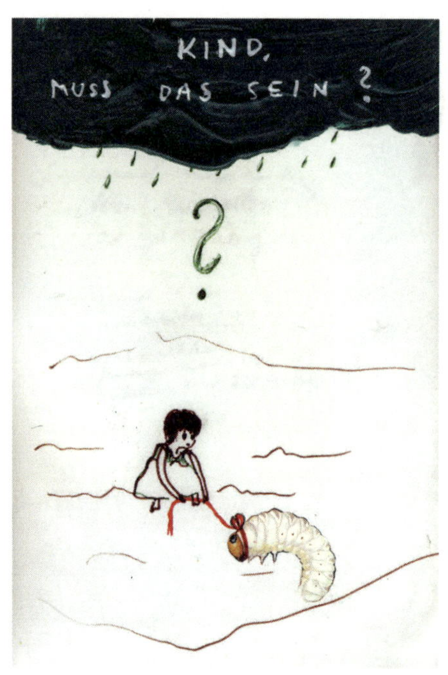

Child, is that really necessary?

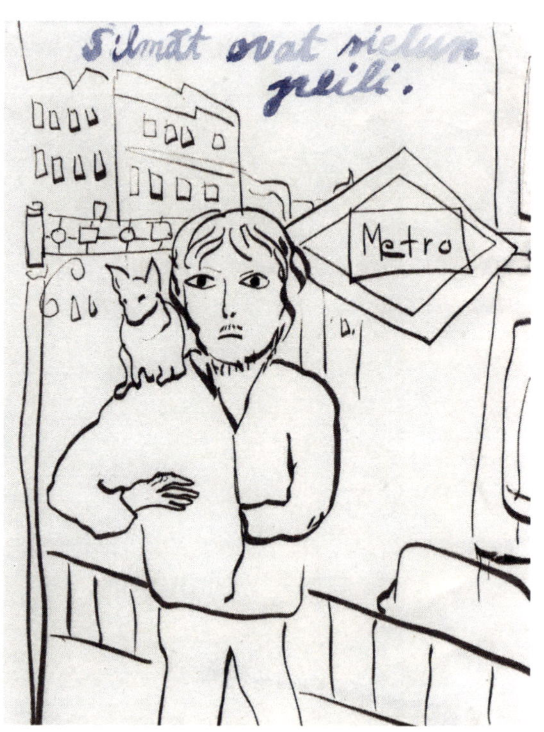

The eyes are the windows to the soul.

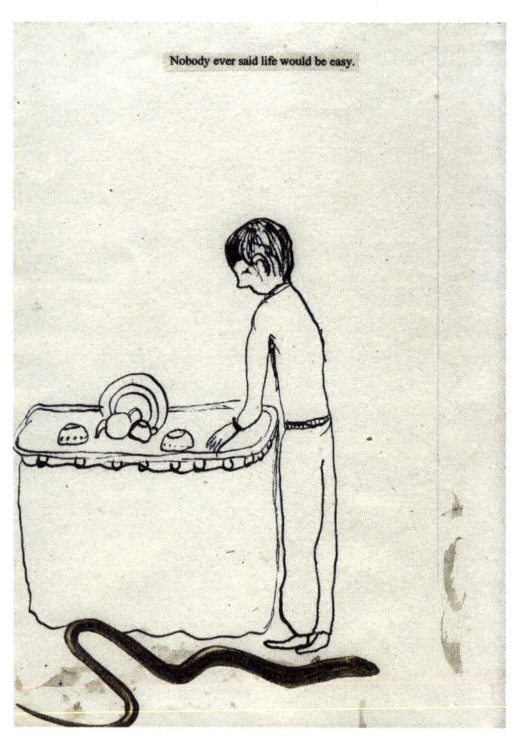

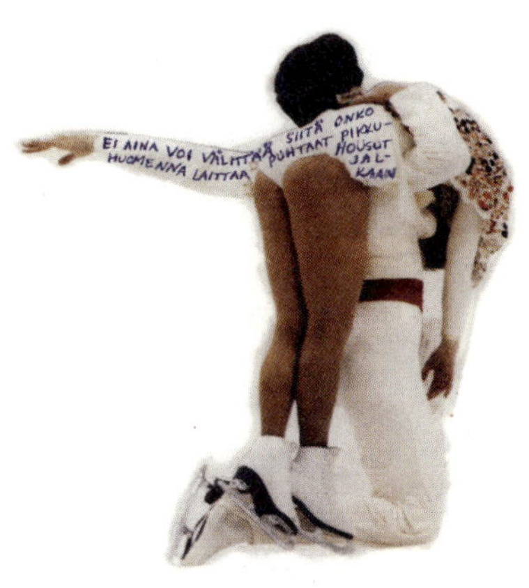

You can't spend all your time wondering
whether or not you're going to have clean
knickers tomorrow.

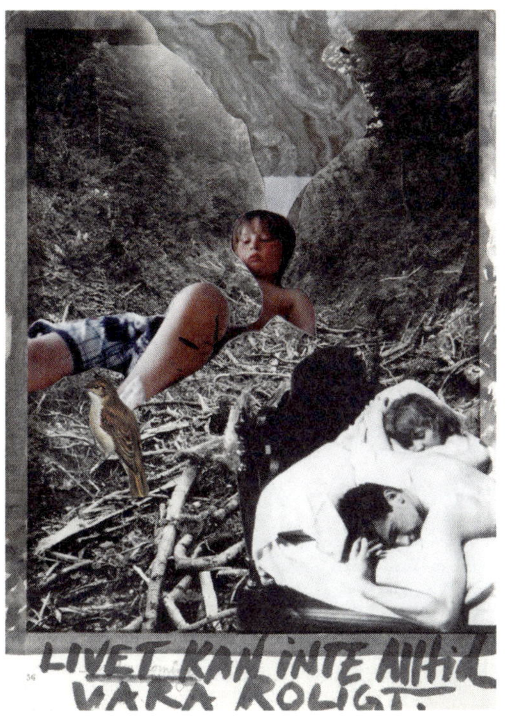

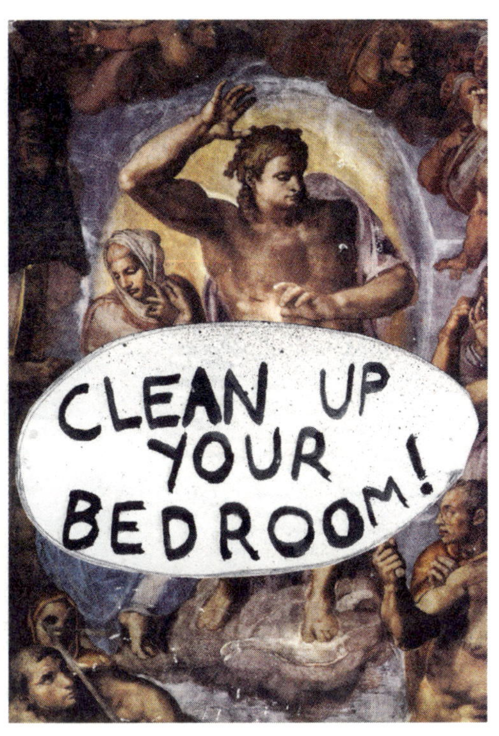

Life isn't always fun.

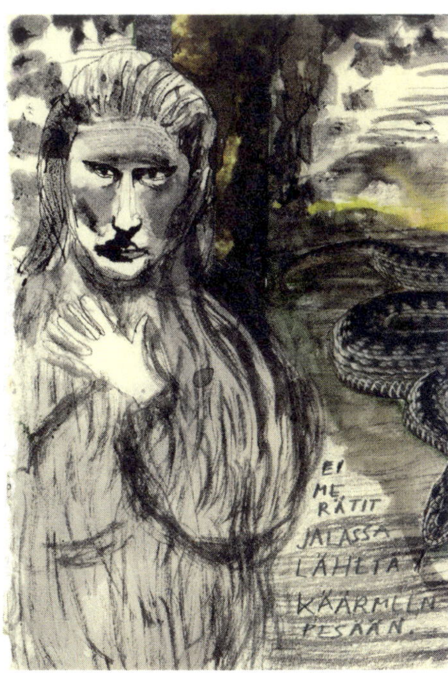

We won´t walk into the snakes nest
with rags on our feet.

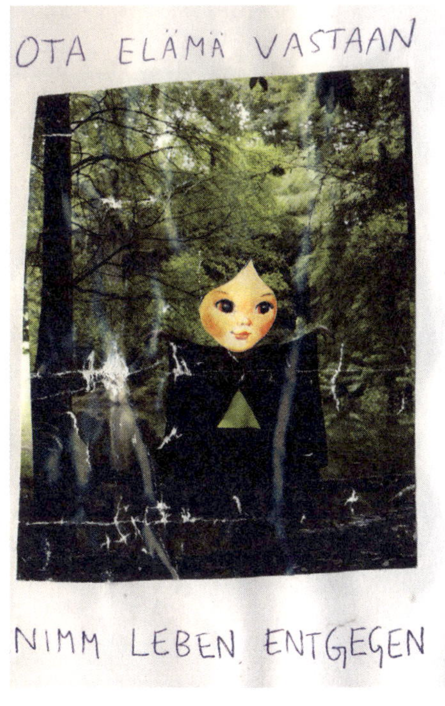

Take life as it comes.

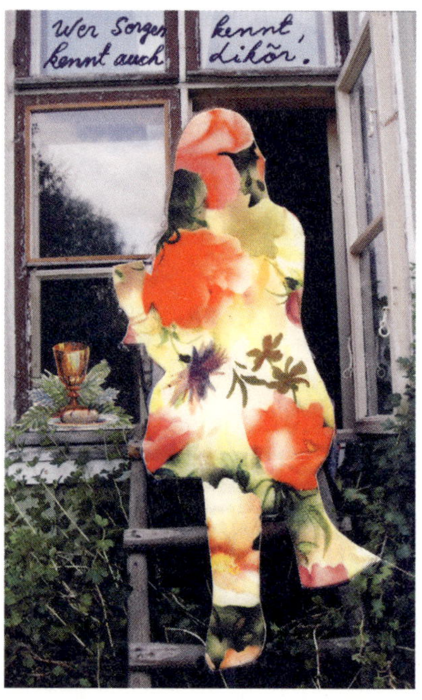

Those who know sorrow also
know liquor.

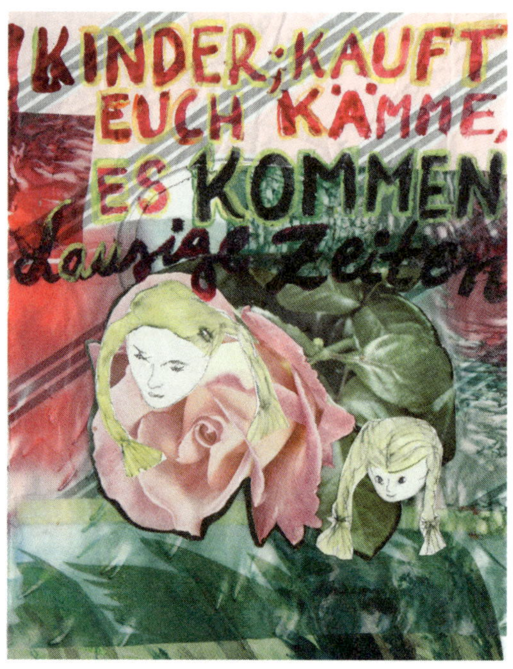

Children, grab your combs.
The lice times are coming.

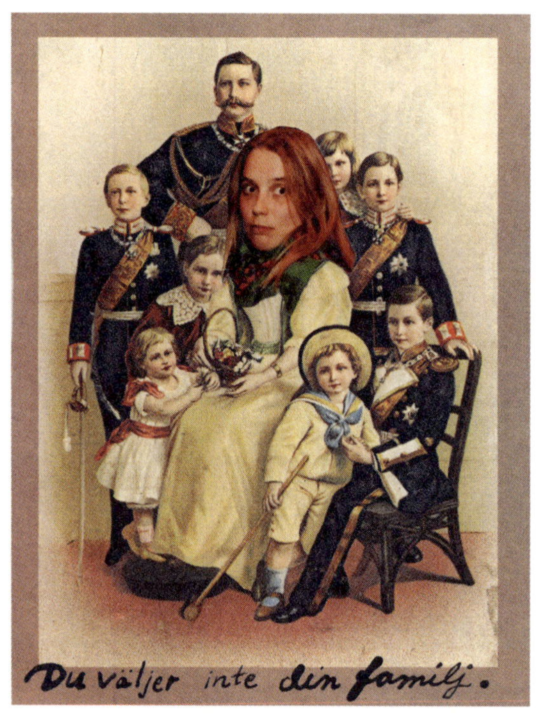

You can't choose family.

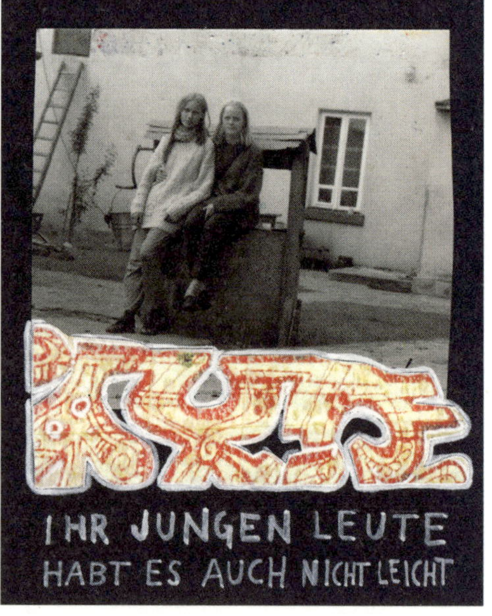

You youngsters haven't got it easy.

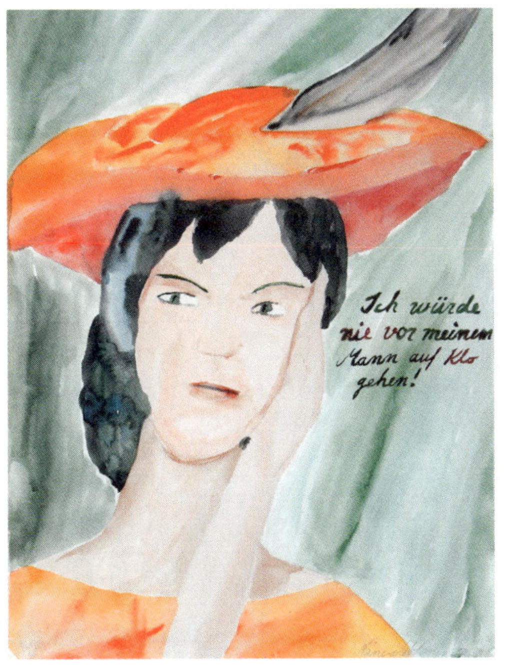

I wouldn't dream of going to the toilet in front of my husband.

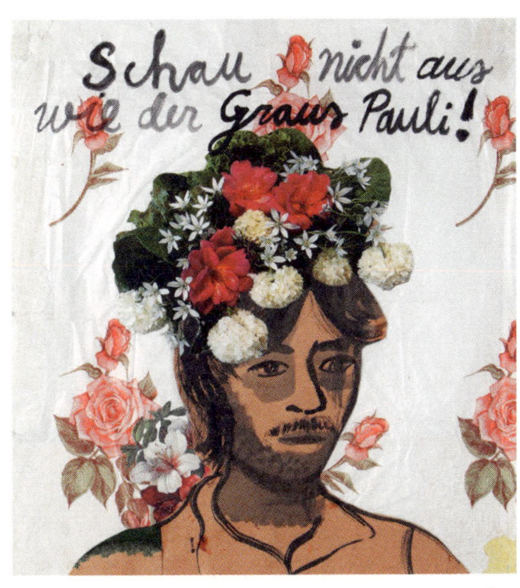

Stop looking like Old Nick!

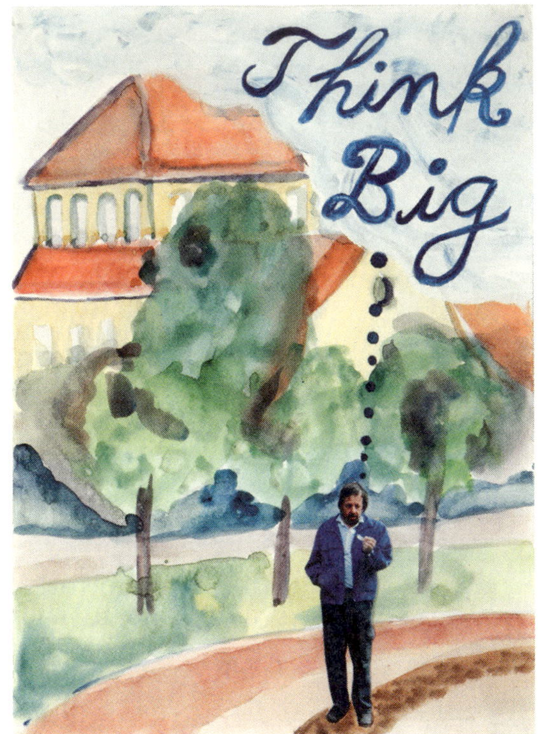

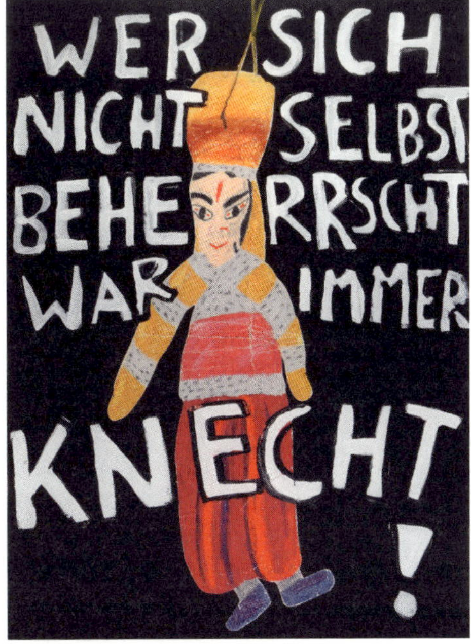

Losing your temper will always hold you back.

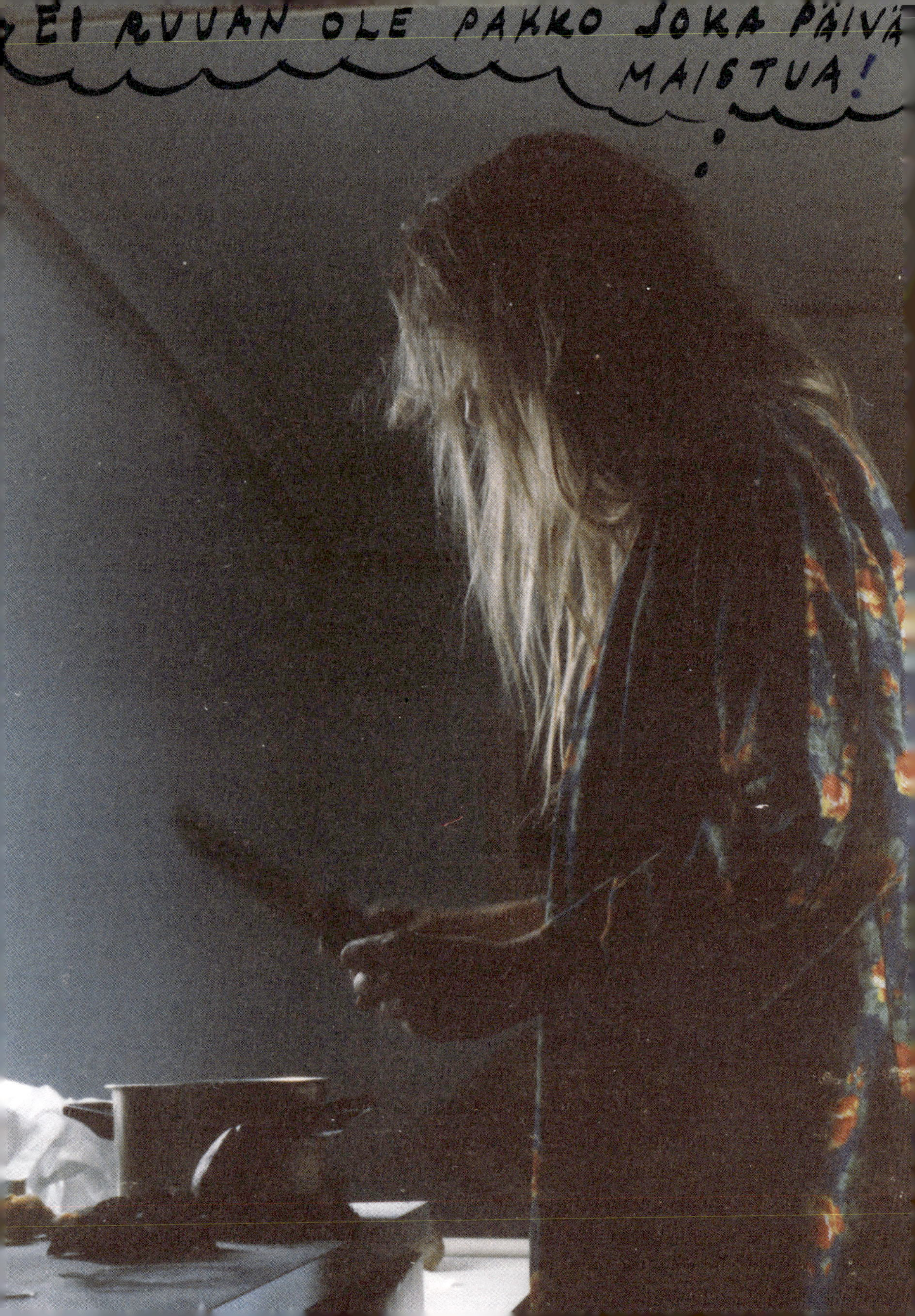

EI RUUAN OLE PAKKO JOKA PÄIVÄ
MAISTUA!

You don't have to enjoy your
meals every day.

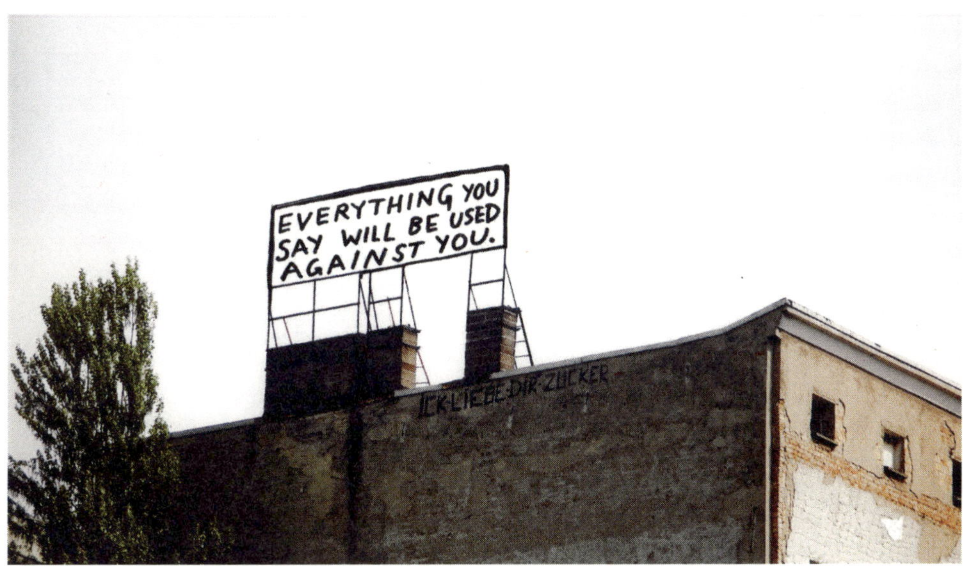

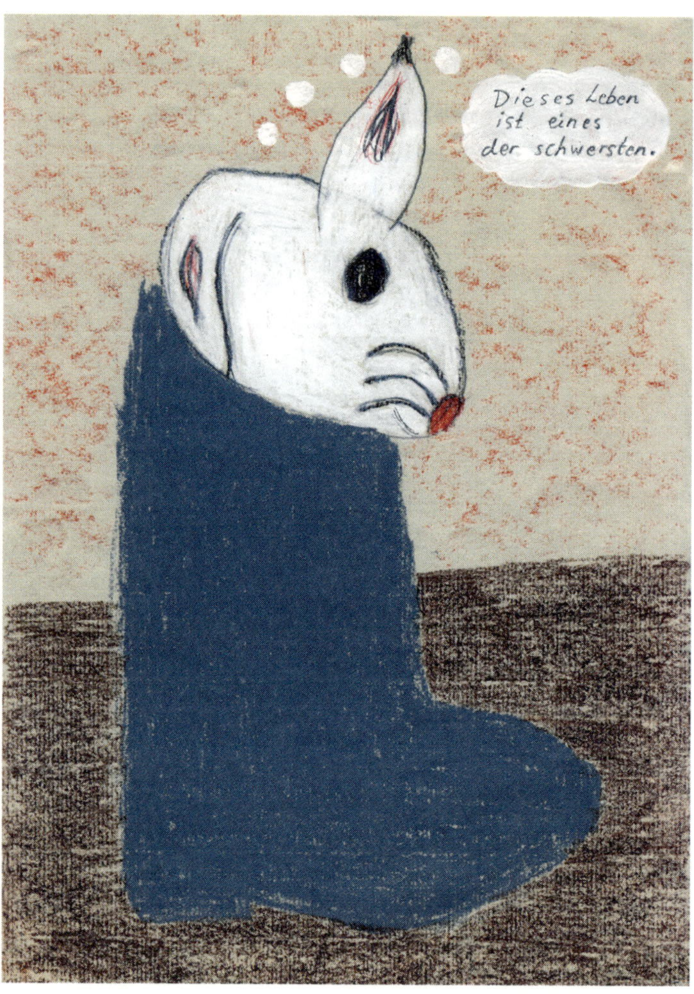

This is one of the most
difficult lives.

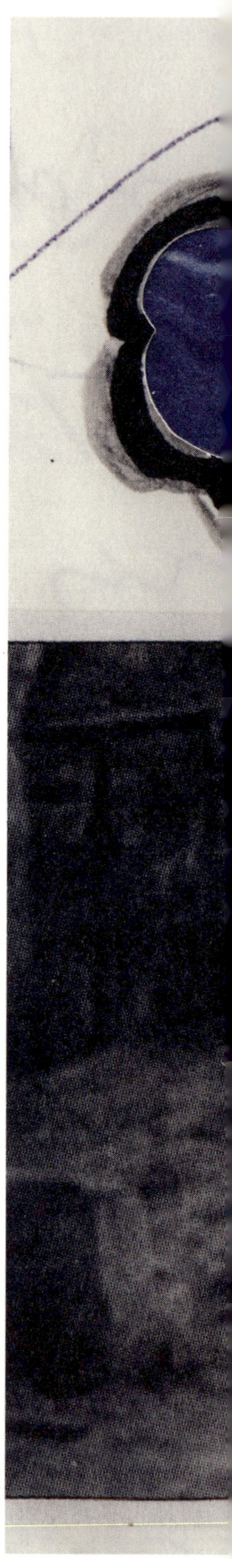

Don't get involved in
wars or accidents.

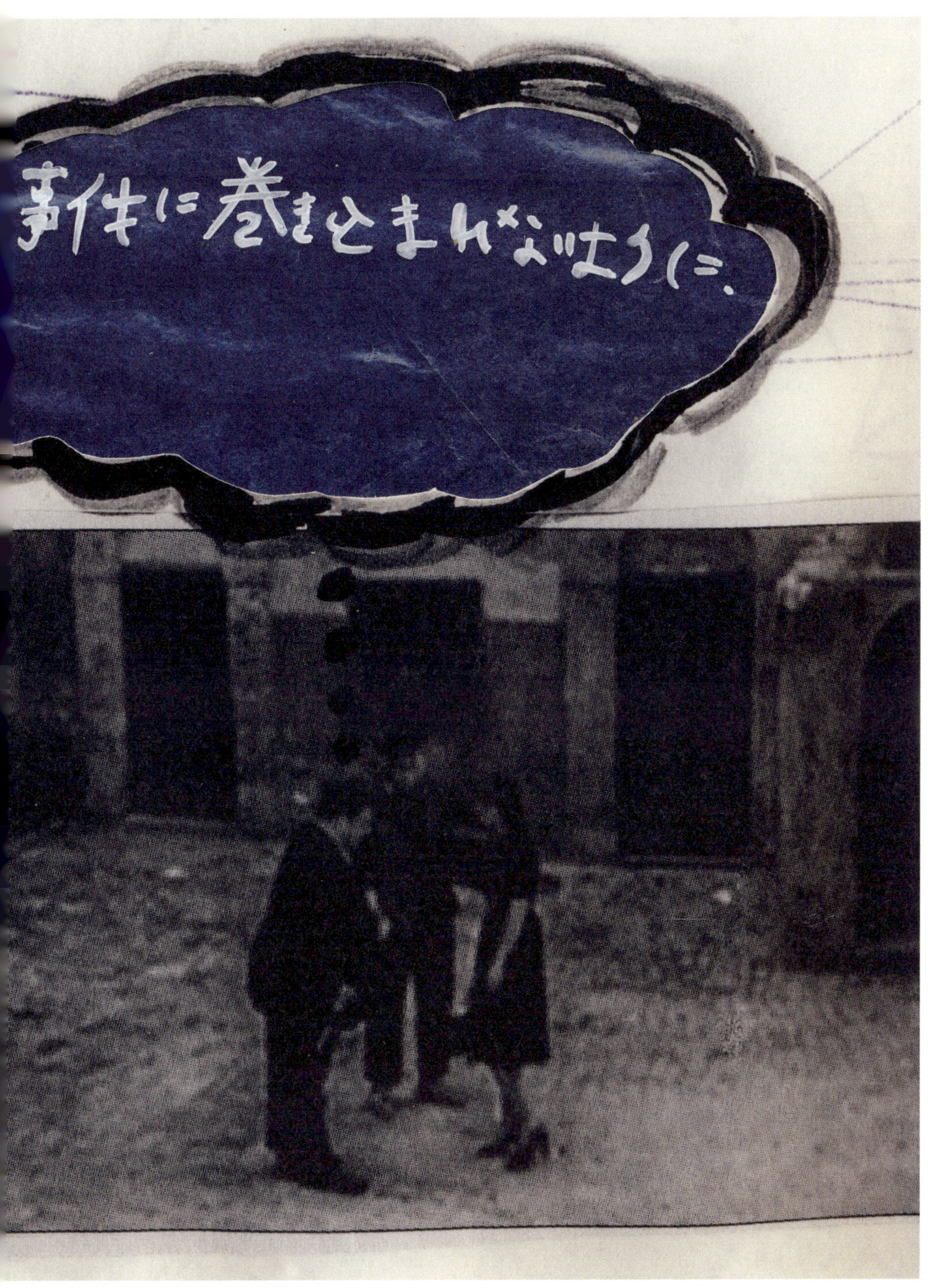
事件に巻きこまれないように。

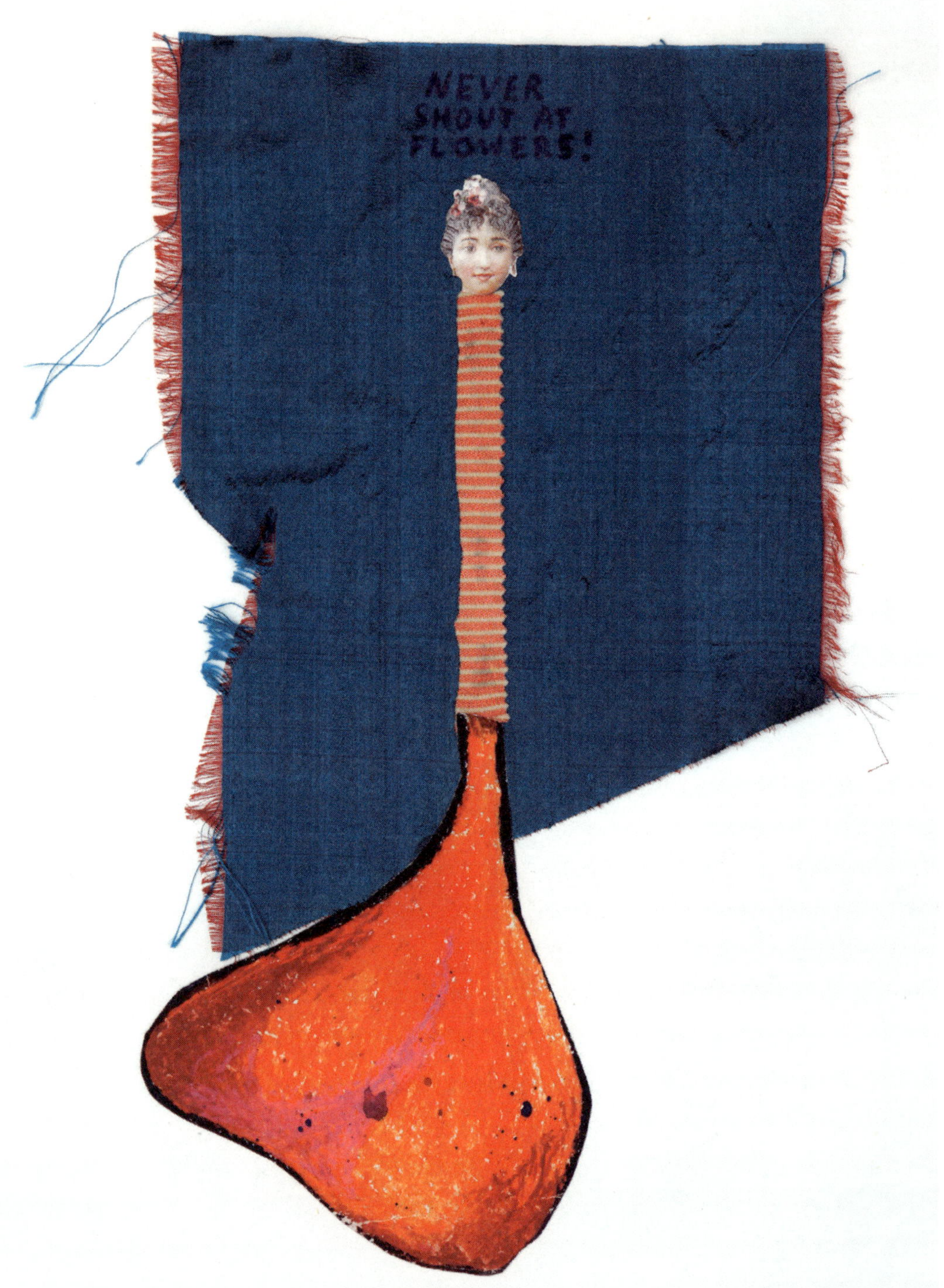

NEVER
SHOUT AT
FLOWERS!

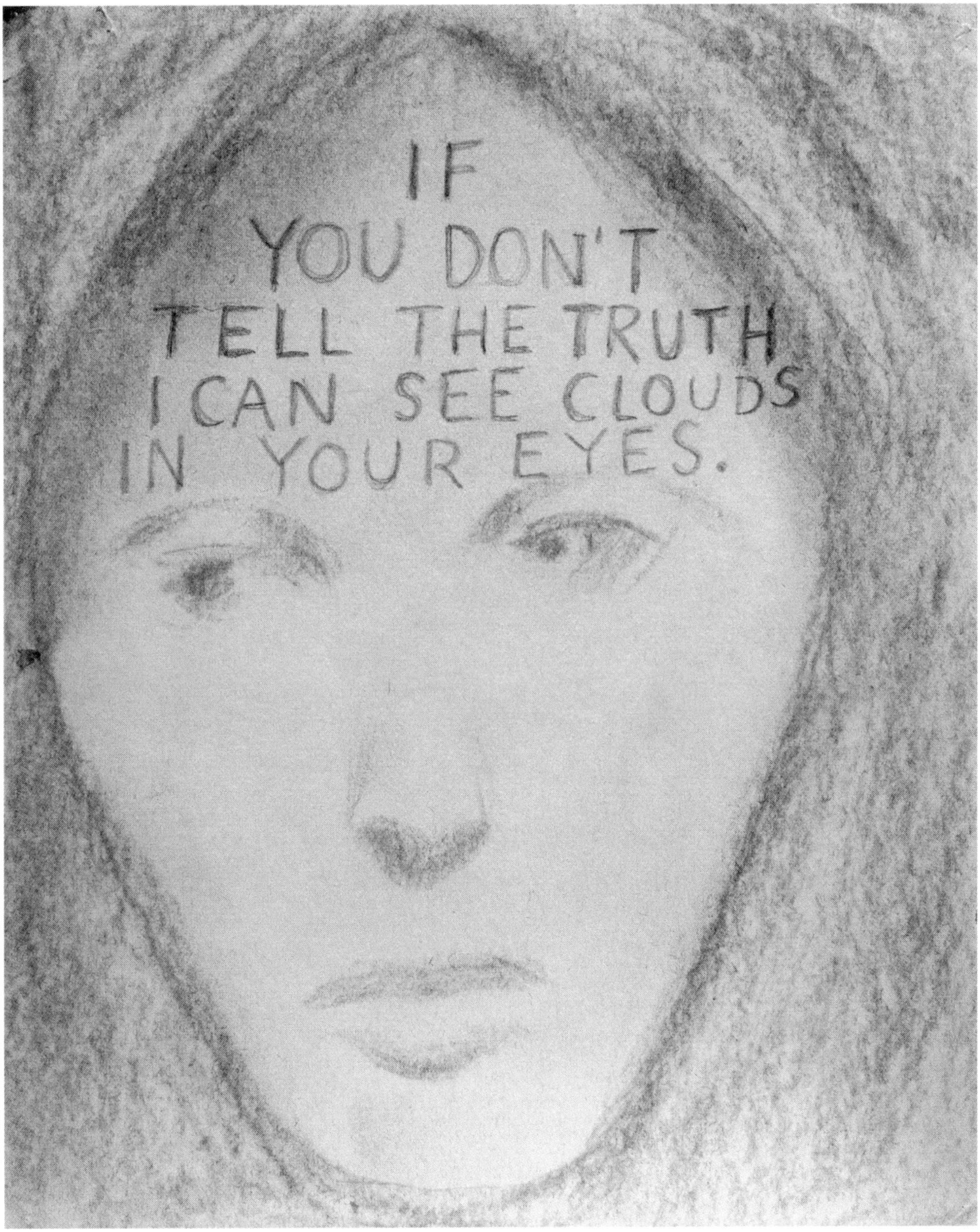

IF
YOU DON'T
TELL THE TRUTH
I CAN SEE CLOUDS
IN YOUR EYES.

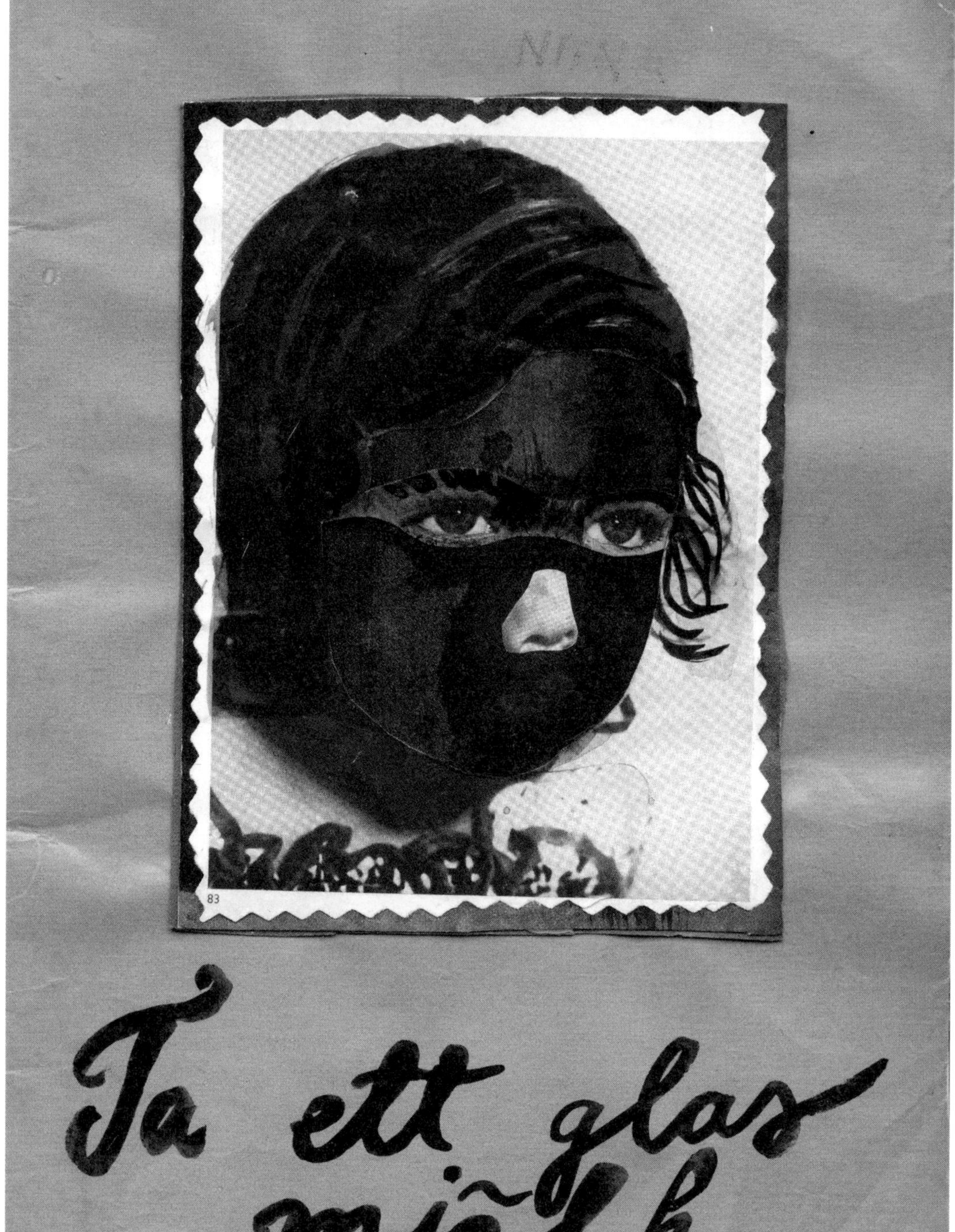

Take a glass of milk.

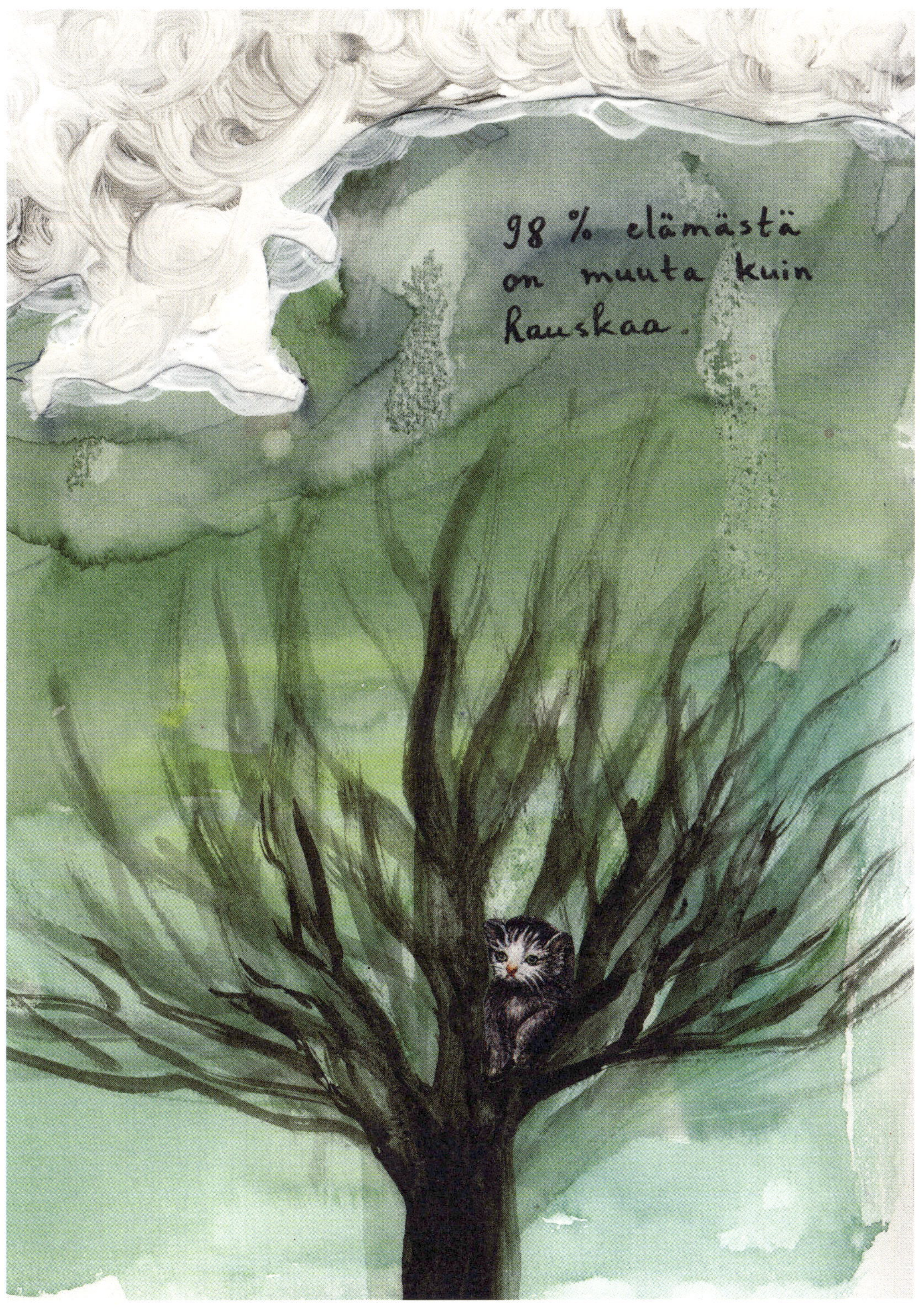

98% of life is something other than fun.

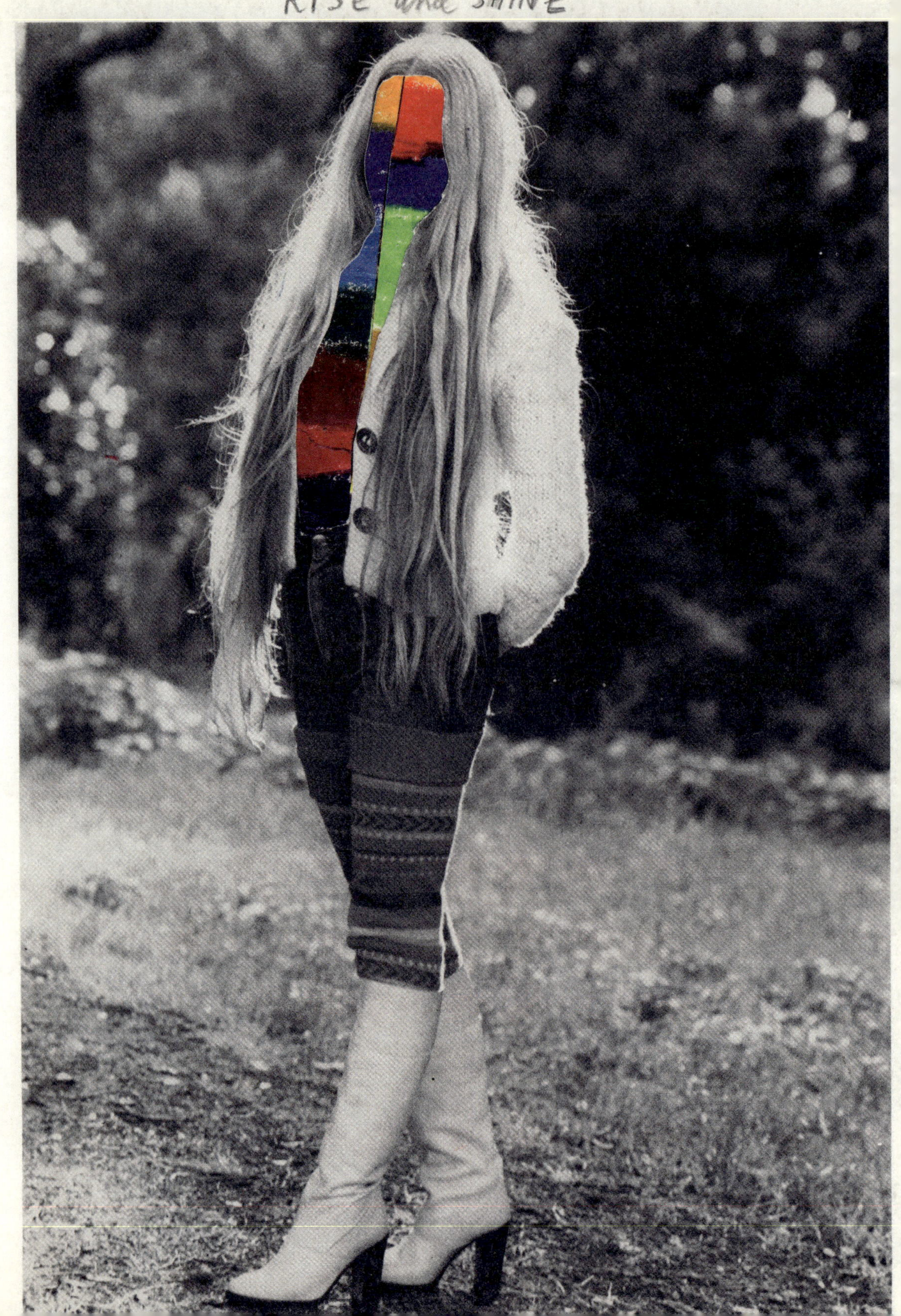

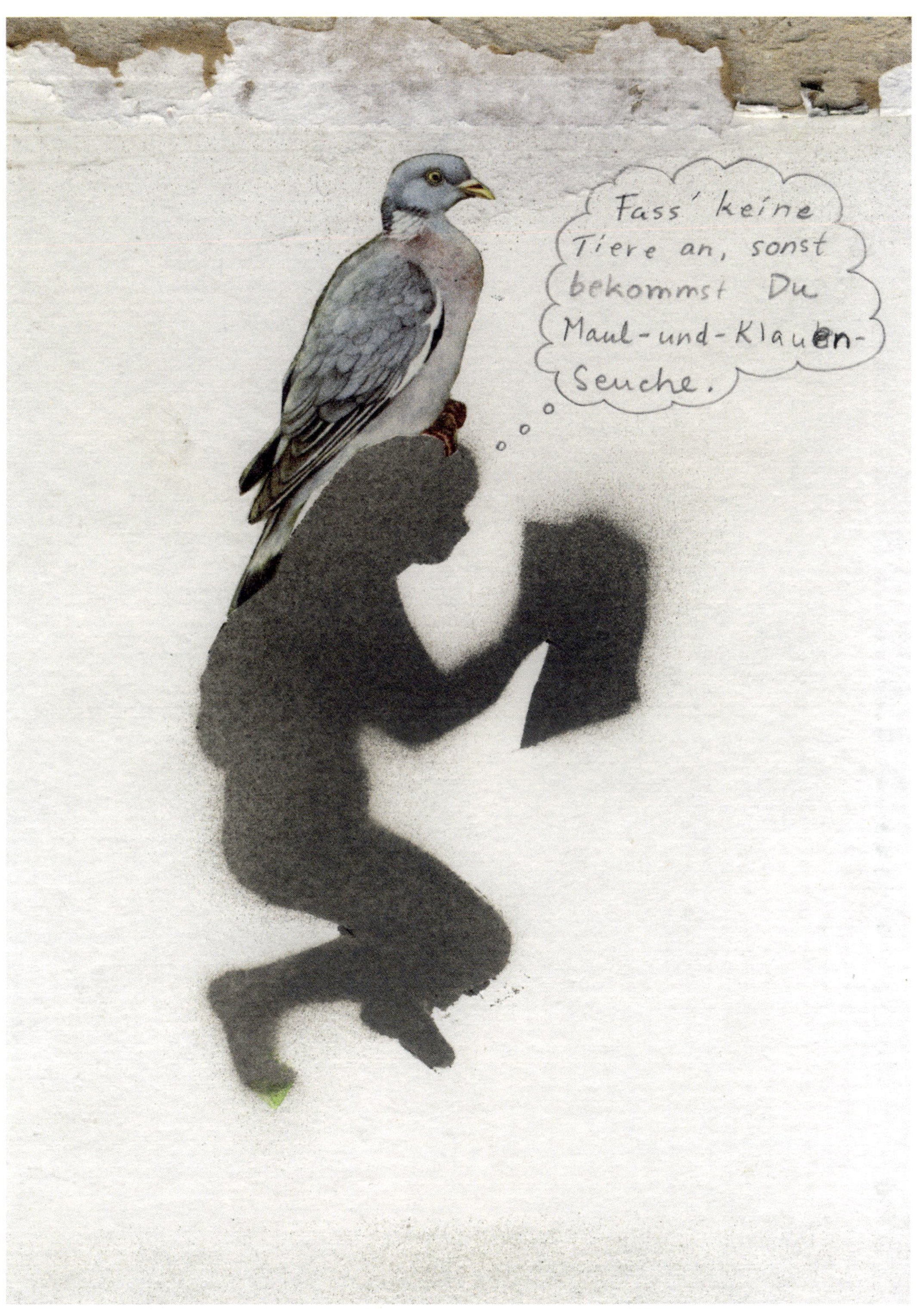

Beware: touching the animals may cause foot-and-mouth disease!

A small problem between your
ears is often big enough.

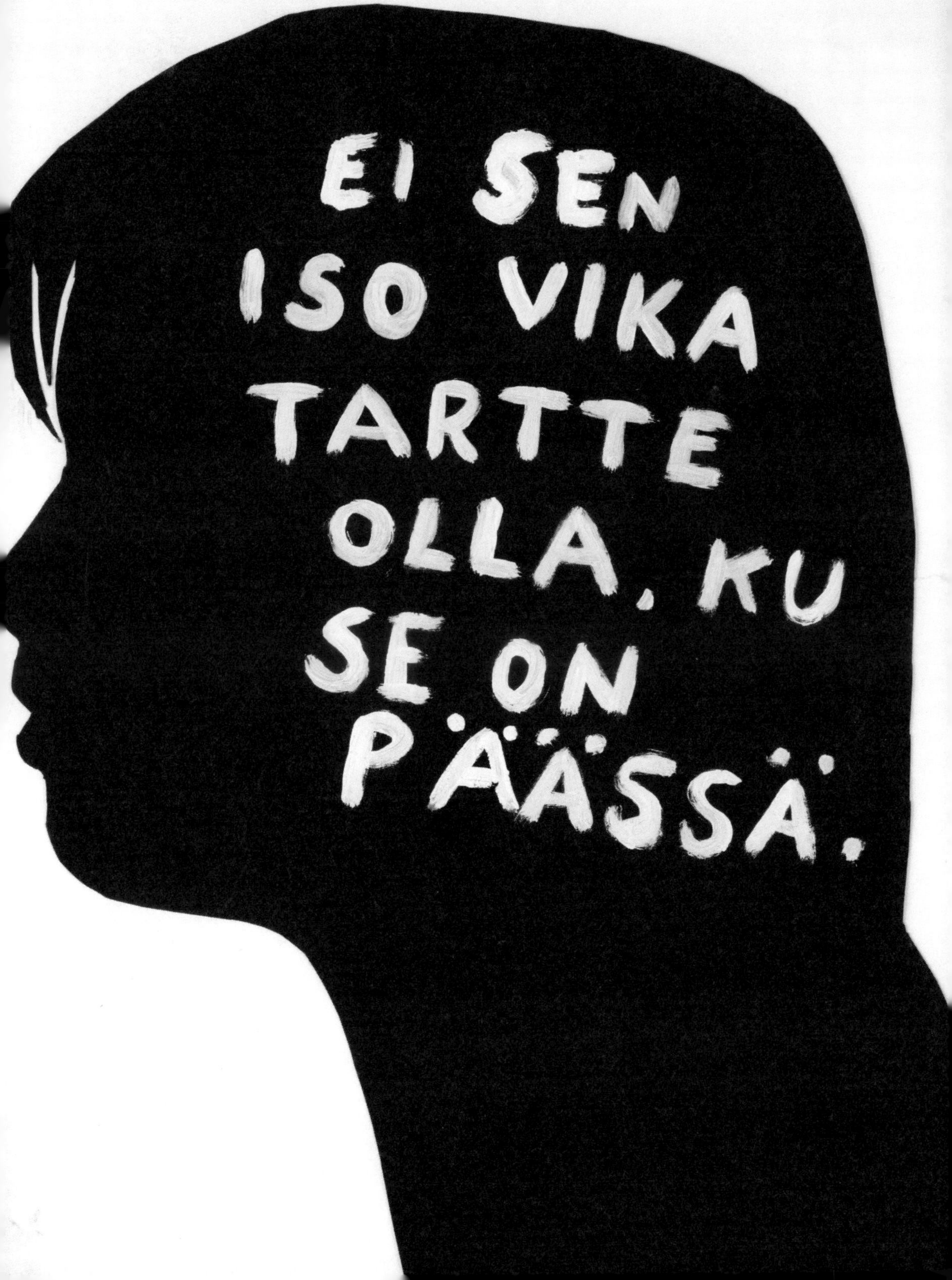

EI SEN
ISO VIKA
TARTTE
OLLA, KU
SE ON
PÄÄSSÄ.

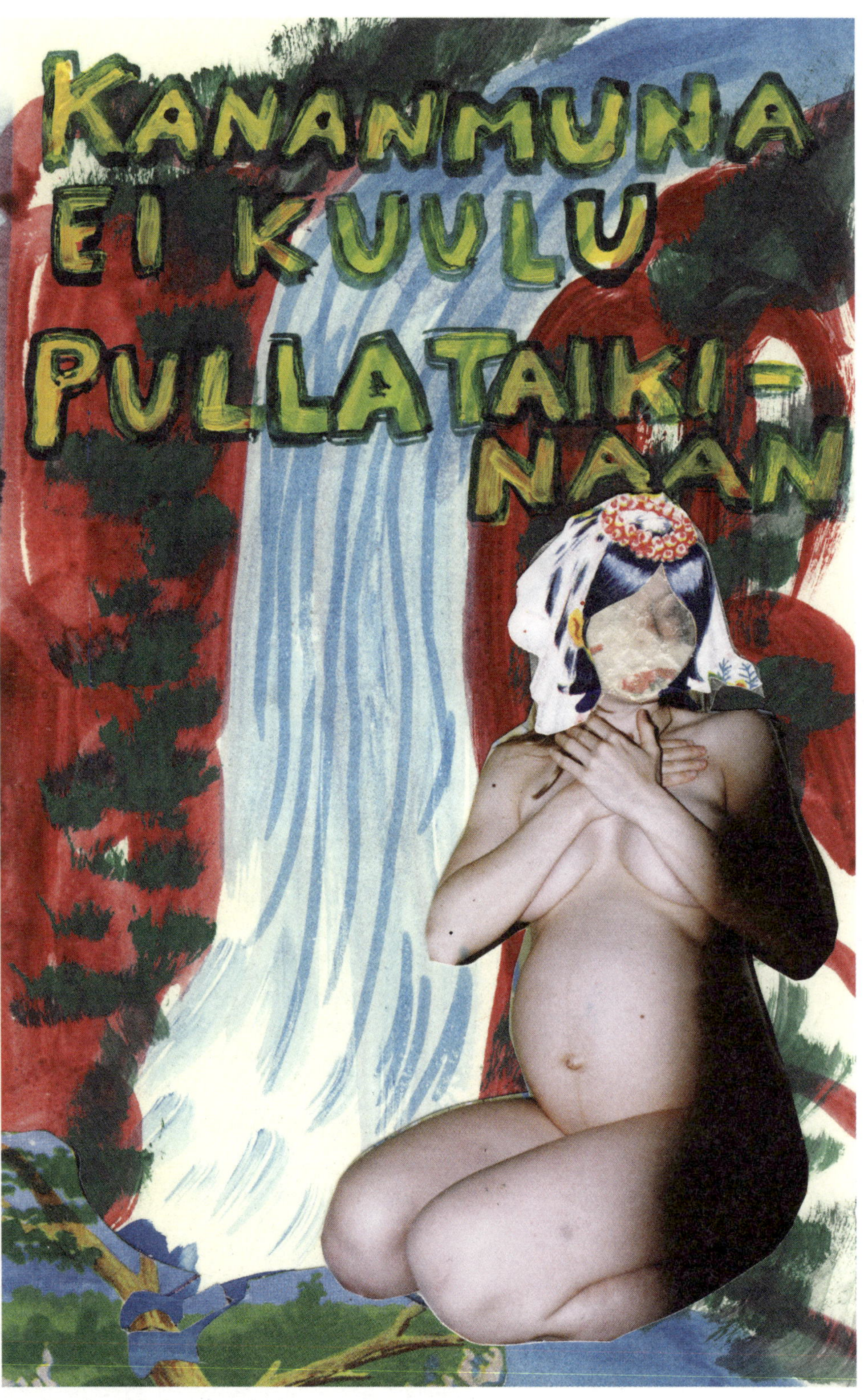

KANANMUNA
EI KUULU
PULLATAIKI-
NAAN

No eggs in a
yeast dough.

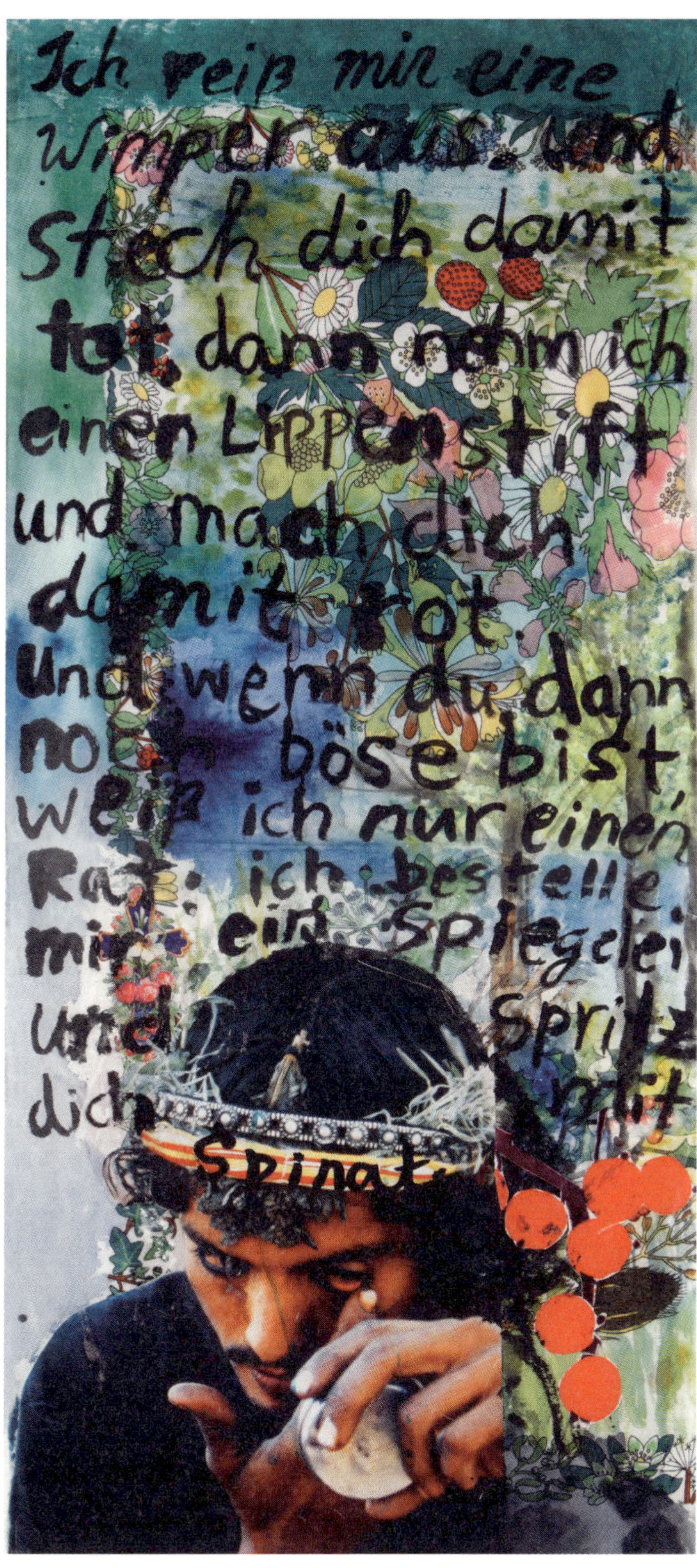
Ich reiß mir eine
Wimper aus und
stech dich damit
tot, dann nehm ich
einen Lippenstift
und mach dich
damit rot.
Und wenn du dann
noch böse bist,
weiß ich nur einen
Rat: ich bestelle
mir ein Spiegelei
und spritz
dich voll mit
Spinat.

I'll rip out an eyelash
and stab you to death
Then I'll take out my lipstick
and paint you all red
And if by that time you
are still being bad
I'll fry eggs and spinach
and scold you with fat

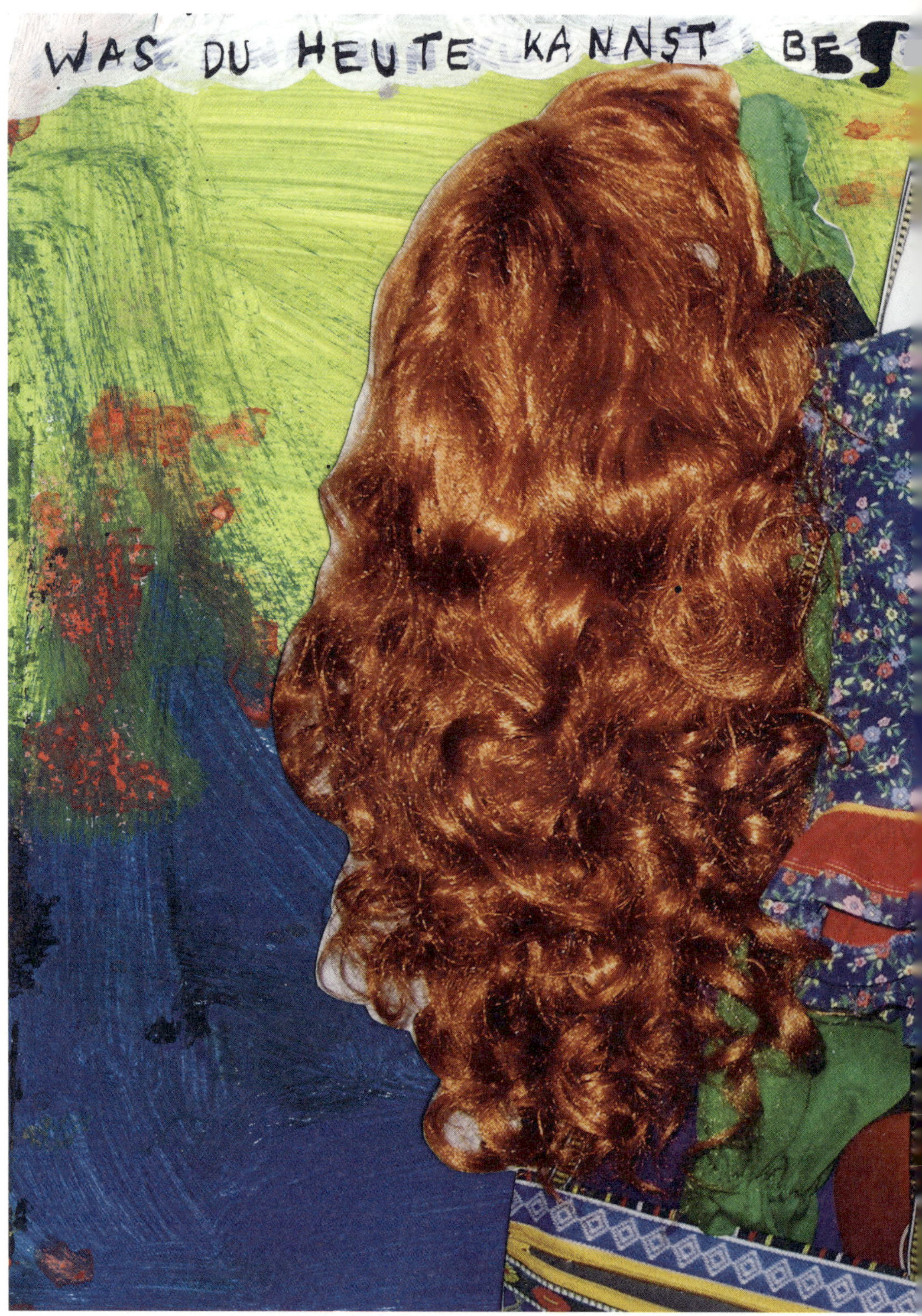

There's no time like the present!

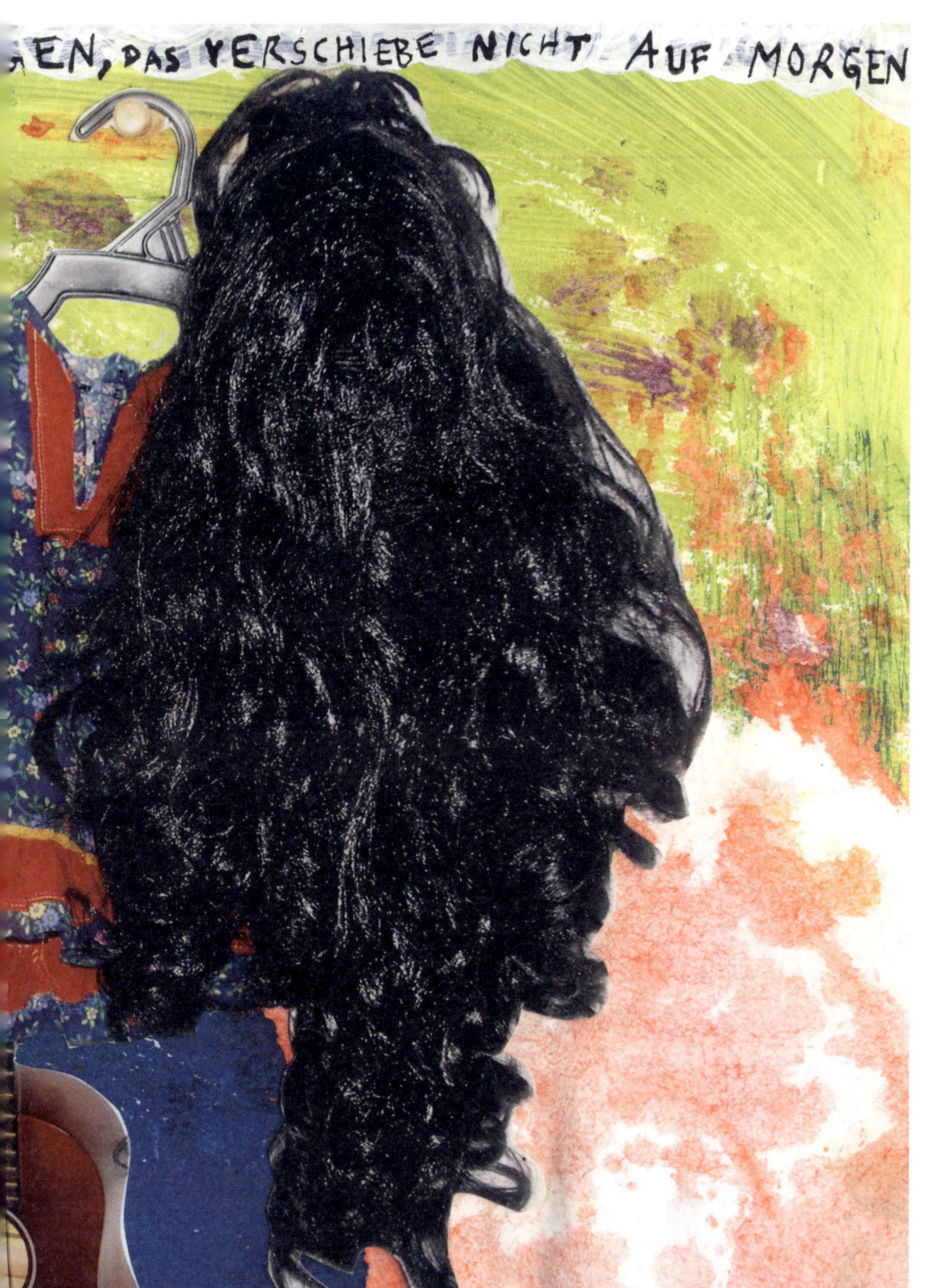
ÄEN, DAS VERSCHIEBE NICHT AUF MORGEN

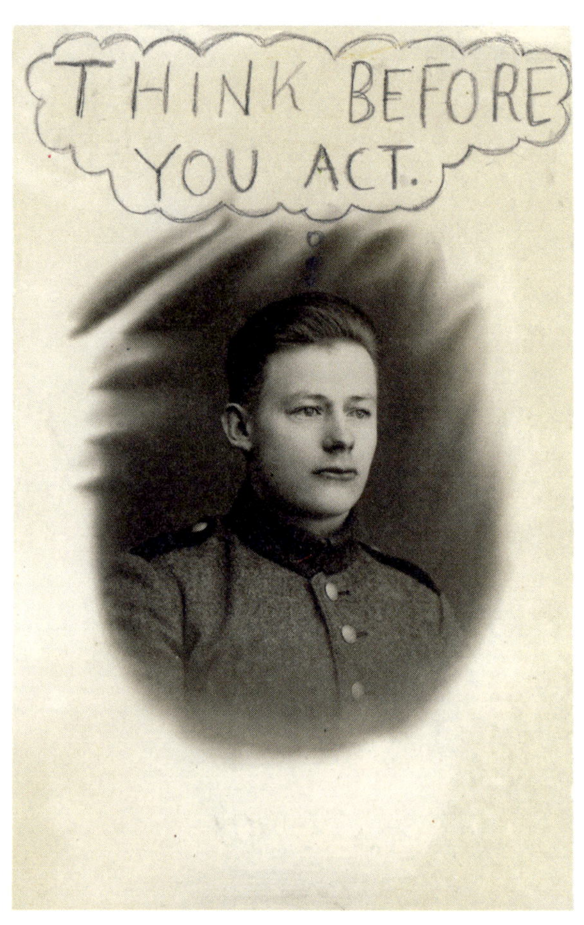
THINK BEFORE YOU ACT.

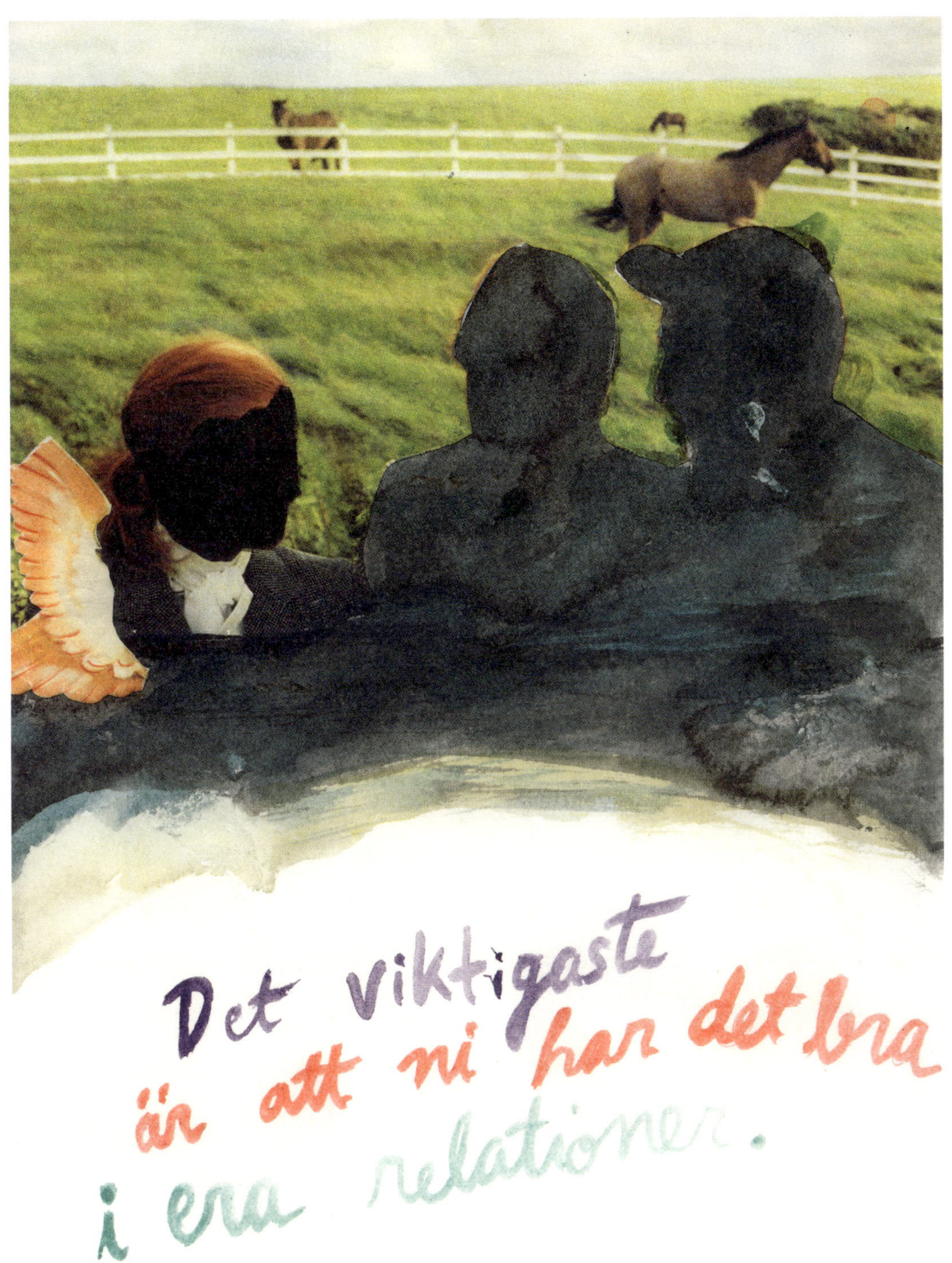

The most important thing is that your relationships are going well.

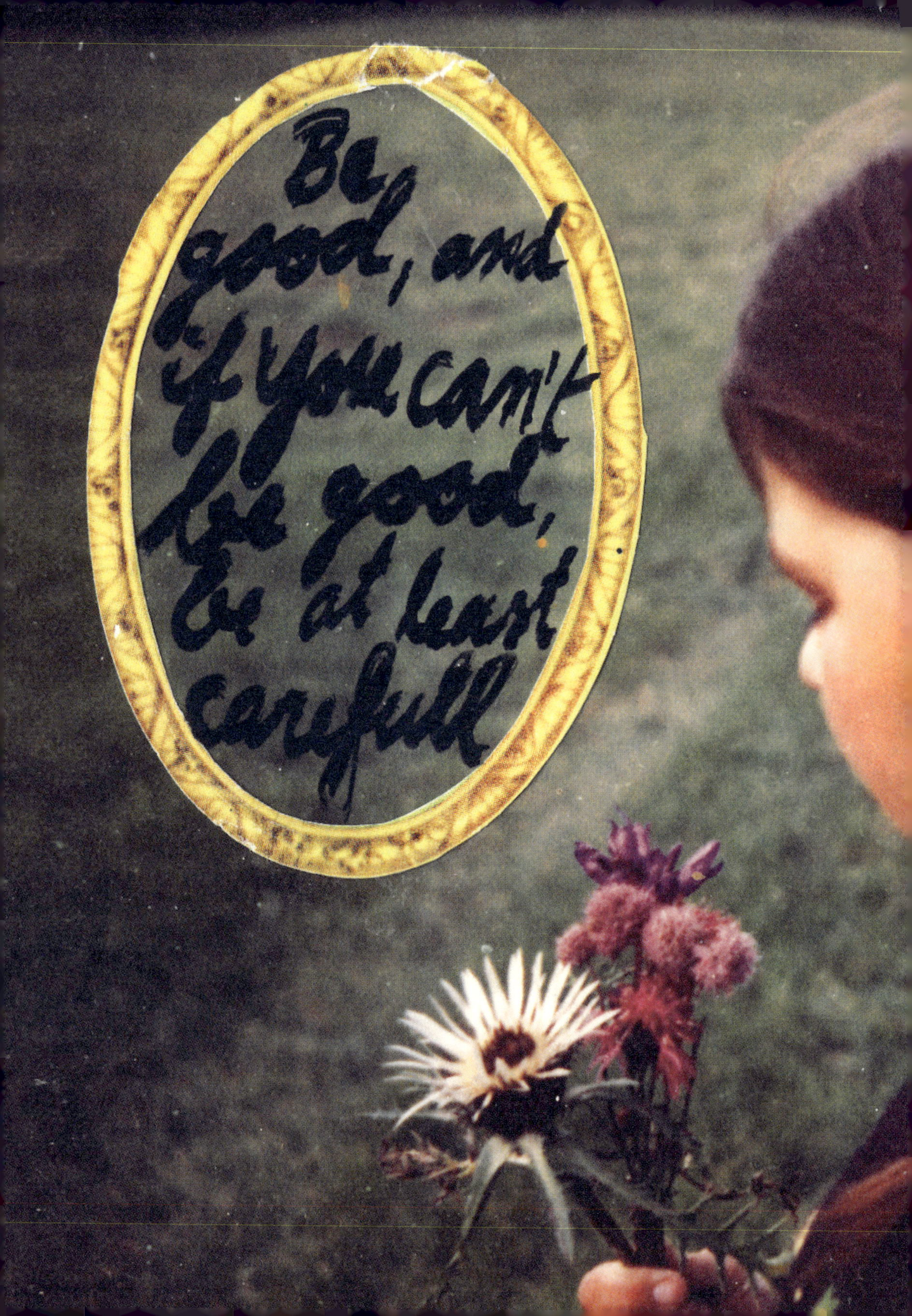

Be
good, and
if you can't
be good,
be at least
carefull

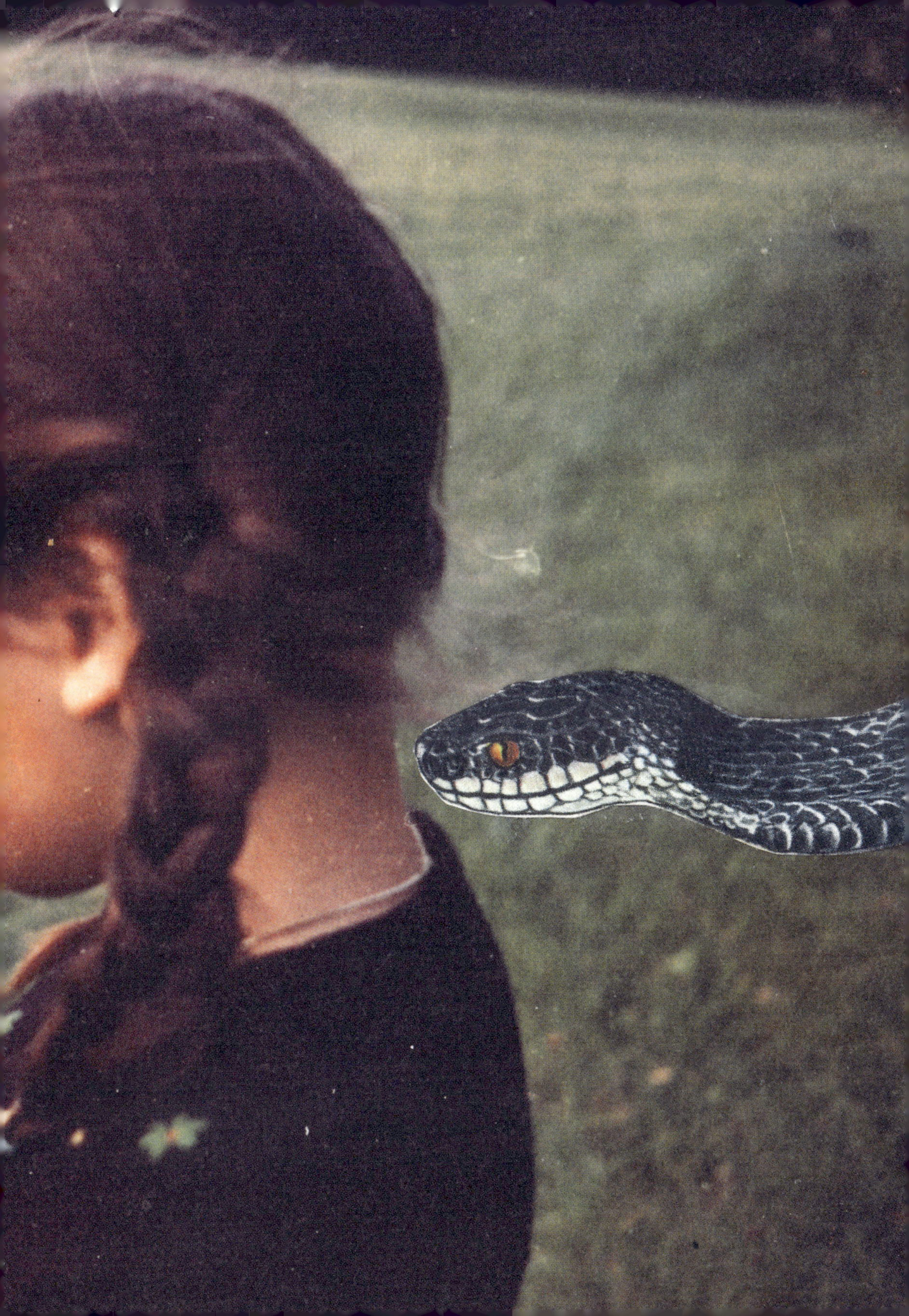

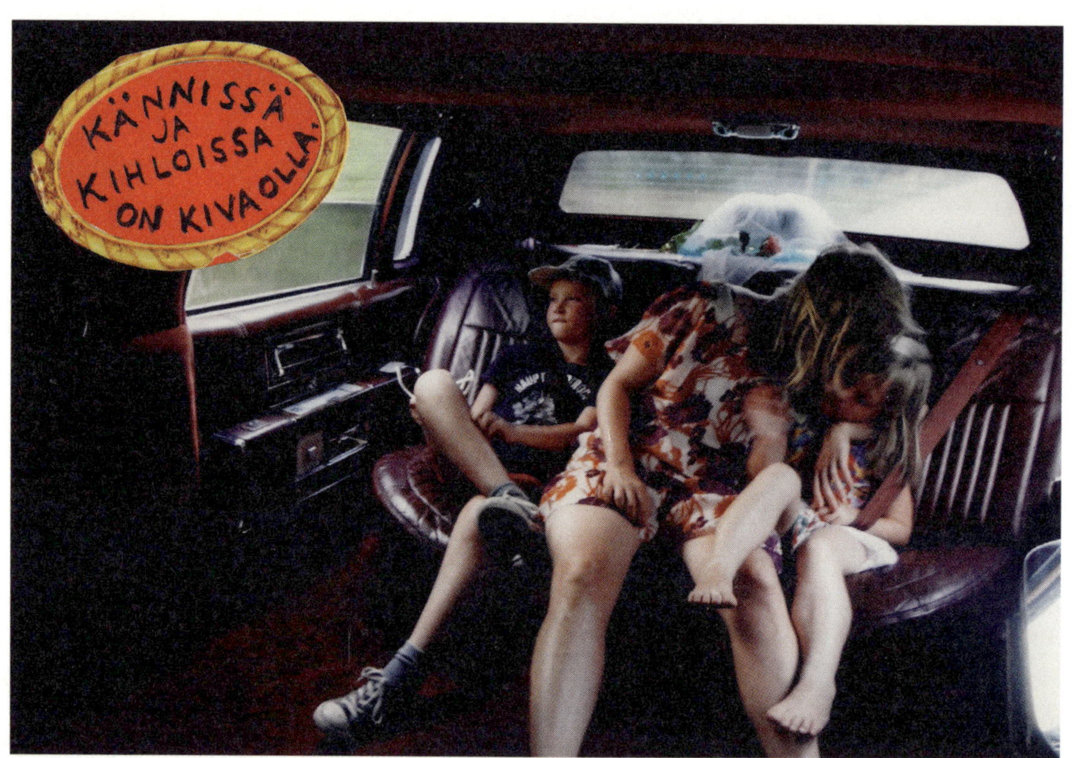

It's fun to be smashed and it's fun to be engaged.

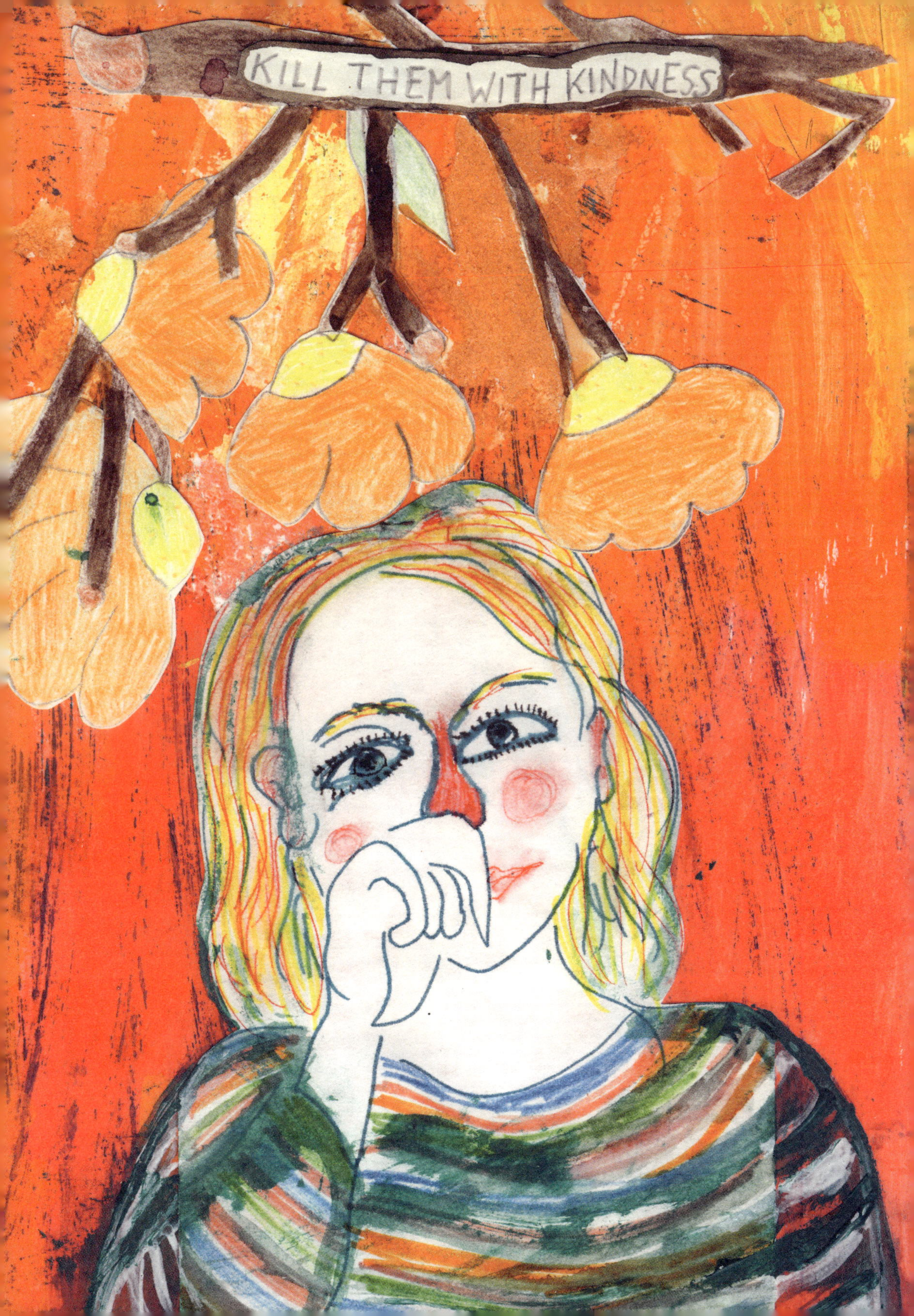
KILL THEM WITH KINDNESS

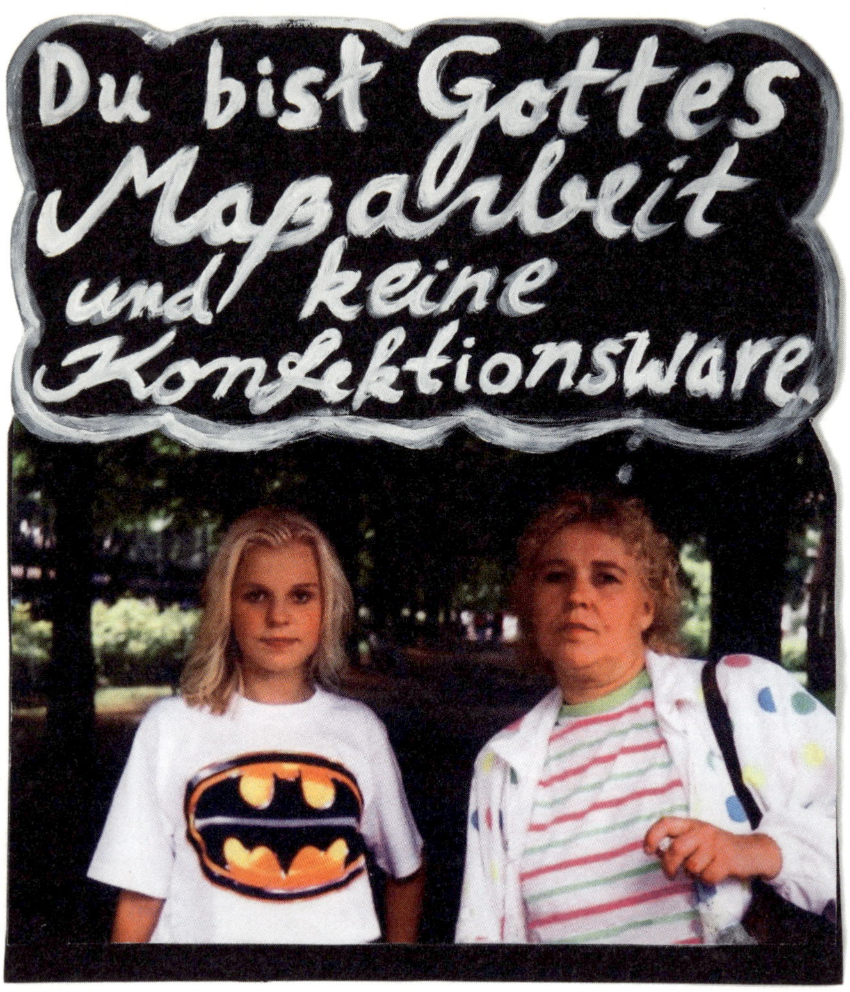

You are God's tailored work, not ready-to-wear.

Better be late for an appointment
than late for life.

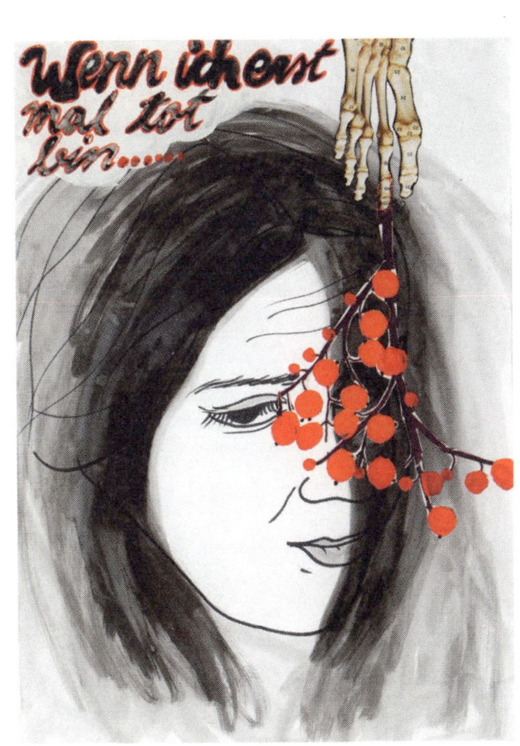

Wenn ich erst mal tot bin......

Once I'm dead...

Parempi myöhästyä sieltä minne on menossa
kuin elämästä!

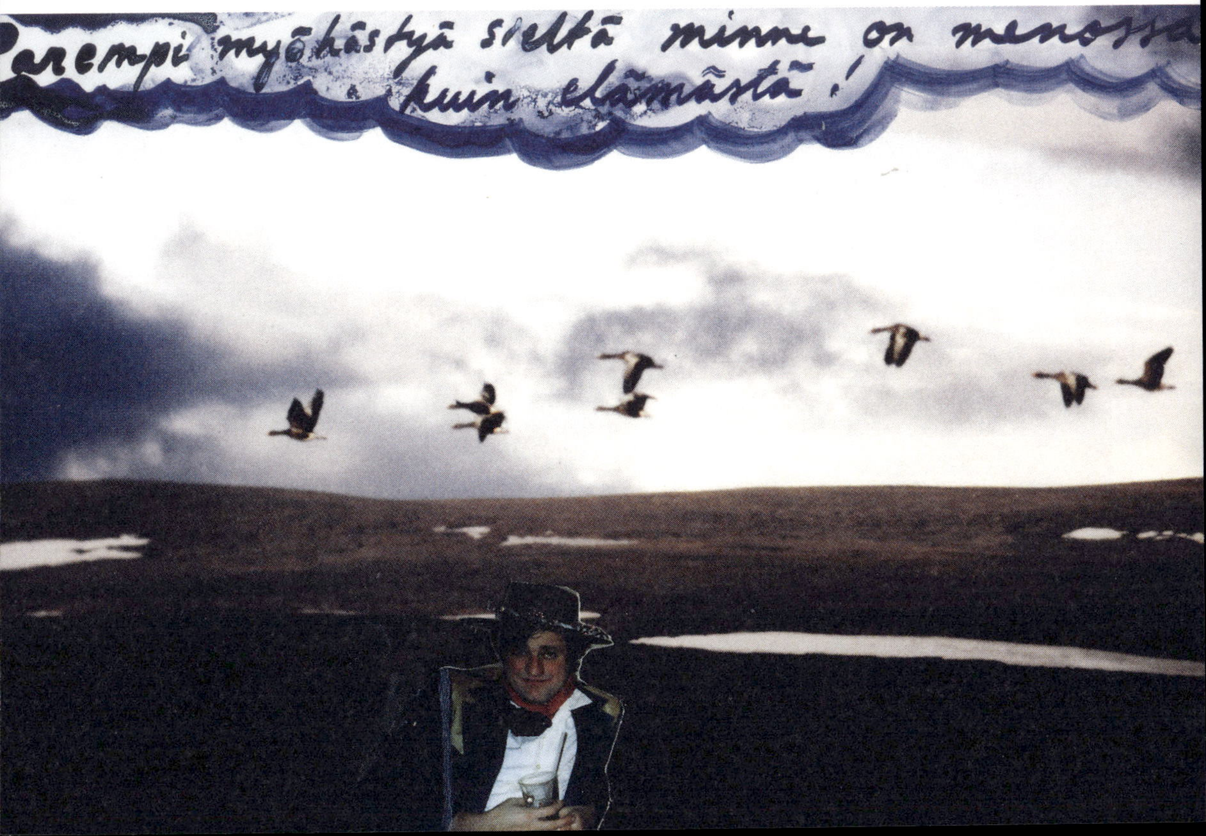

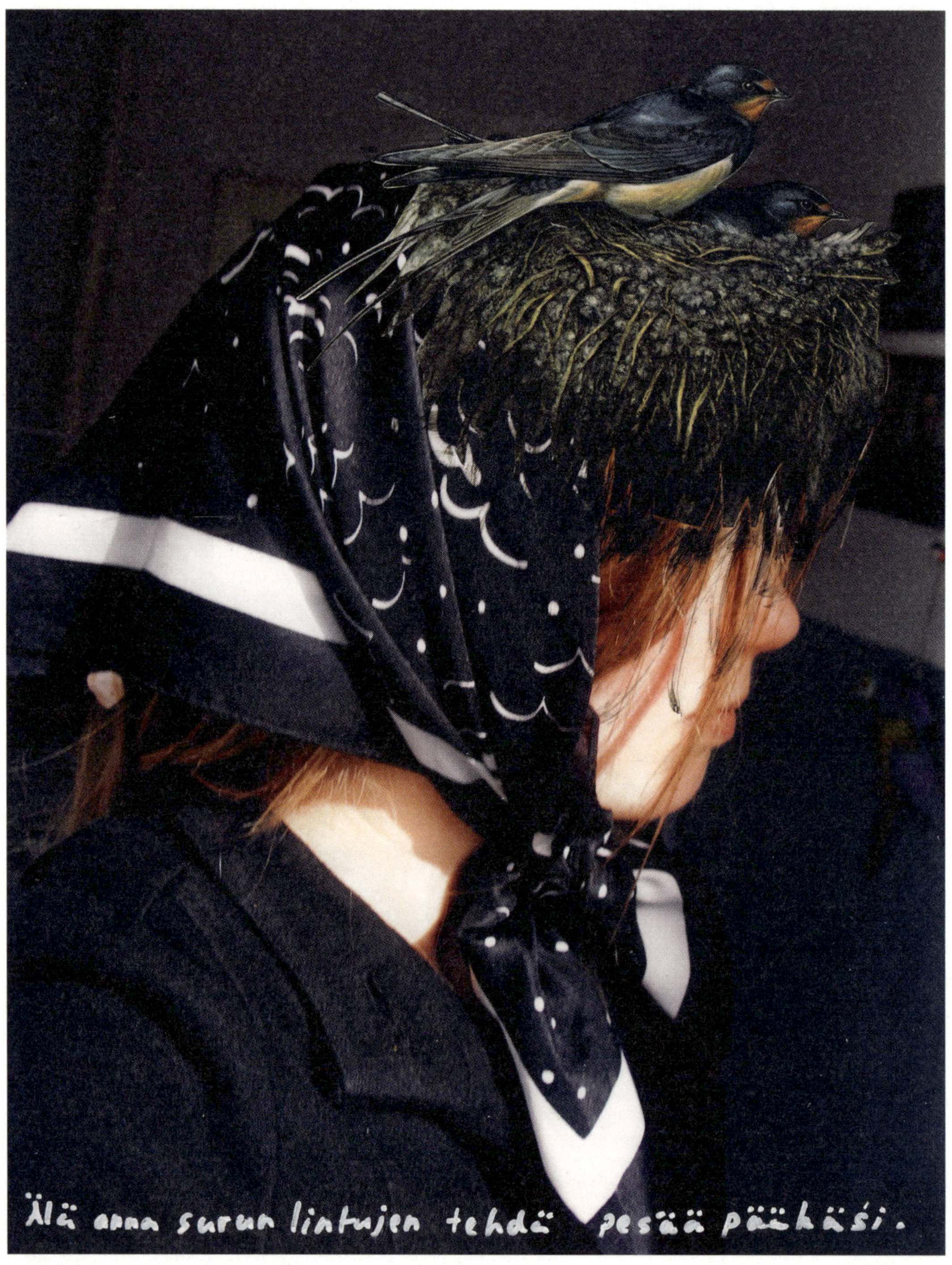

Don't let the birds of sadness nest in your head.

The devil is a little red squirrel.

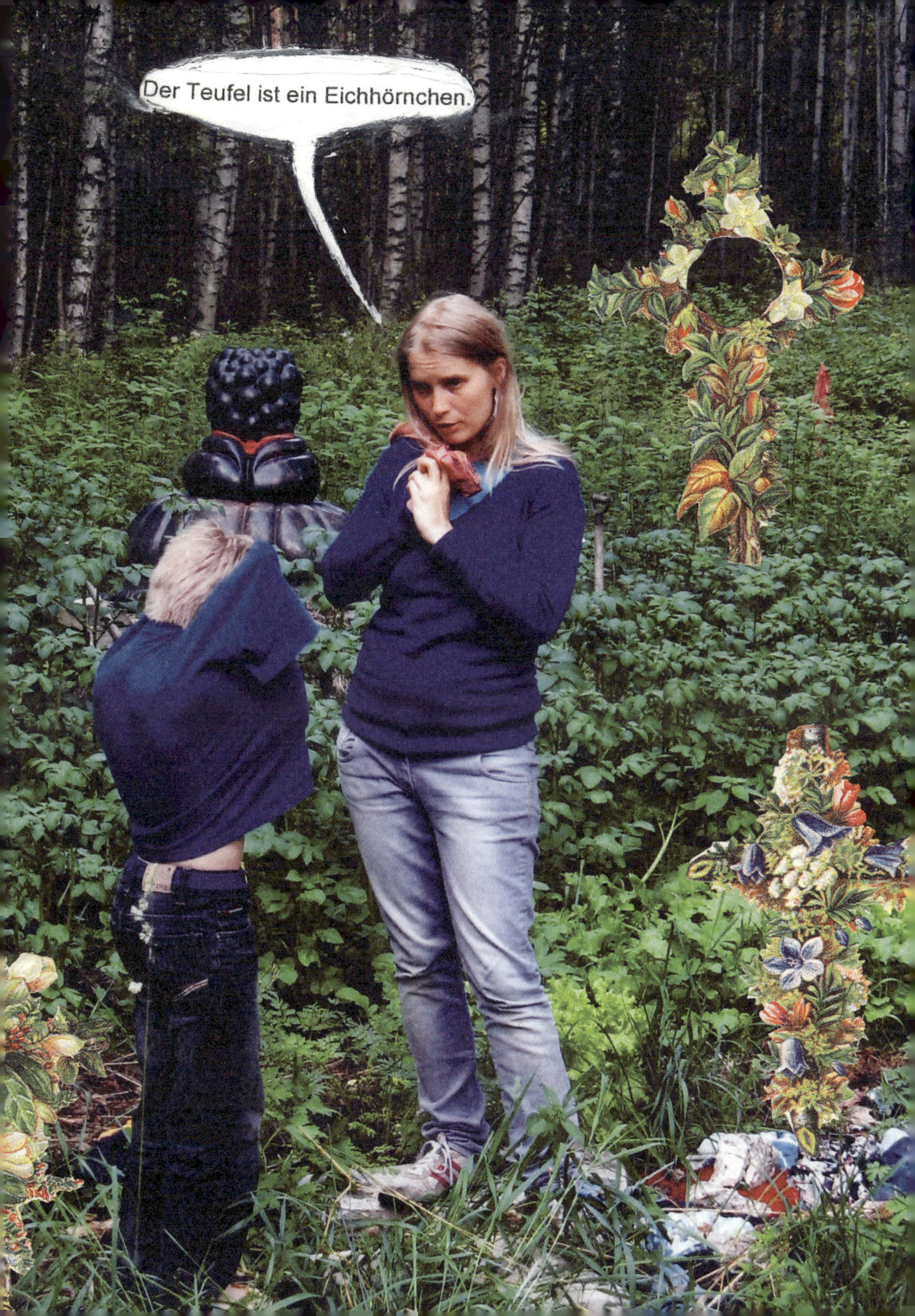

Der Teufel ist ein Eichhörnchen.

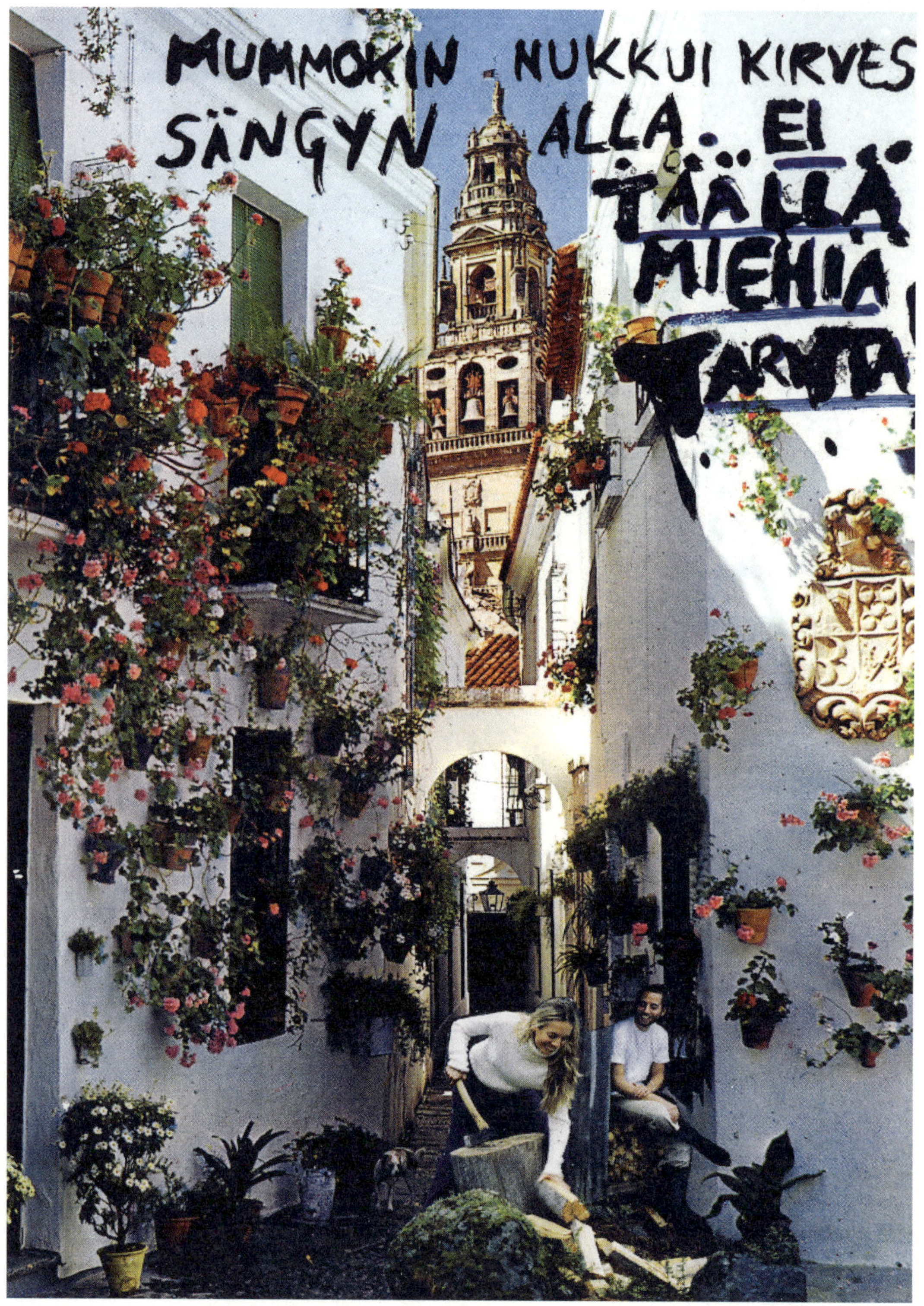

Grandma always slept with an axe under her bed. We don't need any men here.

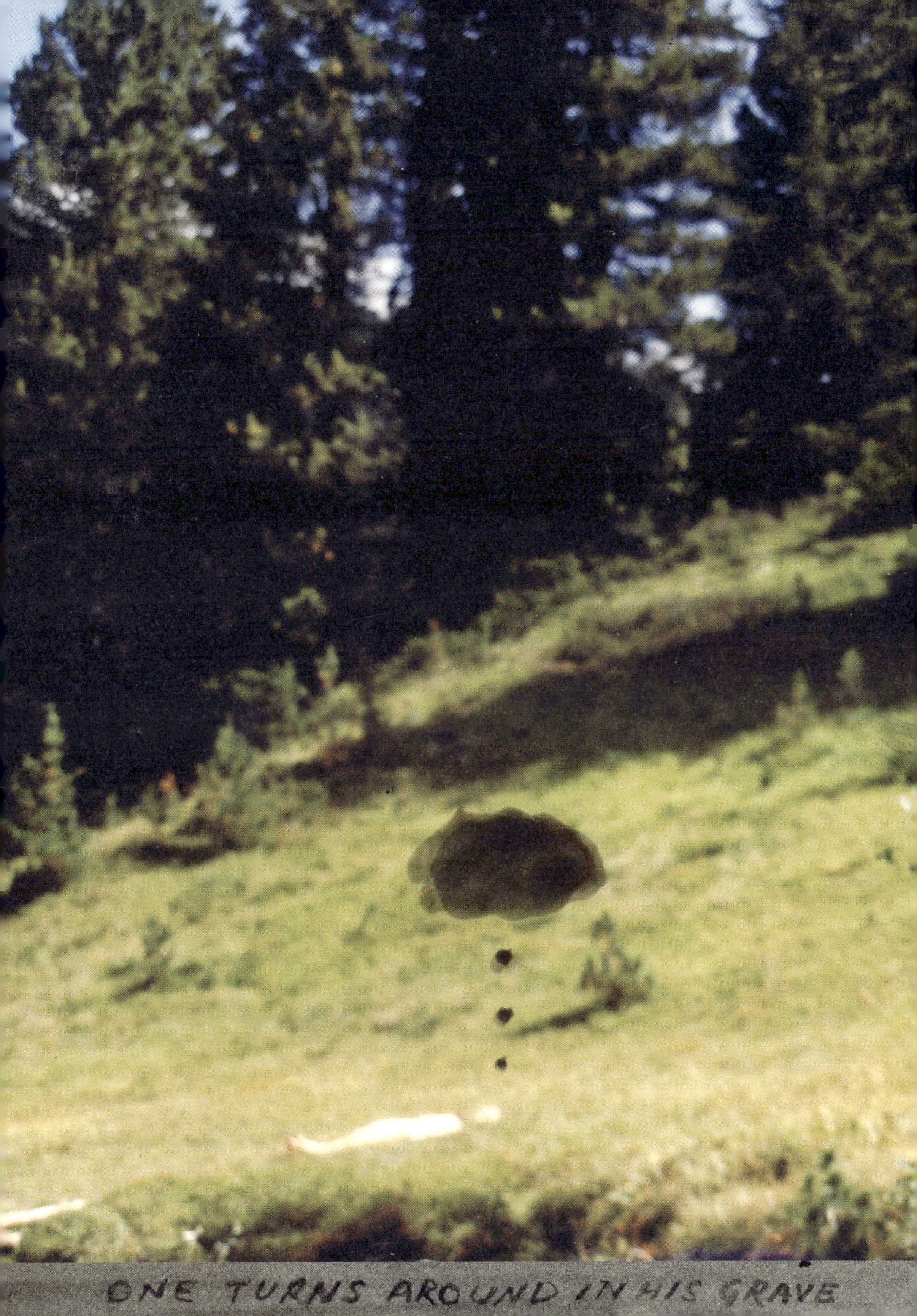
ONE TURNS AROUND IN HIS GRAVE

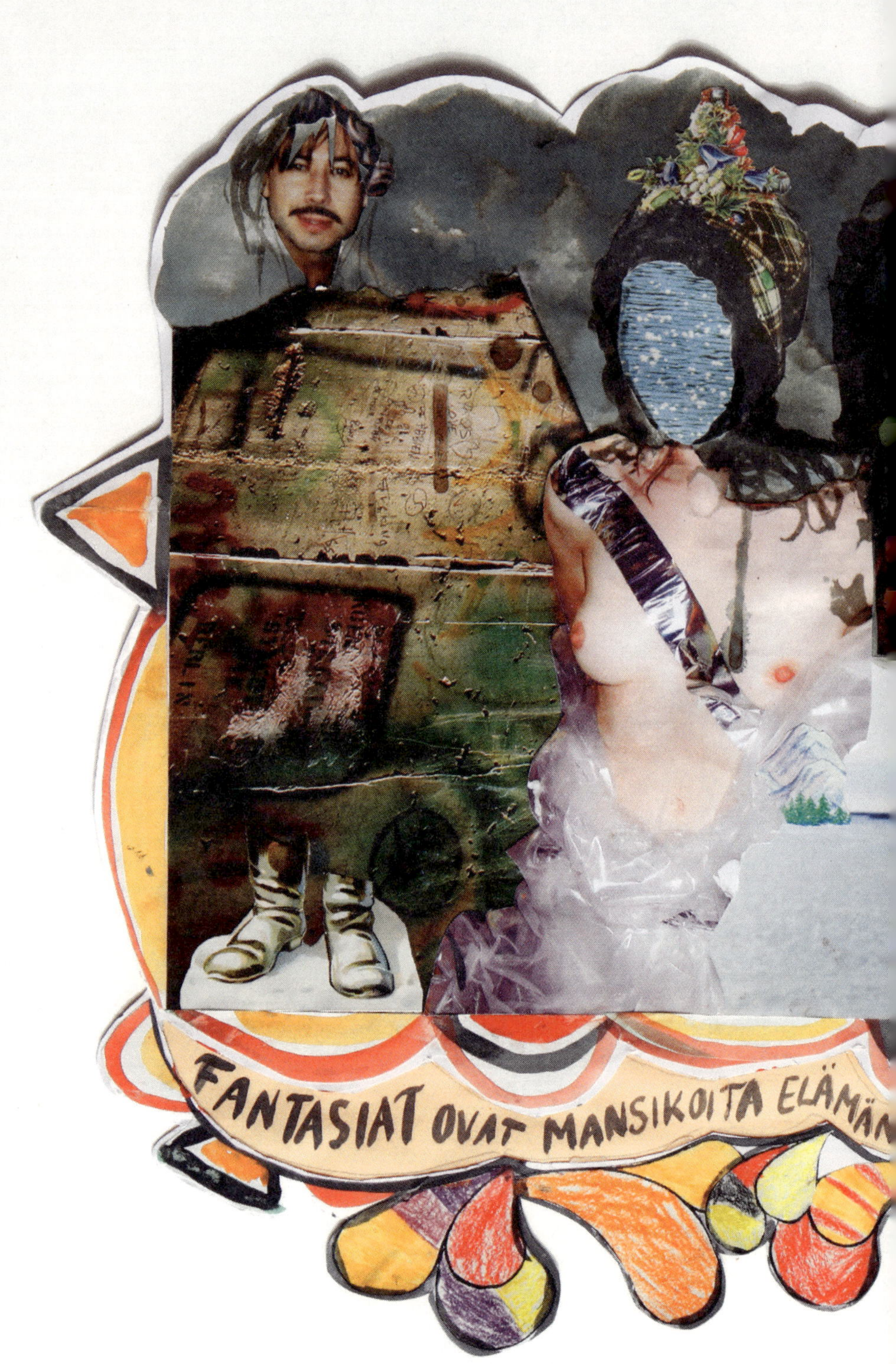
FANTASIAT OVAT MANSIKOITA ELÄMÄ

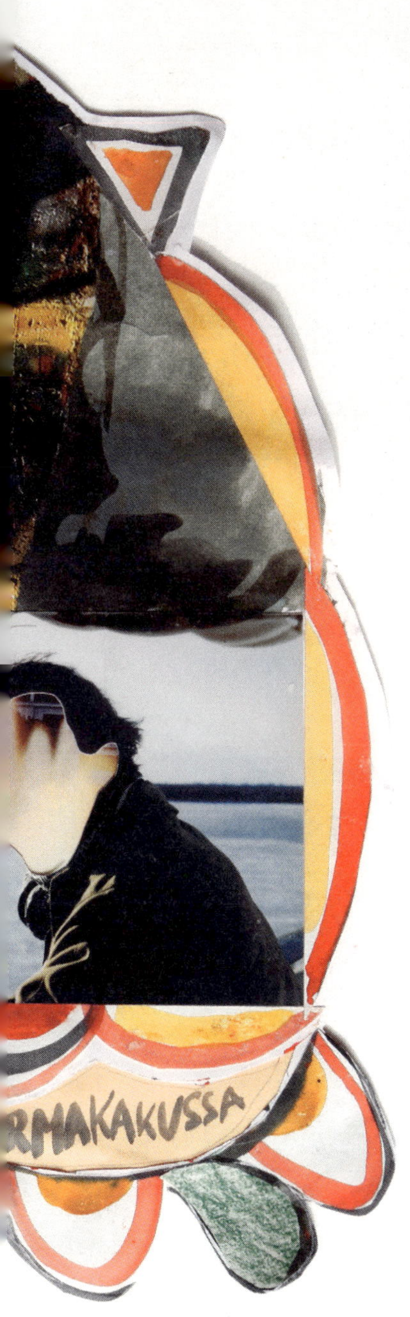

Fantasies are the strawberries in life's cream cake.

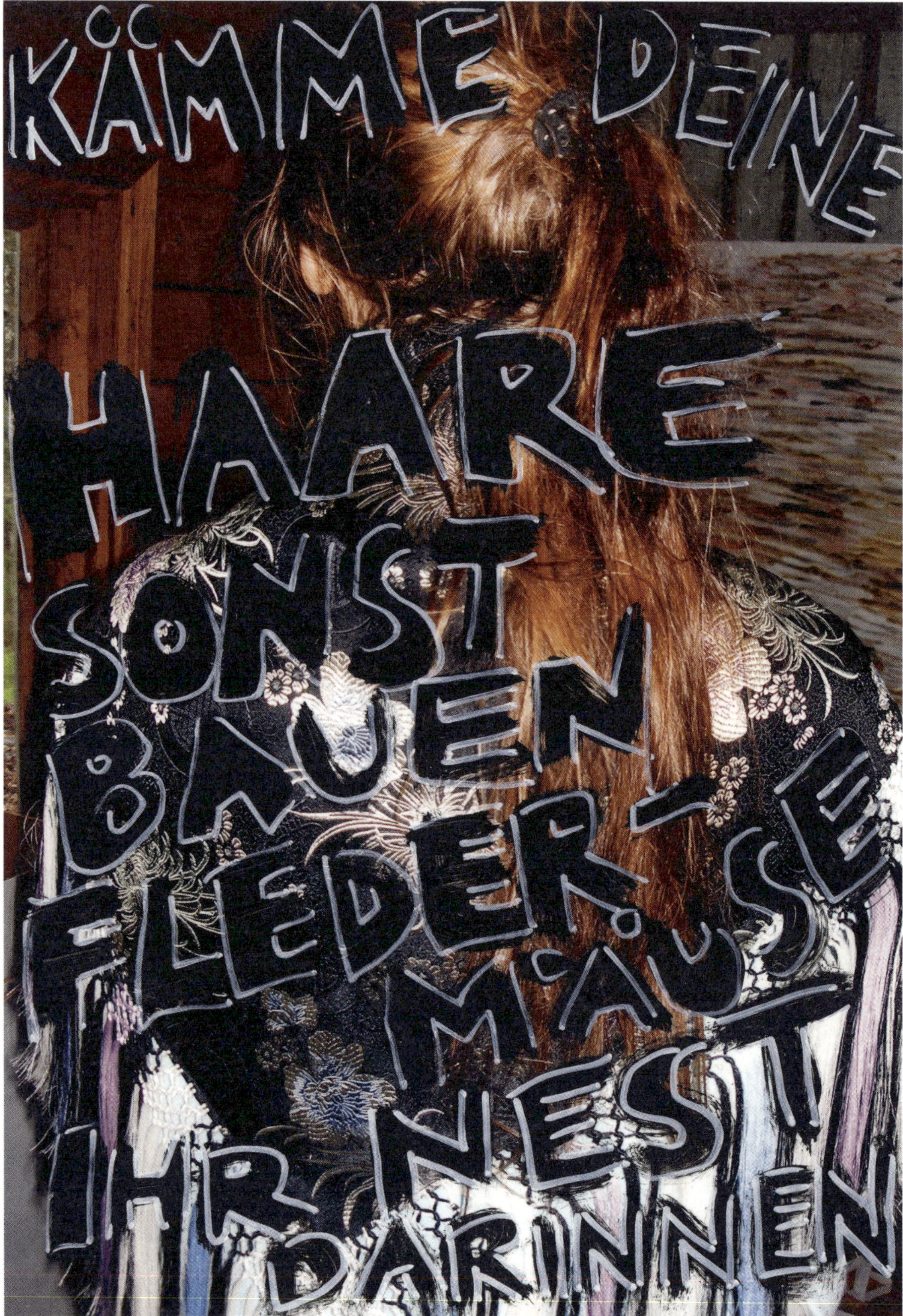
KÄMME DEINE
HAARE
SONST
BAUEN
FLEDER-
MÄUSE
IHR NEST
DARINNEN

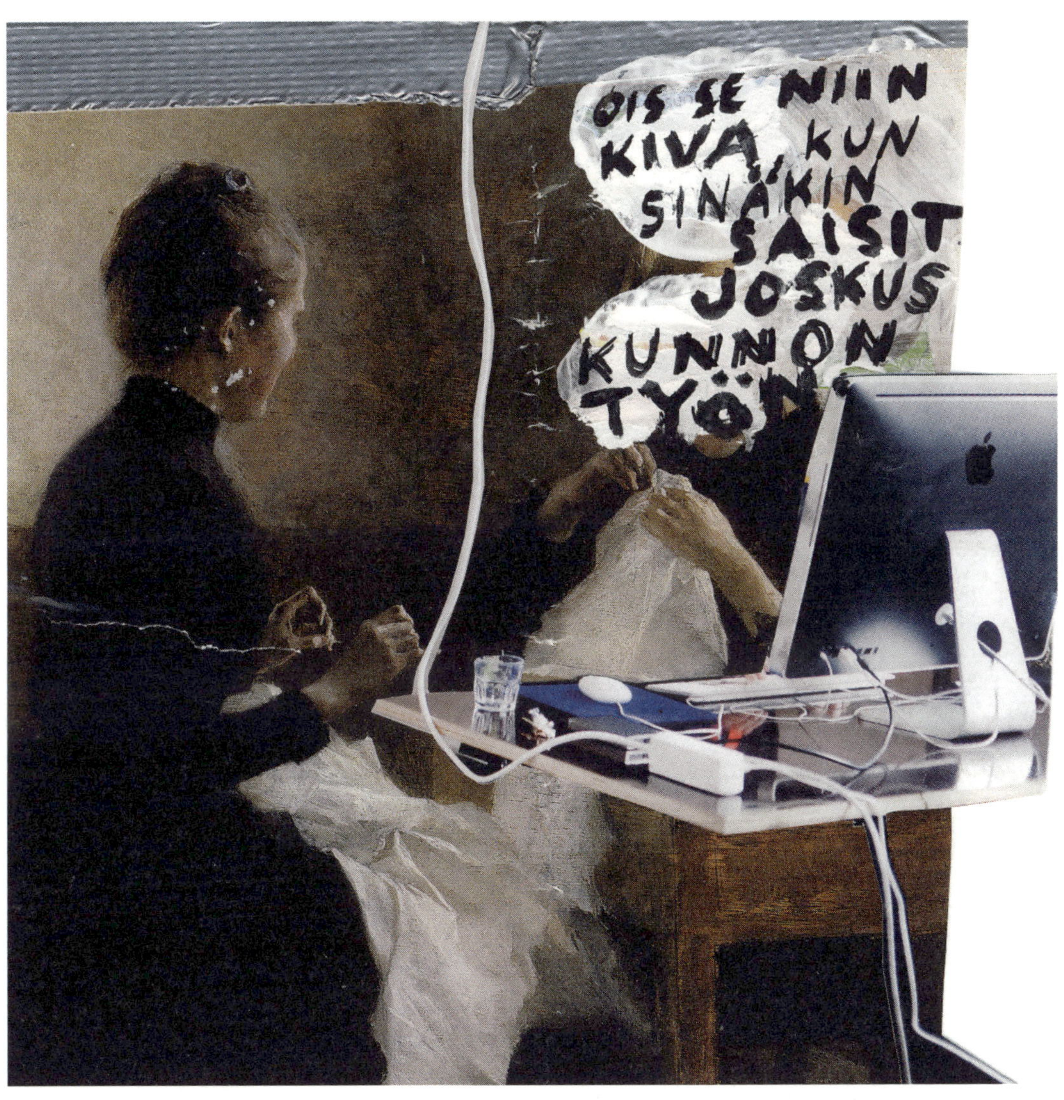

It would be nice if one day
you could get a proper job.

If you don't comb your hair,
bats will start nesting in it.

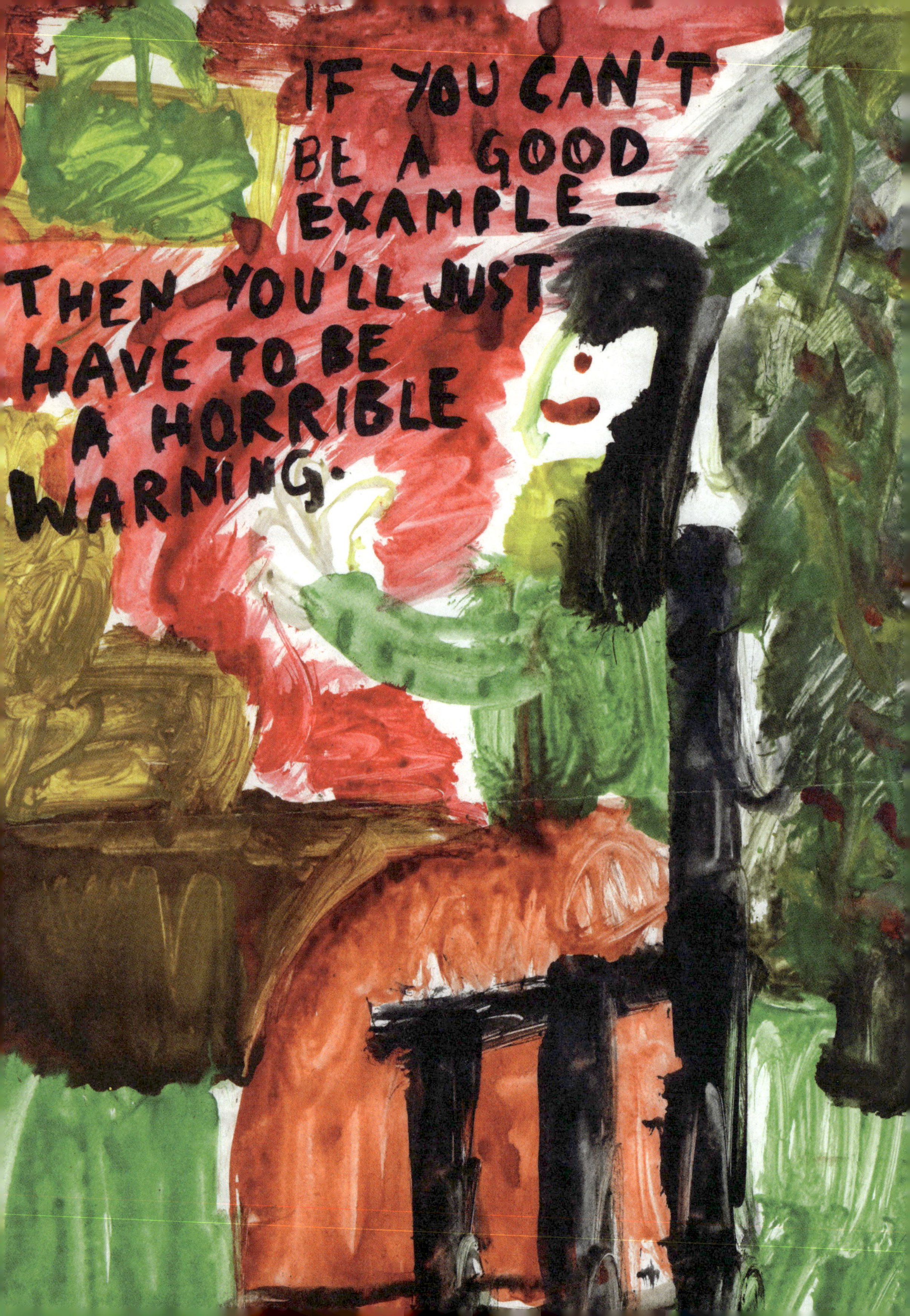

IF YOU CAN'T
BE A GOOD
EXAMPLE —
THEN YOU'LL JUST
HAVE TO BE
A HORRIBLE
WARNING.

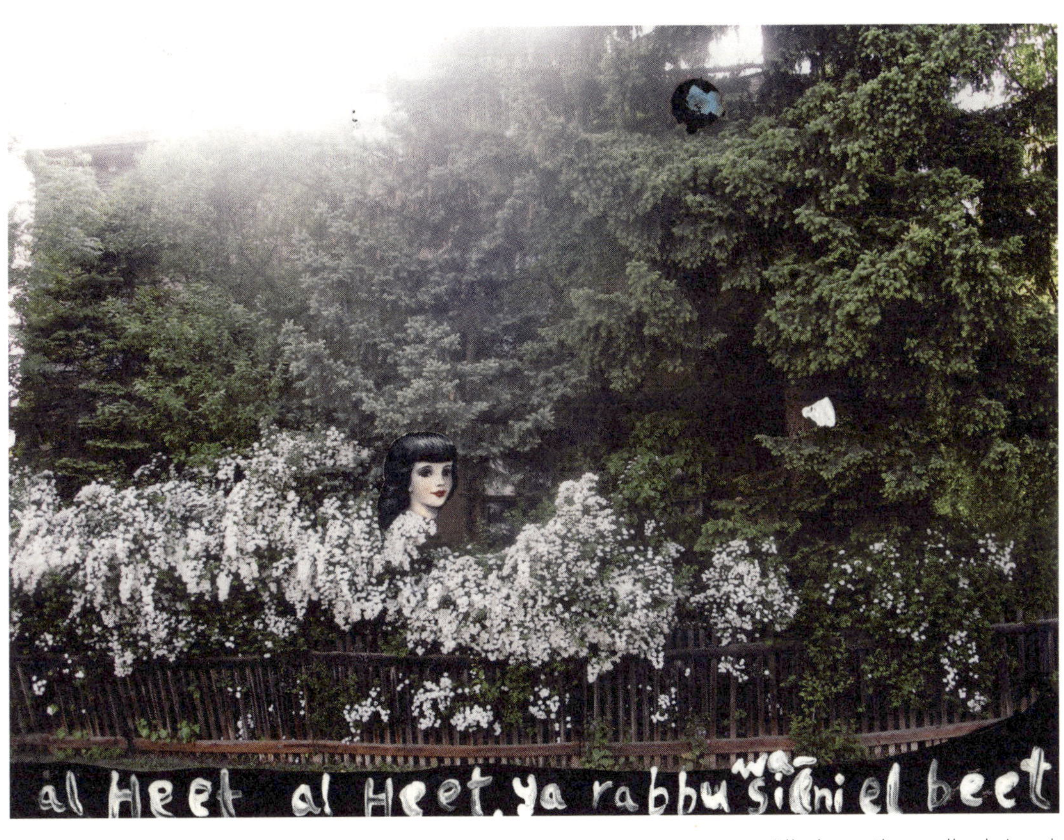

All along the wall, oh Lord,
get me home safely.

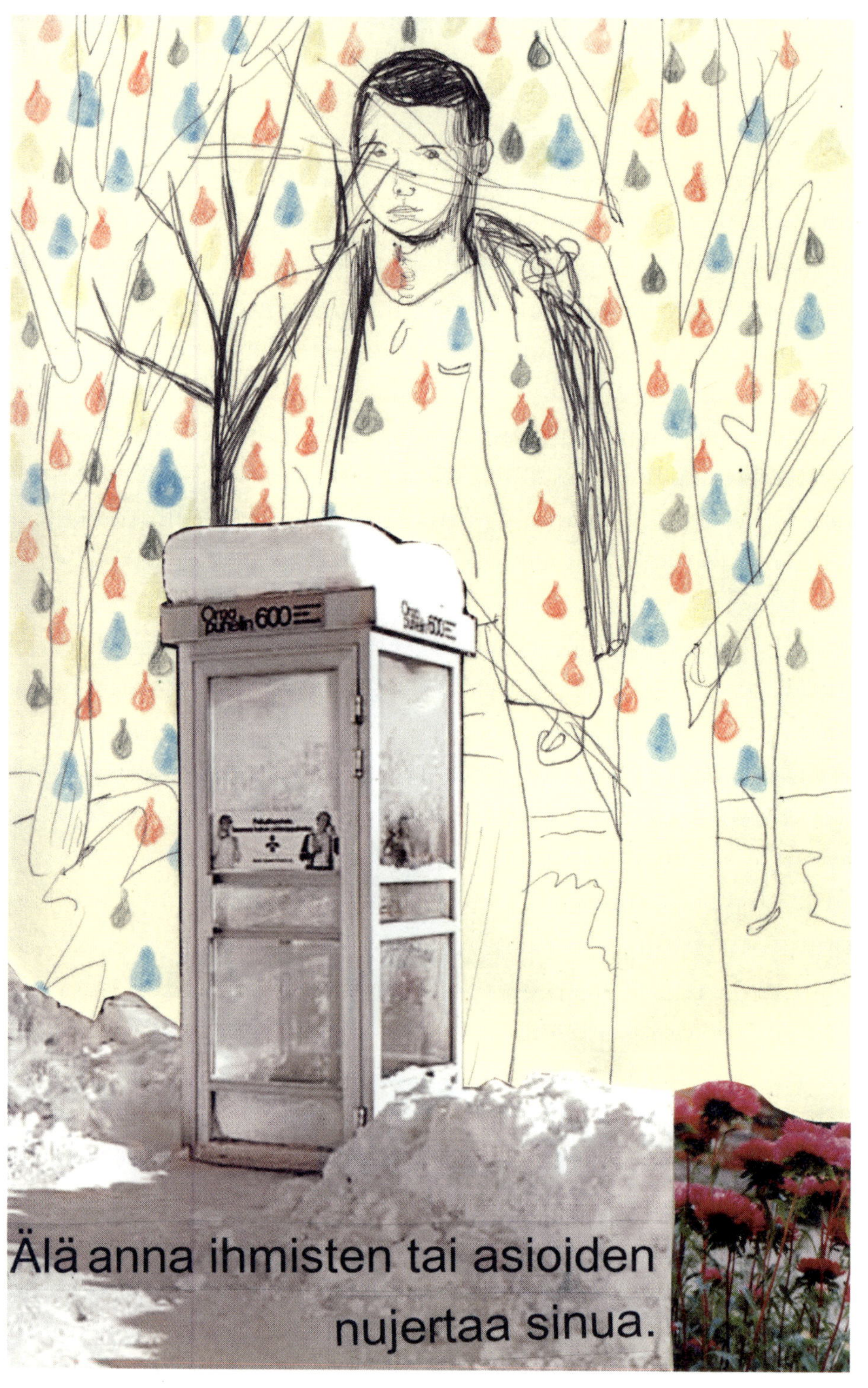

Don't let people or things get you down.

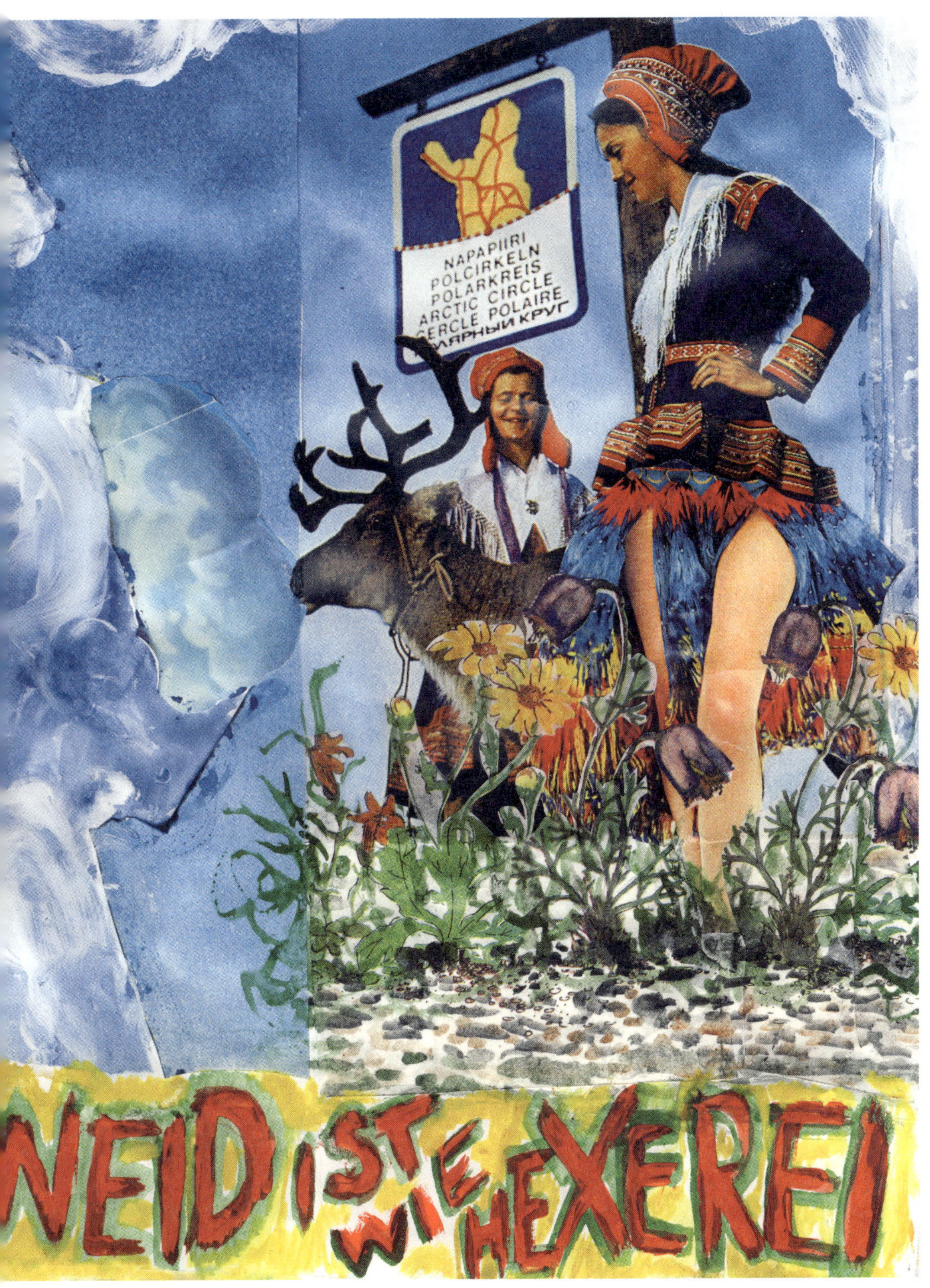

Envy is like witchcraft.

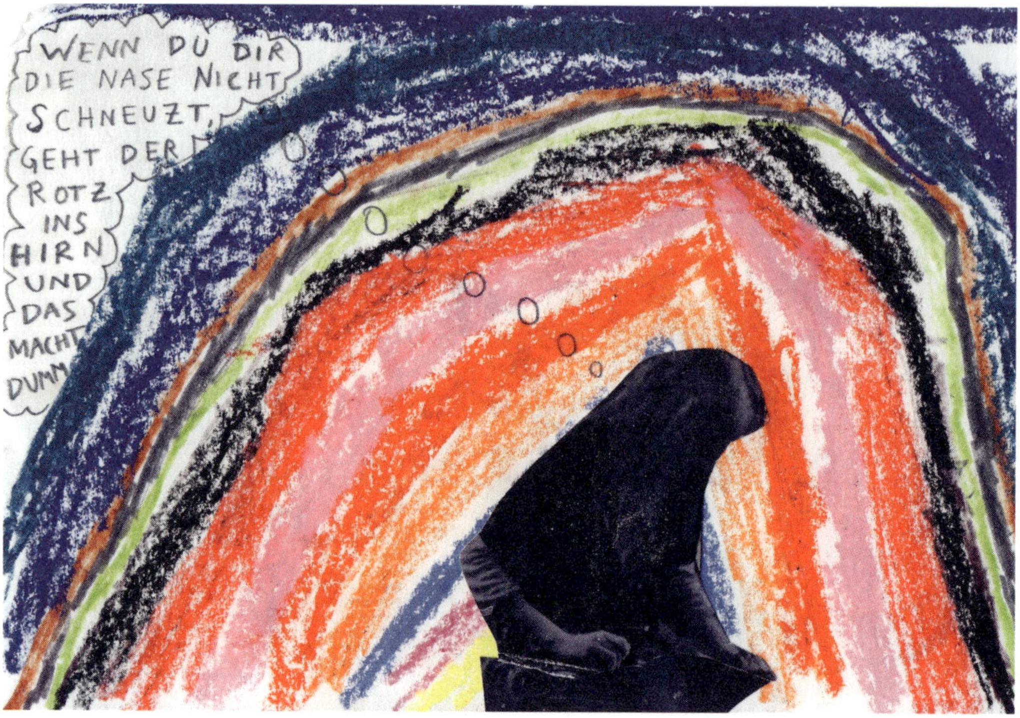

If you don't blow your nose, the snot will enter your brain and make you stupid.

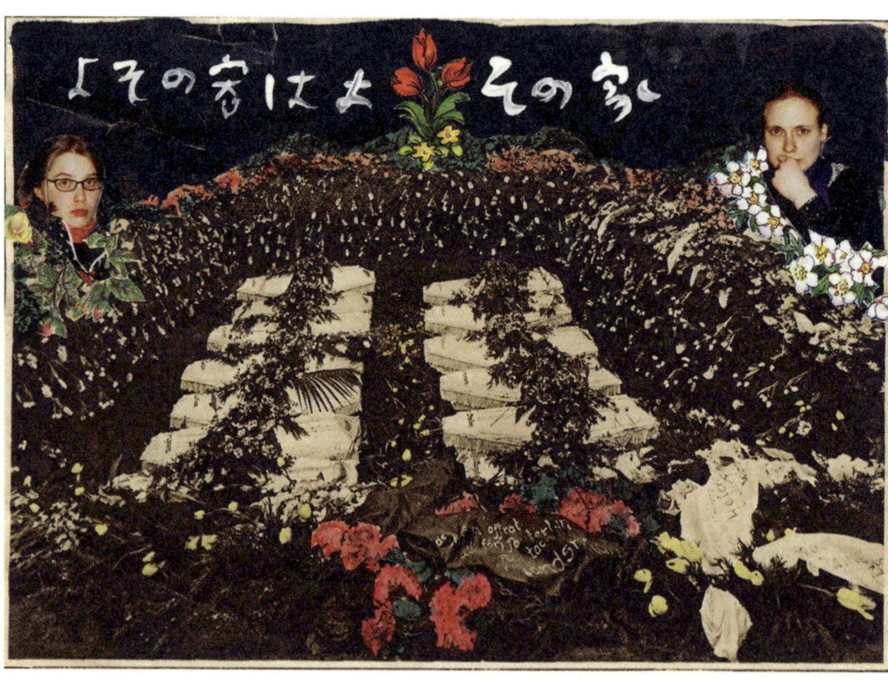

That's them, this is us.

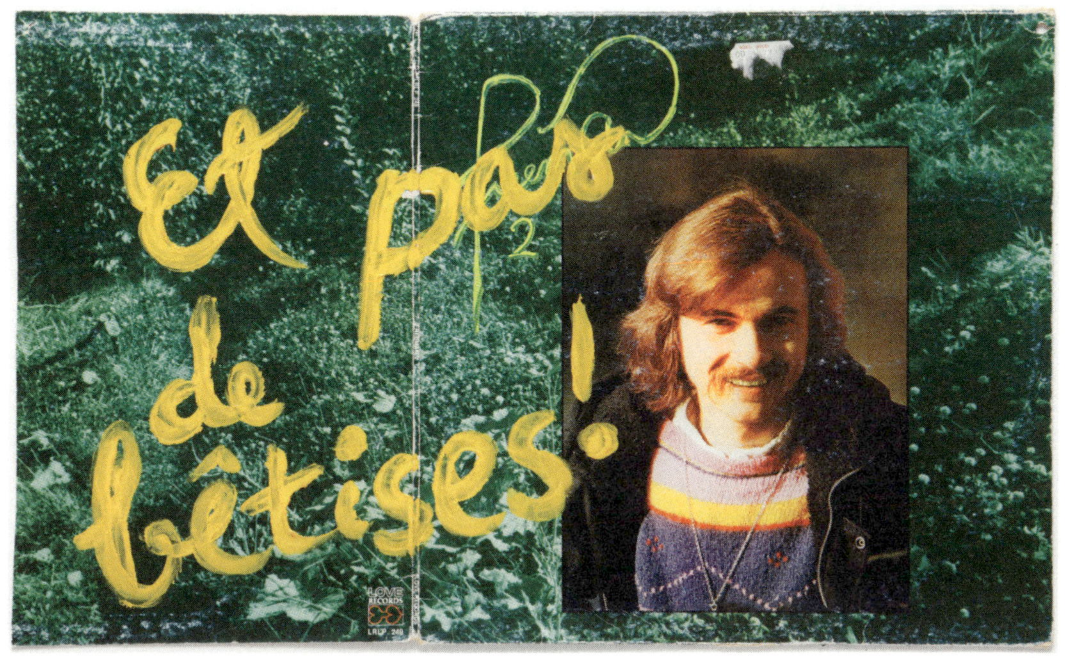

No stupid things!

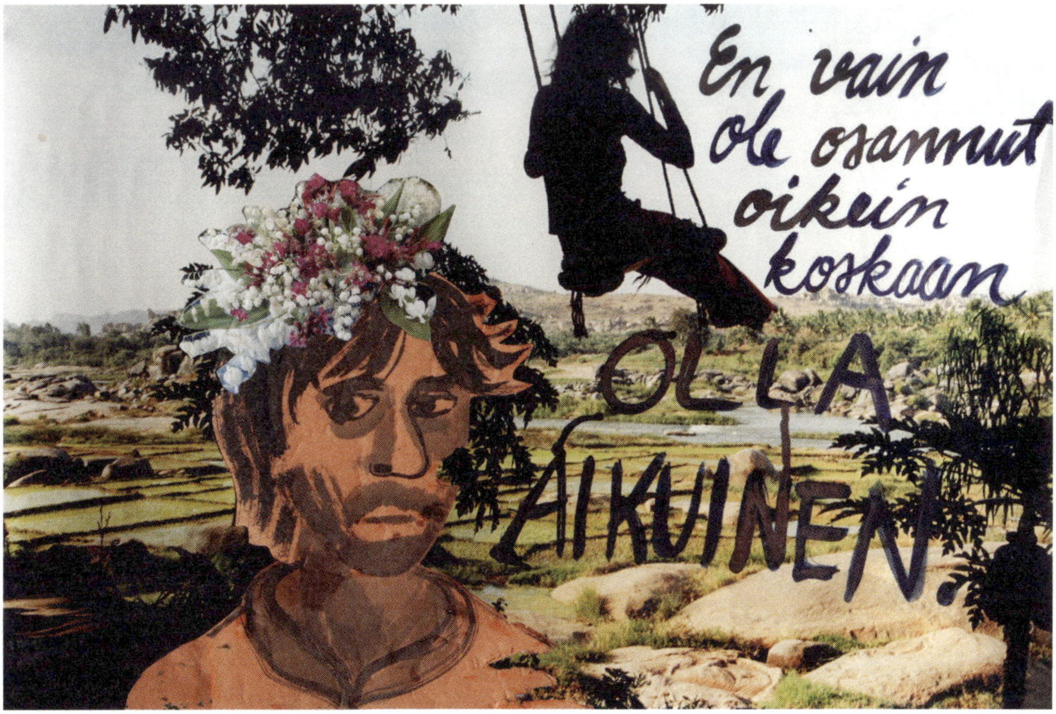

I never learnt to be a grown-up.

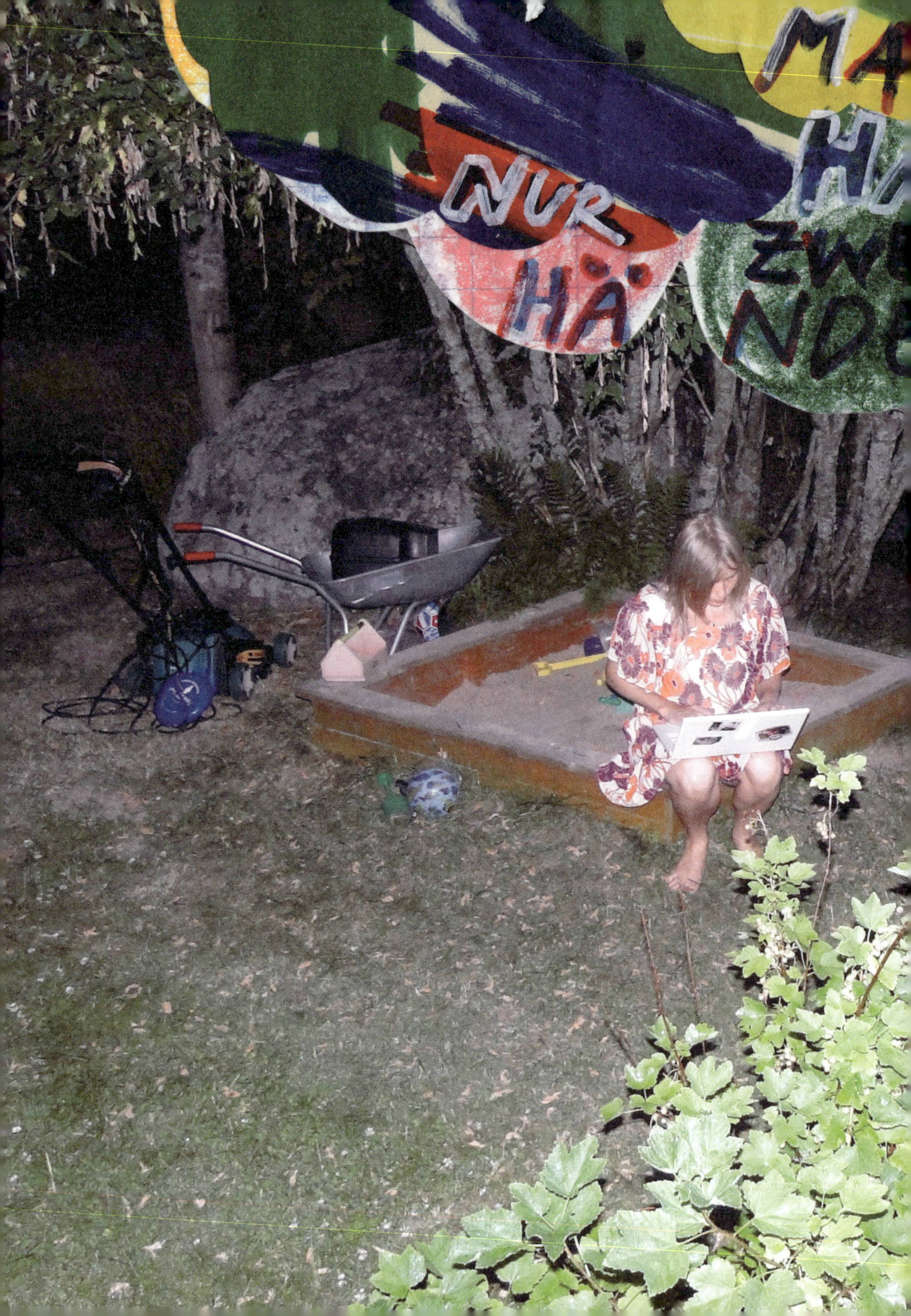

NUR
HÄ
MA
HU
ZW
NO

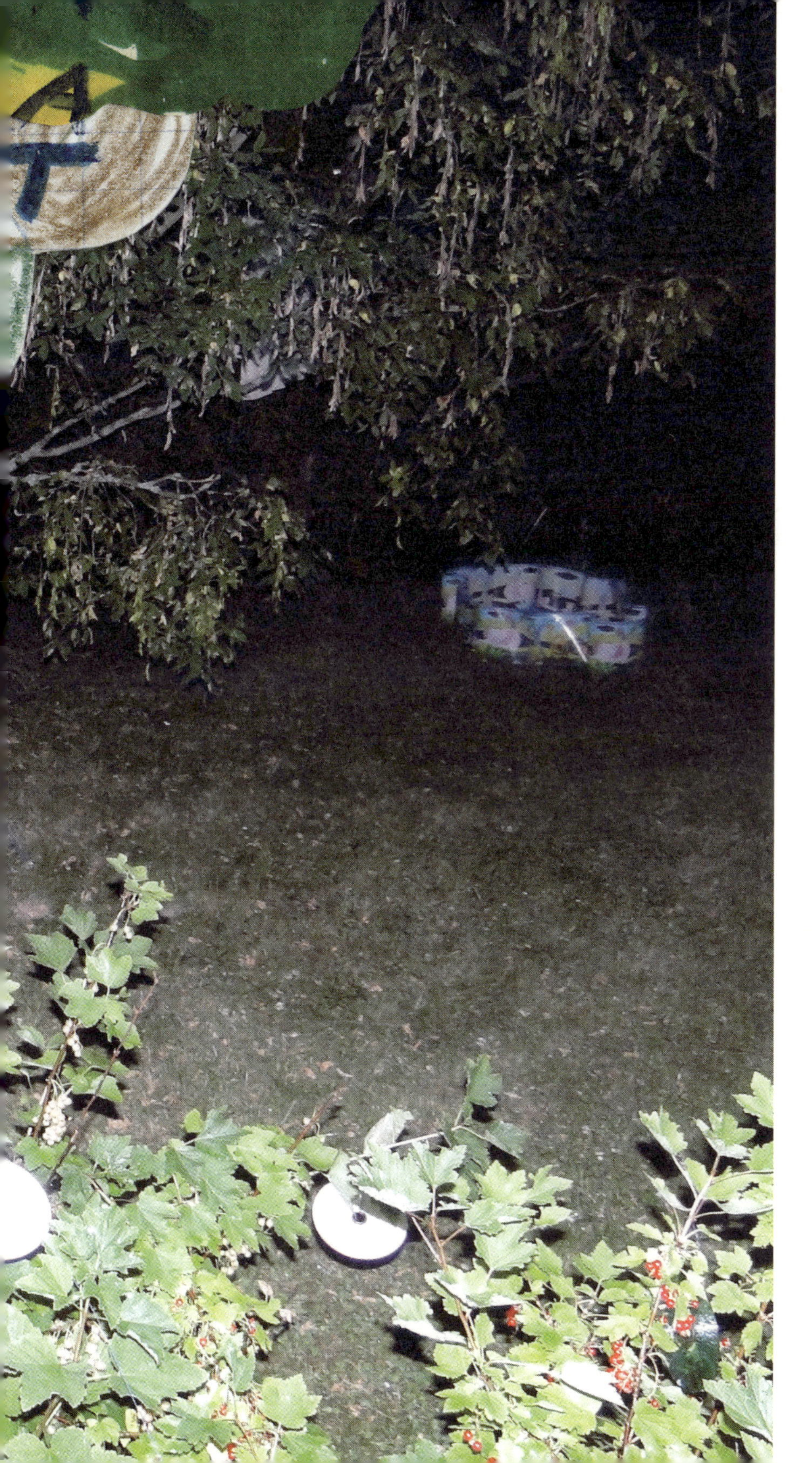

Mother only
has one pair
of hands.

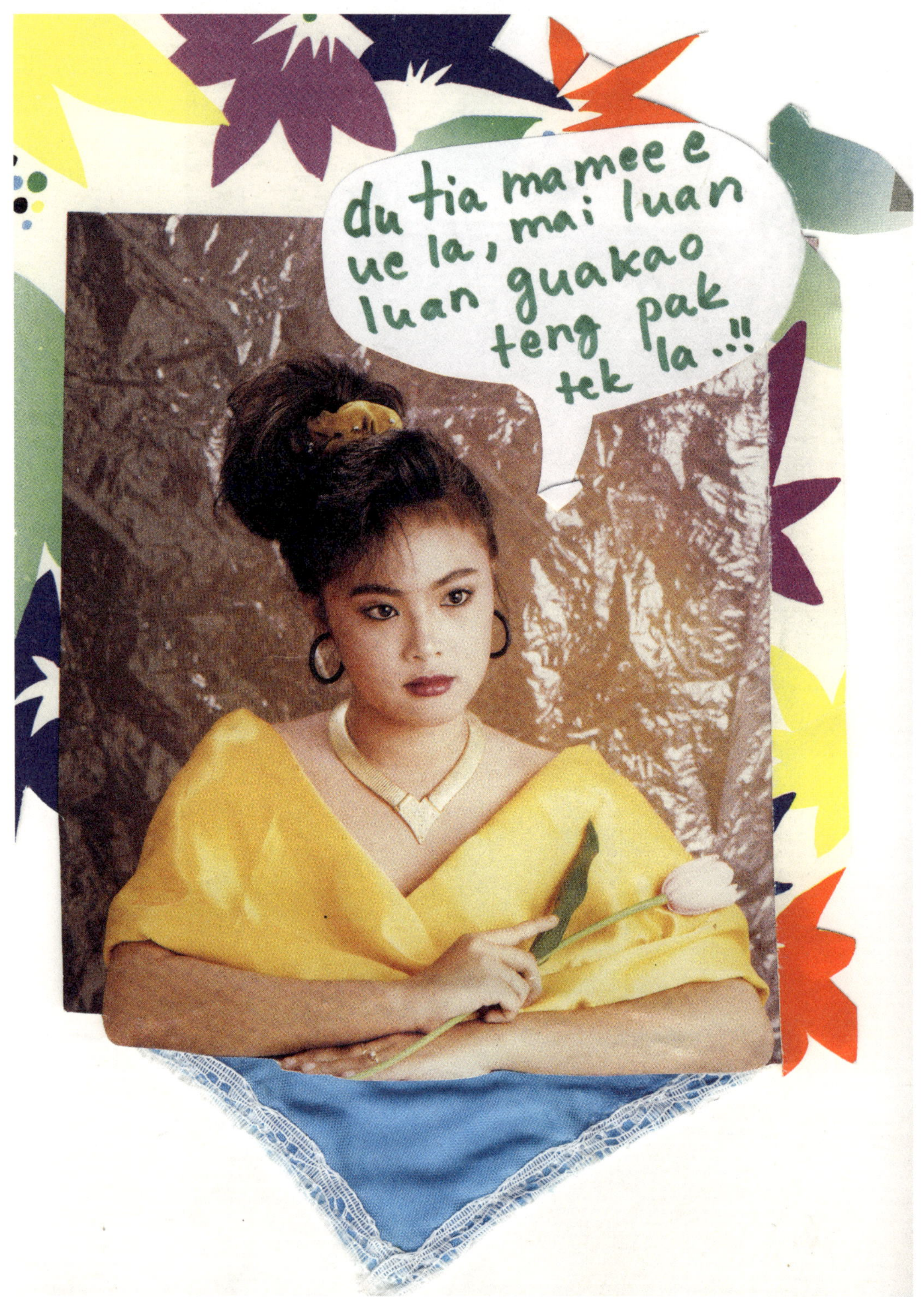

Listen to what your mother says - don't take your clothes off in public.

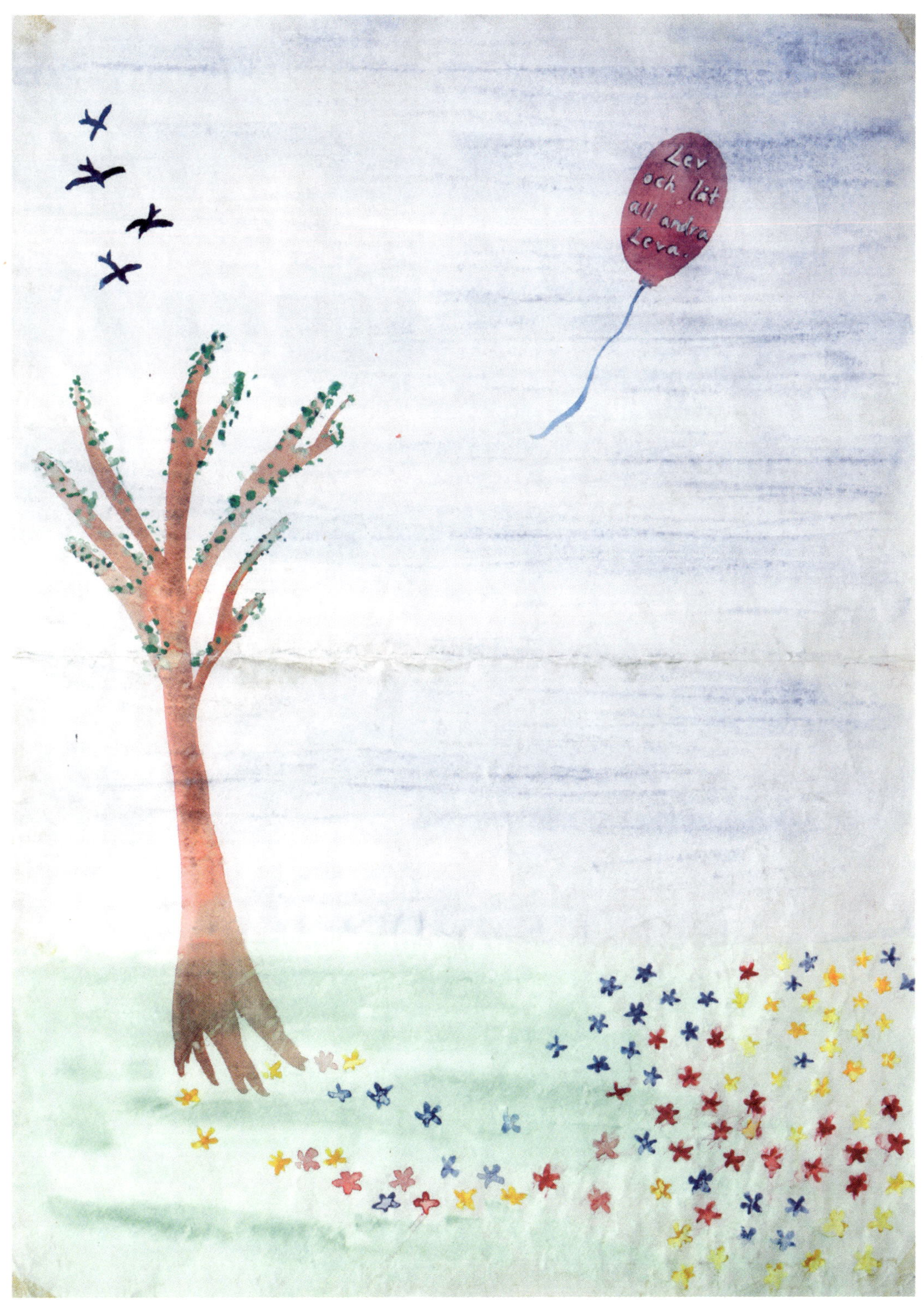

Live and let live.

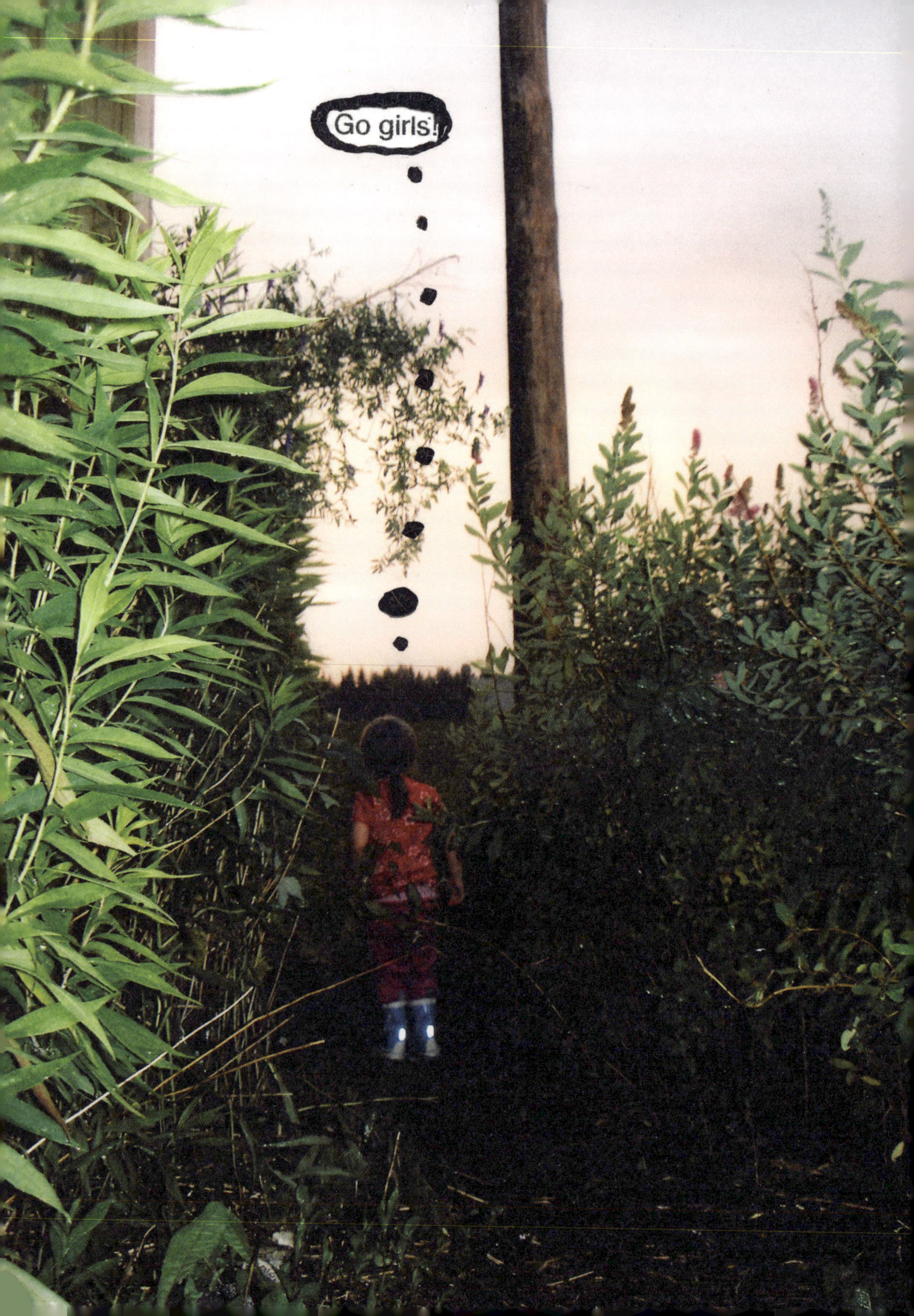

Go girls!

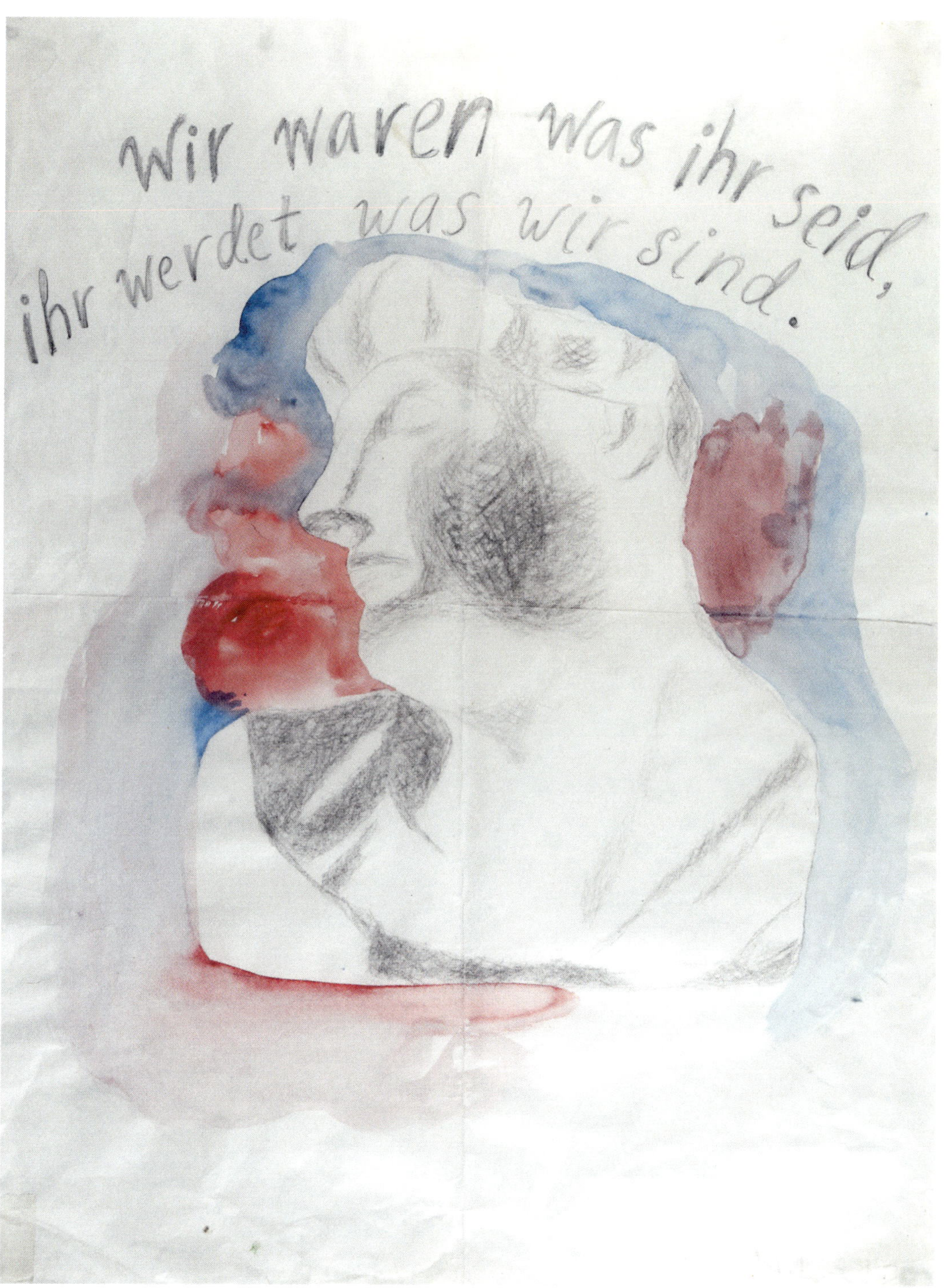

We were like you – and you'll become like us.

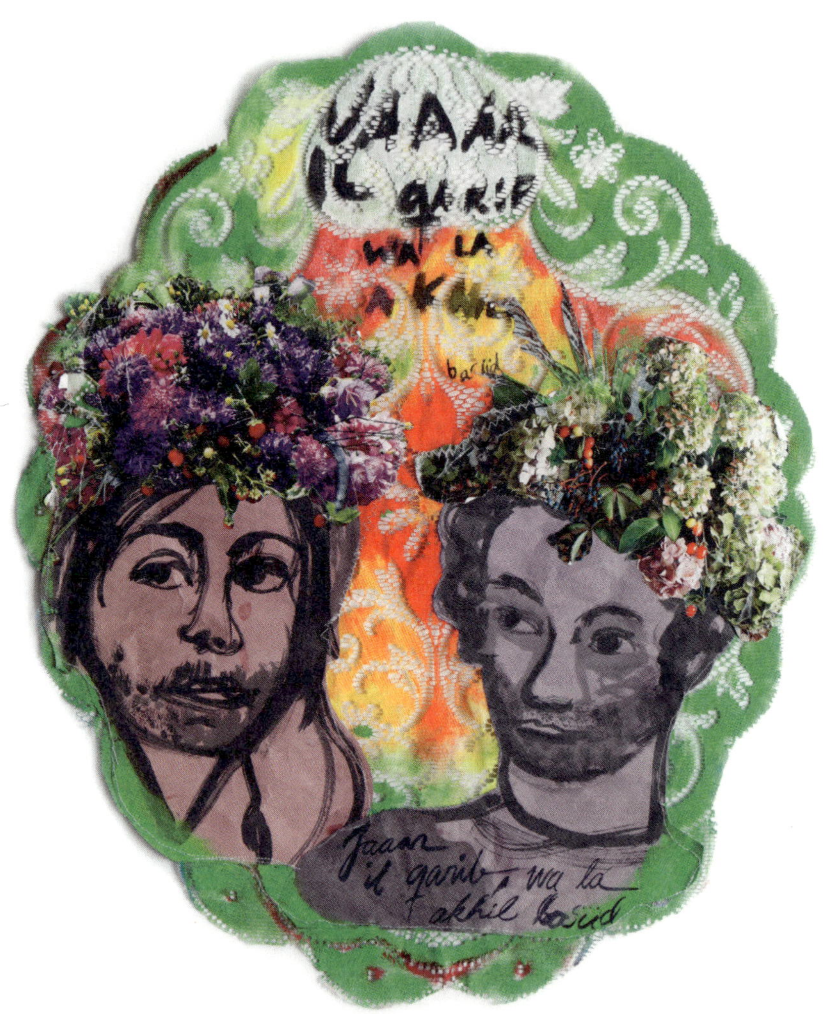

Better a nearby neighbour than
a far-away brother.

Don't put your hand on the hot stove.

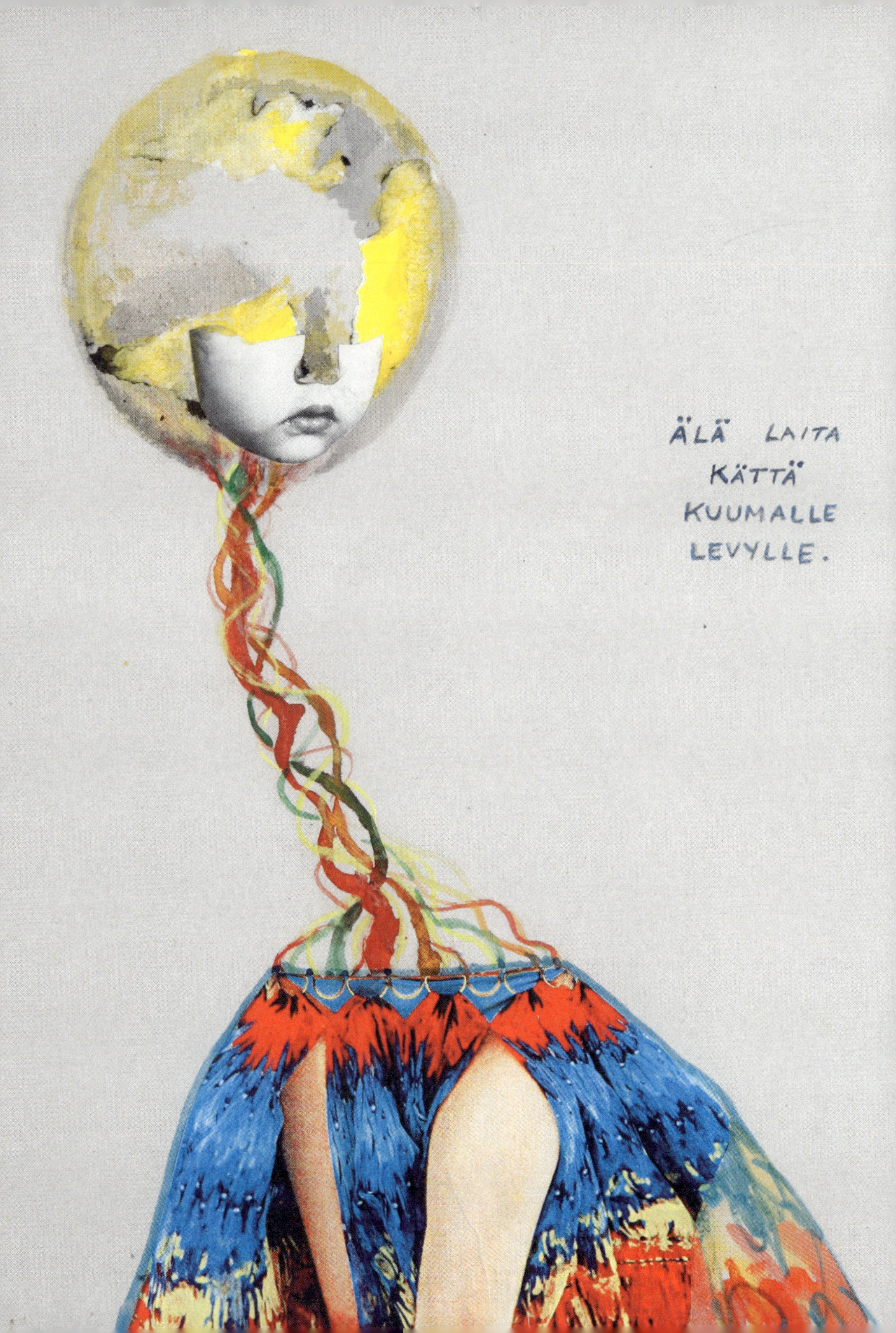

ÄLÄ LAITA
KÄTTÄ
KUUMALLE
LEVYLLE.

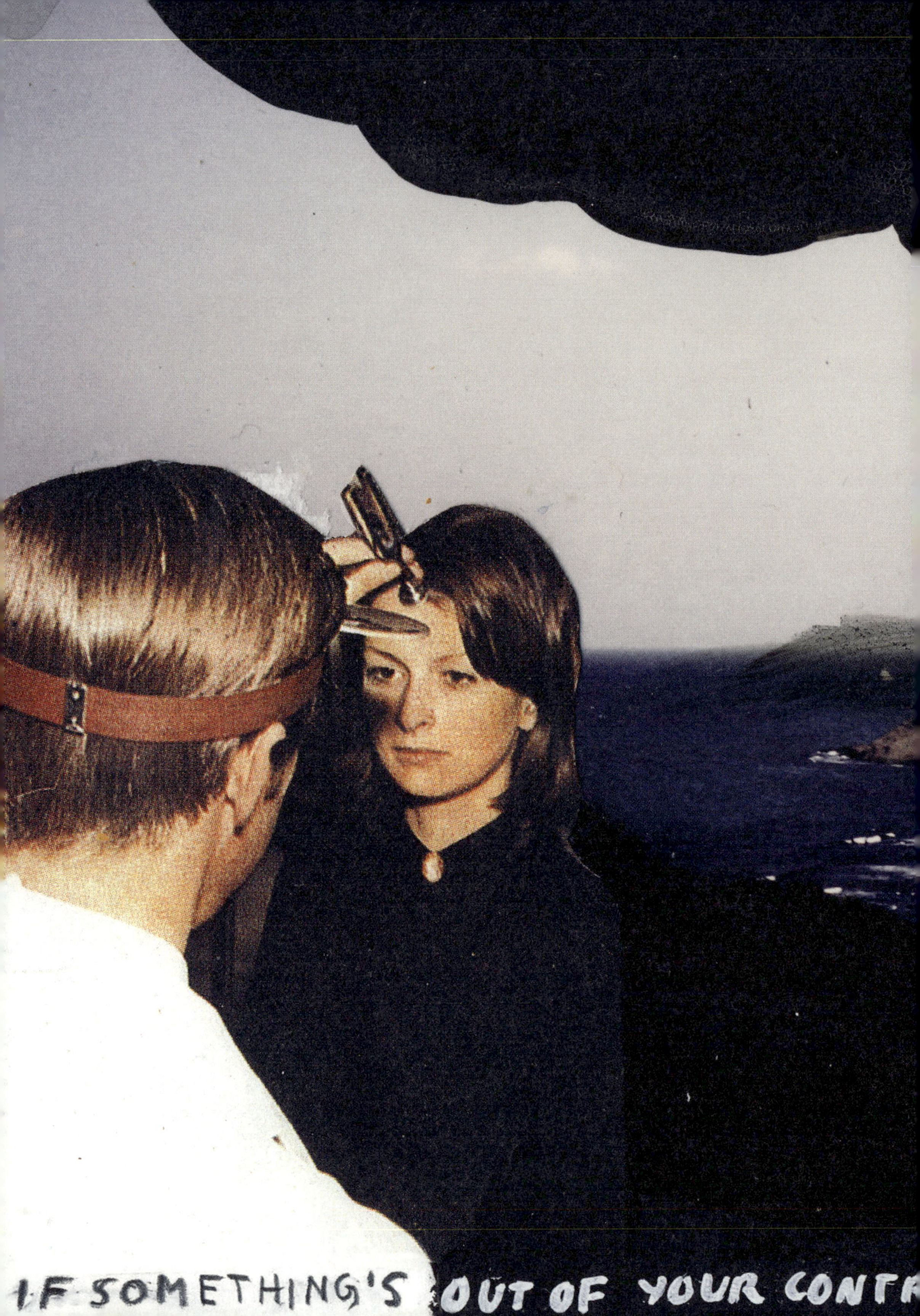
IF SOMETHING'S OUT OF YOUR CONTR

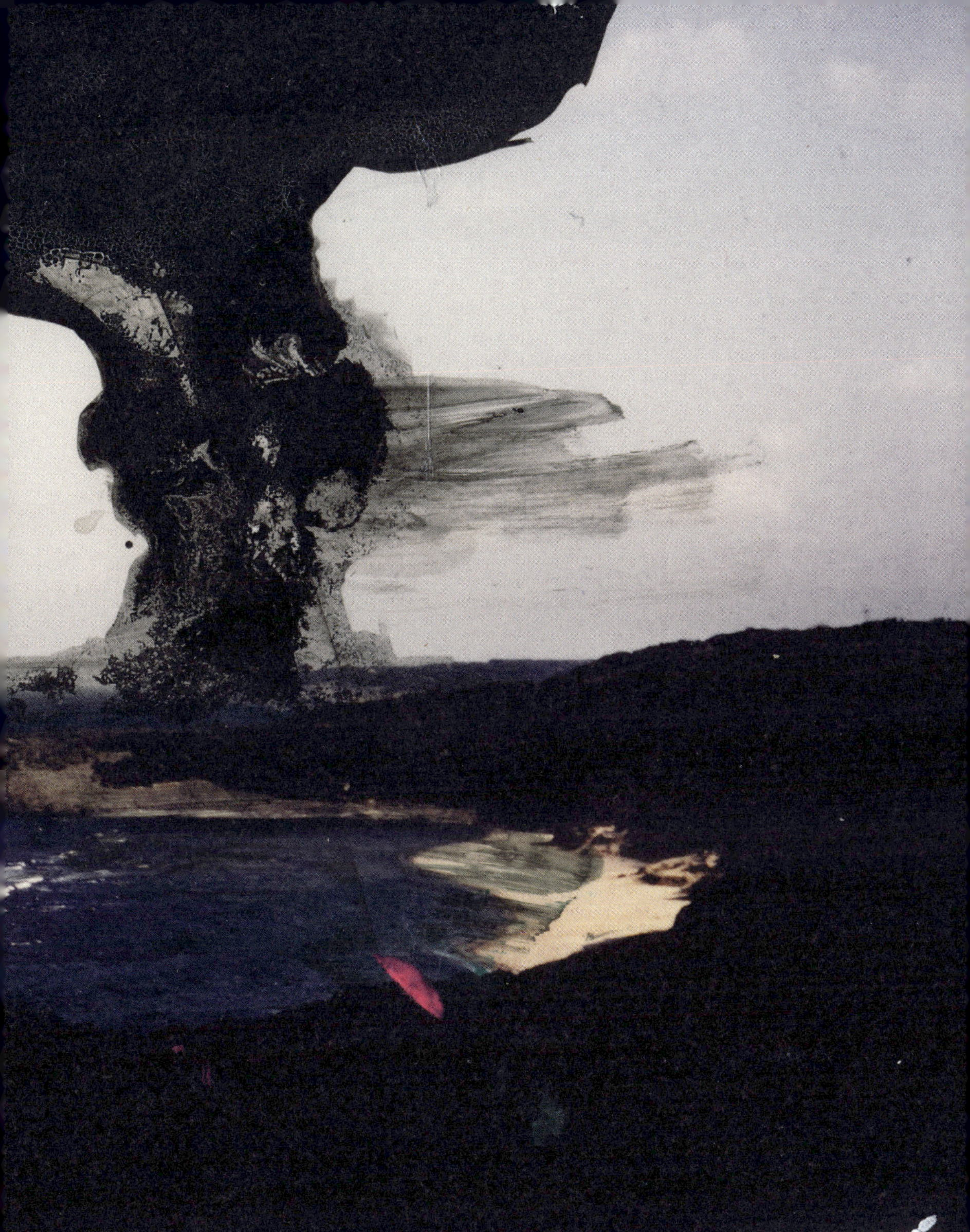
OL, JUST LET IT BE AND HOPE FOR THE BEST

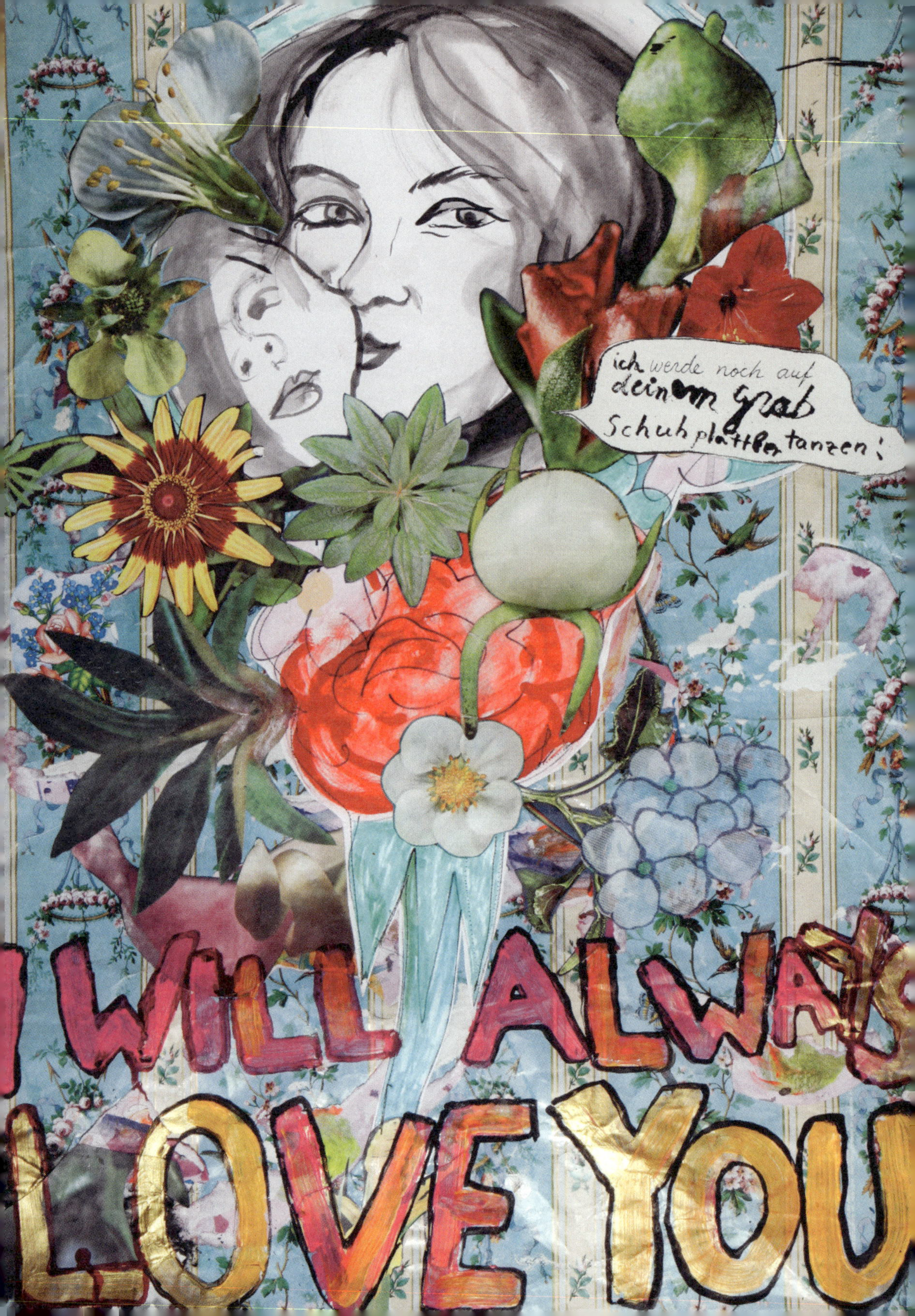

ich werde noch auf deinem Grab Schuhplattler tanzen!
I WILL ALWAYS LOVE YOU

I'll do the Schuhplattler on
your grave one day.

IMAGE INDEX

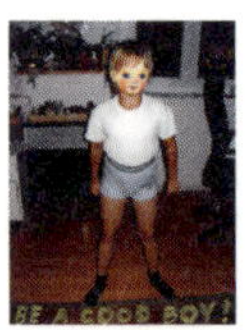

BE A GOOD BOY
collage on photograph
16.5 x 12.5 cm, 2010

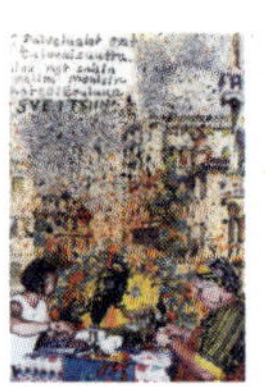

PALVELUALAT OVAT
TULEVAISUUTTA.
JOS NYT SAISIN
VALITA MENISIN
HOTELLIKOULUUN
SVEITSIIN
collage on postcard
15.5 x 10.5 cm, 2009

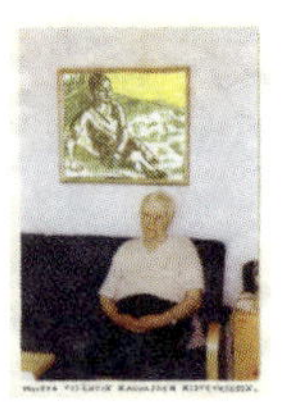

MUISTA PYSÄHTYÄ
KAUHAJOEN
RISTEYKSESSÄ
collage on paper
29.5 x 20.5 cm, 2012
original drawing in the
collage by Mirka Raito

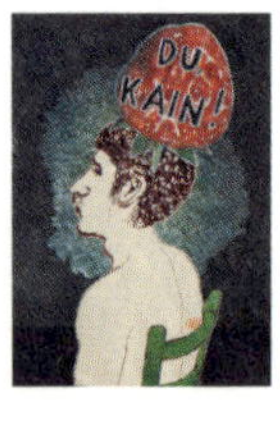

DU KAIN
collage on paper
35 x 25 cm, 2010

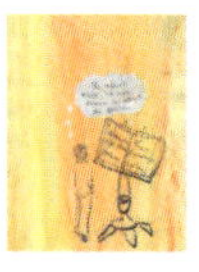

IHR MÜSST NICHT
IMMER DENKEN IHR
WÄRET DIE GÖTTER
ink, pencil, watercolour
and acrylic on paper
27 x 20.5 cm, 2009

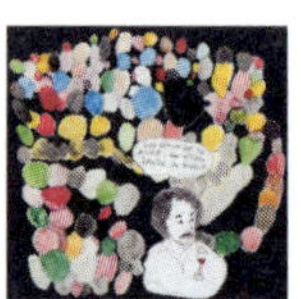

DAS LEBEN IST ZU KURZ
UM OFFENE WEINE ZU
TRINKEN
collage on paper
29.5 x 29.5 cm, 2009

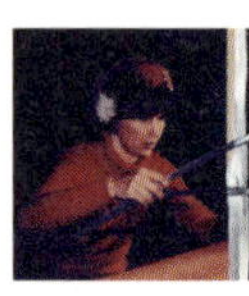

JOS KOHTAAT ITSESI
UNESSA NUKKUVANA ÄLÄ
HERÄTÄ ITSEÄSI
acrylic on photograph
20 x 29 cm, 2009

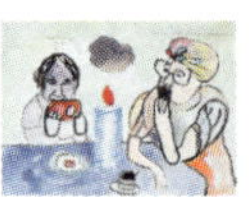

KÖYHYYS EI OLE KIVAA
MUTTA SIINÄ ON OMA
CHARMINSA
watercolour and collage
on paper
30 x 39.5 cm, 2009

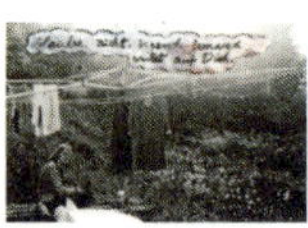

GLAUBE NICHT IRGEND
JEMAND WARTET AUF
DICH
ink and acrylic on
photograph
20 x 30 cm, 2009

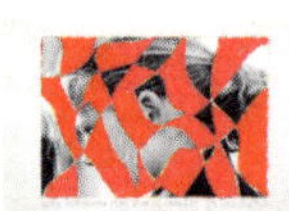

WAS IST SCHON EINE
MATHE-ARBEIT IM
VERGLEICH ZUR
EWIGKEIT
collage on paper
41.5 x 29.5, 2009

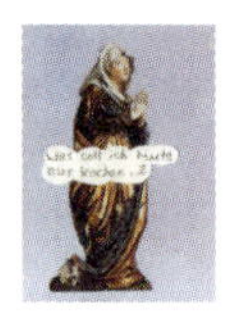

WASS SOLL ICH HEUTE
NUR KOCHEN
collage on postcard
15 x 10.5 cm, 2010
private collection

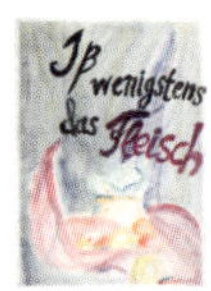

ISS WENIGSTENS DAS
FLEISCH
watercolour on paper
69.5 x 49 cm, 2010

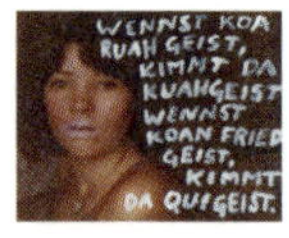

WENNST KOA RUAH
GEIST KIMMT DA
KUAHGEIST WENNST
KOAN FRIED GEIST
KIMMT DA QUIGEIST
acrylic on photograph
9 x 11 cm, 2009

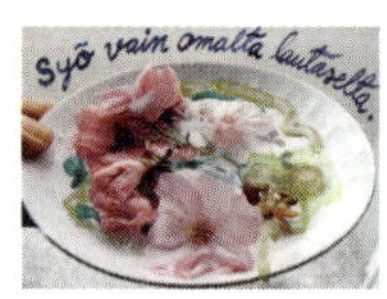

SYÖ VAIN OMALTA
LAUTASELTA
watercolour and acrylic
on photograph
12.5 x 16.5 cm, 2010

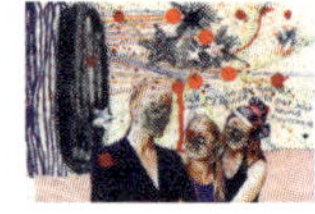

ÄLÄ MAALAA SUN
NAAMAA NIIN PALJON
SÄ OOT NIIN KAUNIS
MUUTENKIN
collage on paper
15 x 21 cm, 2010

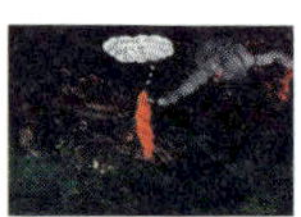

JUNGE MÄDCHEN
SOLLEN NICHT AUF DER
STRASSE RAUCHEN
acrylic on paper
21 x 30 cm, 2009

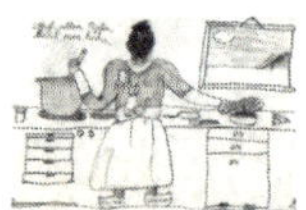

AUF ALTEN TÖPFEN
LERNT MAN KOCHEN
pencil on paper
21 x 29.5 cm, 2009

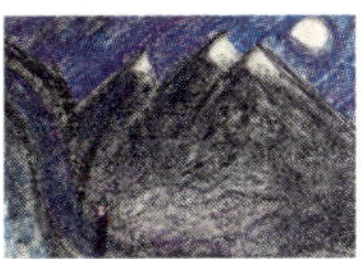

JUST DO WHAT YOU
NEED TO DO
*crayon and collage on
paper
29.5 x 41 cm, 2010*

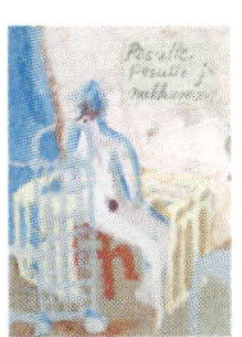

PISULLE PESULLE JA
NUKKUMAAN
*gouache and pencil on
paper
33 x 23.5 cm, 2010*

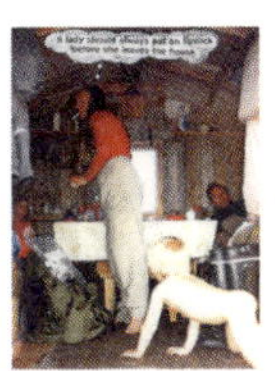

A LADY SHOULD ALWAYS
PUT ON LIPSTICK BEFORE
SHE LEAVES THE HOUSE
*collage and acrylic on
photograph
18.5 x 13 cm, 2009*

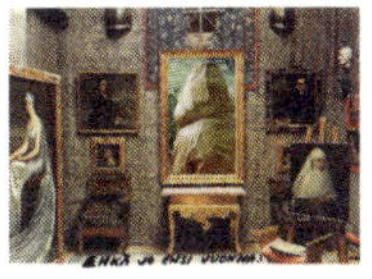

EHKÄ JO ENSI VUONNA
*collage on printed image
15 x 20 cm, 2011*

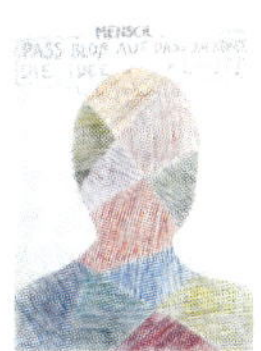

MENSCH PASS BLOSS AUF
DAS DIR KEINER DIE IDEE
KLAUT

*pencil and coloured
pencil on paper
42 x 29.5 cm, 2009*

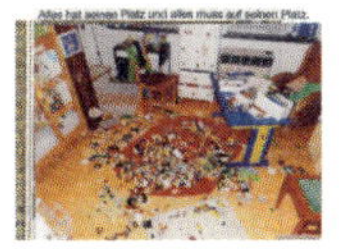

ALLES HAT SEINEN
PLATZ UND ALLES MUSS
AUF SEINEN PLATZ
*collage on photograph
11.5 x 16 cm, 2012*

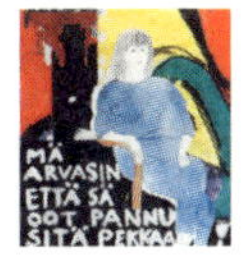

MÄ ARVASIN ETTÄ SÄ
OOT PANNU SITÄ PEKKAA
*gouache, acrylic and
collage on paper
56.5 x 50 cm, 2011*

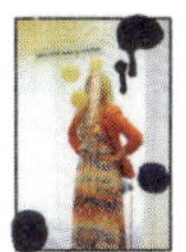

LECKE NICHT BEVOR ES
RUNTERFÄLLT
*collage on magazine
28.5 x 21.5 cm, 2010*

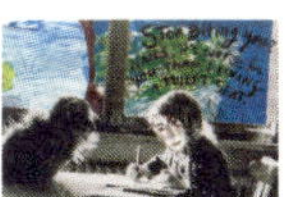

STOP BITING YOUR NAILS,
IT'S WORSE FOR YOU
THAN LICKING A TOILET
SEAT
*collage on paper
30 x 45 cm, 2012*

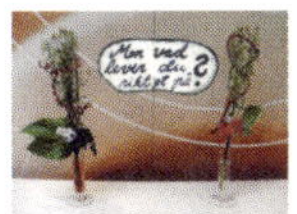

MEN VAD LEVER DU
RIKTIGT PÅ
*acrylic and ink on
photograph,
20 x 27 cm, 2013*

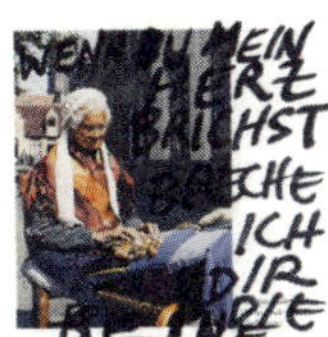

WENN DU MEIN HERZ
BRICHST BRECHE ICH
DIR DIE BEINE
*permanent marker on
printed image
16.5 x 16 cm, 2010*

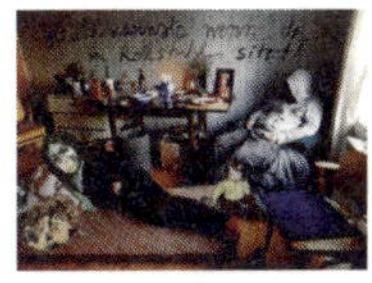

HEULEN KANNSTE WENN
DU IM ROLLSTUHL SITZT
*collage on photograph
20 x 26.5 cm, 2012*

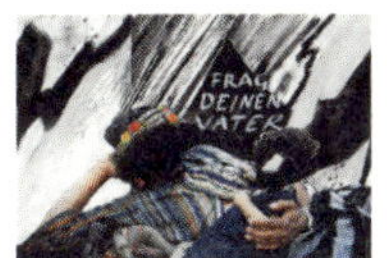

FRAG DEINEN VATER
*collage and gouache on
paper
41.5 x 58 cm, 2009*

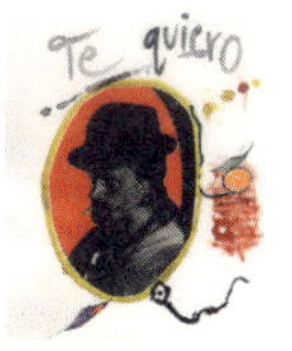

TE QUIERO
*collage on paper
28 x 21 cm, 2011
original photograph by
Harri Aiho ‚What about
jazz in Finland‘, 1990*

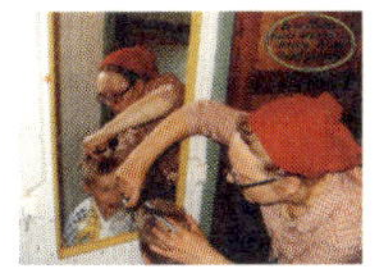

EINE MUTTER FÜHLT
WENNS IHREM KIND
NICHT GUT GEHT
*collage on photograph
20 x 27 cm, 2010*
original photograph by
Teemu Tuonela

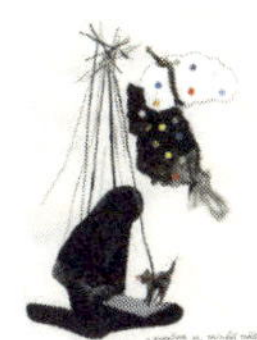

MAALAA SE MINKÄ NÄET
*collage and ink on paper
29.5 x 21 cm, 2012*

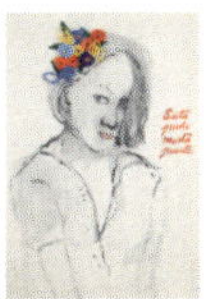

SIITÄ PUHE MISTÄ
PUUTE
*watercolour, ink and wool
on paper
42 x 29.5 cm, 2010*

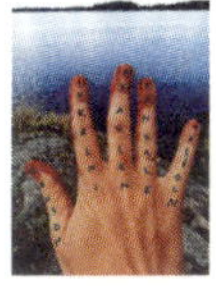

EI KENENKÄÄN KANSSA
VOI OLLA ONNELLINEN
*permanent marker on
photograph
27 x 20 cm, 2013*

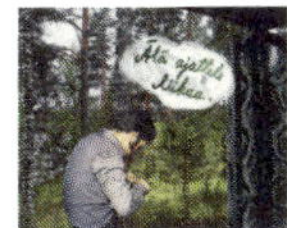

ÄLÄ AJATTELE LIIKAA
*collage on photograph
20 x 25 cm, 2010*

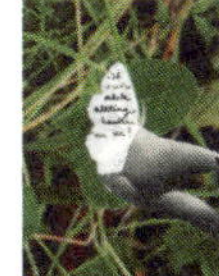

SÅ VARFÖR MÅSTE
ALLTTING HANDLA OM
SEX
collage on photograph
30 x 20 cm, 2012

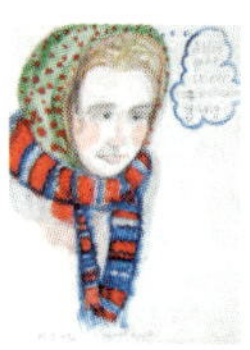

ALLES GEHT SEINEN
SOZIALISTISCHEN GANG
pencil and watercolour
on paper
40 x 28.5 cm, 2009
original drawing by
Samuel Kivijärvi, 1996

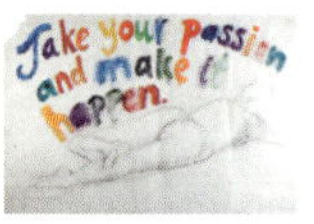

TAKE YOUR PASSION AND
MAKE IT HAPPEN
pencil and watercolour
on paper
72 x 103 cm, 2009

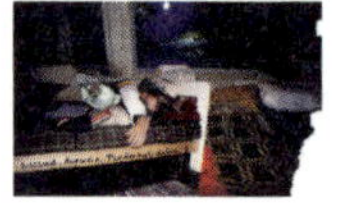

SCHLÜSSEL, AUSWEIS,
TASCHENTUCH DABEI
collage on printed image
13.5 x 21 cm, 2013
original photograph in
the collage by Teemu
Tuonela

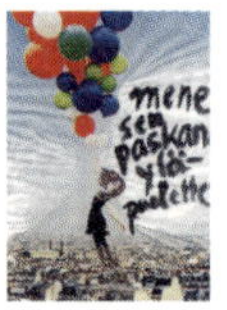

MENE SEN PASKAN
YLÄPUOLELLE
collage on magazine
28 x 20 cm, 2010

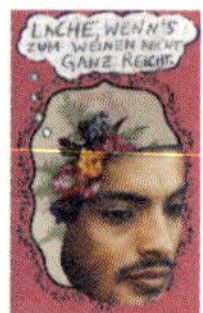

LACHE WENN'S ZUM
WEINEN NICHT GANZ
REICHT
collage on postcard
17.5 x 10.5 cm, 2009

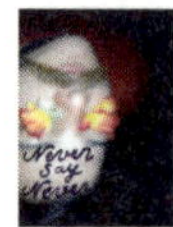

NEVER SAY NEVER
watercolour on
photograph
20 x 14.5 cm, 2010

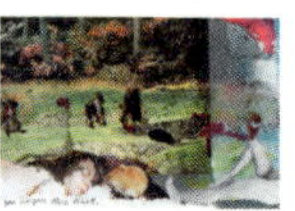

GOD MORGON HERR
HÄST
collage on paper
30.5 x 42 cm, 2012

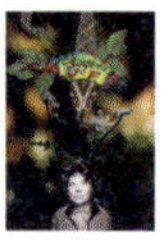

AUGEN AUF
collage on photograph
19 x 12.5 cm, 2010

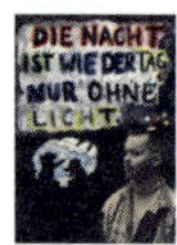

DIE NACHT IST WIE DER
TAG NUR OHNE LICHT
collage on paper
29.5 x 21 cm, 2009
original photograph by
Harri Aiho 'What about
jazz in Finland', 1990

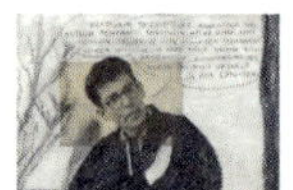

VARSINKIN
POIKAYSTÄVÄT
KANNATTAA
HOUKUTELLA
PELAAMAAN
MONOPOLIA...
pencil and collage on
paper, 30 x 42 cm, 2010
Finnish State Art
Collection

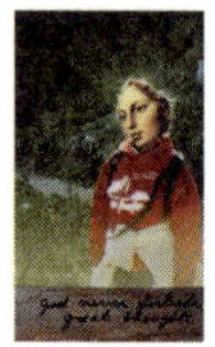

GOD NEVER FORBADE
GREAT THOUGHTS
collage on postcard
16 x 10 cm, 2012

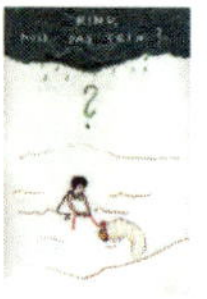

KIND, MUSS DAS SEIN
acrylic and collage on
paper
30.5 x 19 cm, 2010

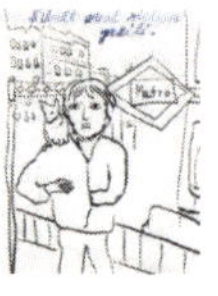

SILMÄT OVAT SIELUN
PEILI
ink and watercolour on
paper
27 x 20.5 cm, 2009

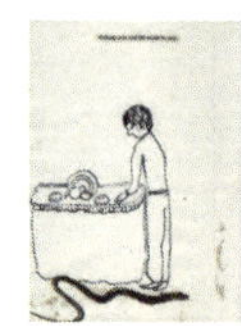

NOBODY EVER SAID LIFE
WOULD BE EASY
ink and collage on paper
29.5 x 21 cm, 2012

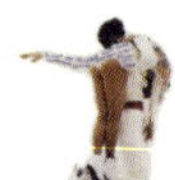

EI AINA VOI VÄLITTÄÄ
SIITÄ ONKO HUOMENNA
LAITTAA PUHTAAT
PIKKUHOUSUT JALKAAN
collage on paper
30 x 20 cm, 2013

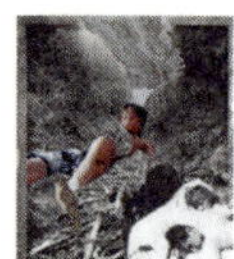

LIVET KAN INTE ALLTID
VARA ROLIGT
collage on printed image
33 x 23.5 cm, 2012

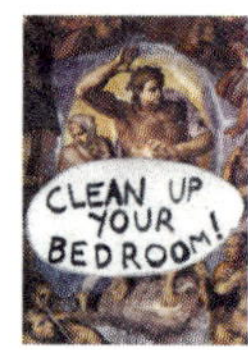

CLEAN UP YOUR
BEDROOM
collage on postcard
15.5 x 10.5 cm, 2010

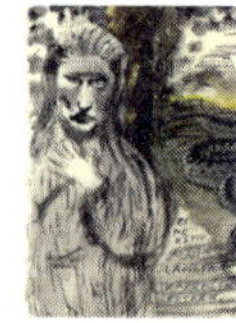

EI ME RÄTIT JALASSA
LÄHETÄ KÄÄRMEEN
PESÄÄN
pencil, ink, watercolour
and collage on paper
19 x 13 cm, 2010
original drawing in the
collage by Mirka Raito

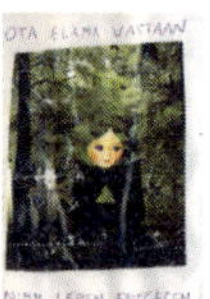

OTA ELÄMÄ VASTAAN/
NIMM LEBEN ENTGEGEN
collage on printed image
27 x 20 cm, 2010

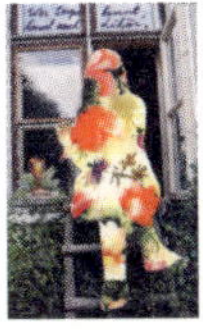

WER SORGEN KENNT,
KENNT AUCH LIKÖR
collage on photograph
15 x 10 cm, 2009

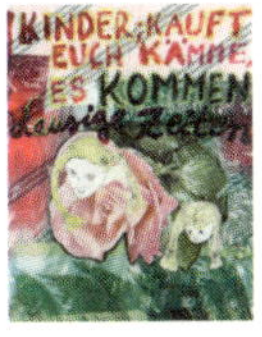

KINDER KAUFT EUCH
KÄMME ES KOMMEN
LAUSIGE ZEITEN
collage on paper and
fabric
36.5 x 24.5 cm, 2010

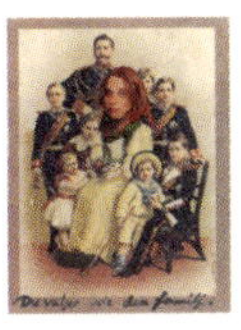

DU VÄLJER INTE DIN
FAMILJ
collage on printed image
19 x 14.5 cm, 2012

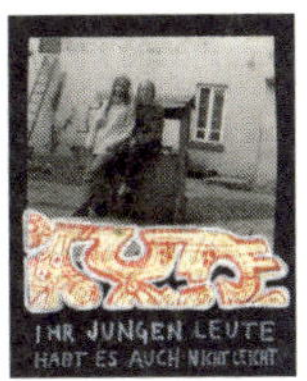

IHR JUNGEN LEUTE
HABT ES AUCH NICHT
LEICHT
collage on paper
17 x 14 cm, 2010

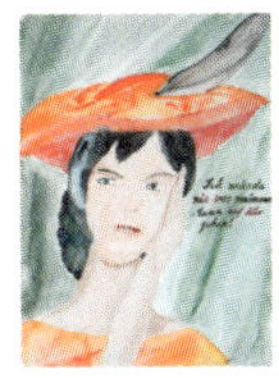

ICH WÜRDE NIE VOR
MEINEM MANN AUF KLO
GEHEN
watercolour on paper
59 x 41 cm, 2010

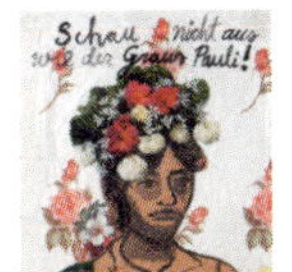

SCHAU NICHT AUS WIE
DER GRAUS PAULI
collage on wrapping
paper
48.5 x 45.5 cm, 2009

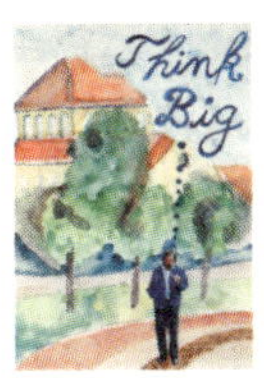

THINK BIG
watercolour and collage
on paper
42 x 29.5 cm, 2010

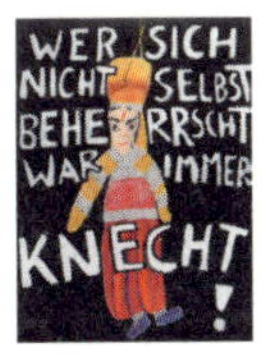

WER SICH NICHT SELBST
BEHERRSCHT WAR
IMMER KNECHT
crayon and acrylic on
paper
69.5 x 49.5 cm, 2009

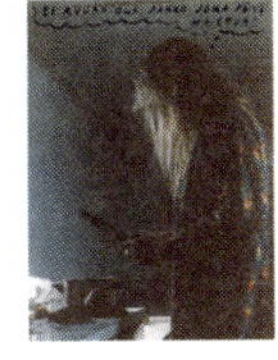

EI RUUAN OLE PAKKO
JOKA PÄIVÄ MAISTUA
collage on phptograph
15 x 10 cm, 2009
original photograph by
Teemu Tuonela

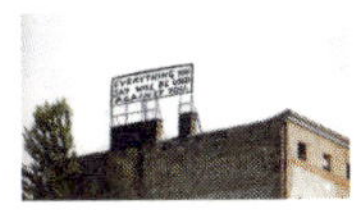

EVERYTHING YOU SAY
WILL BE USED AGAINST
YOU
permanent marker on
photograph
20 x 30 cm, 2013

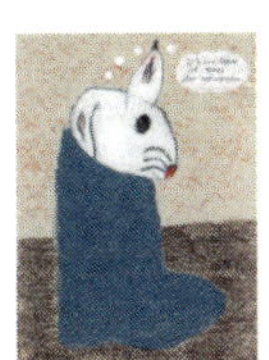

DIESES LEBEN IST EINES
DER SCHWERSTEN
crayon, pencil and acrylic
on paper 29.5 x 21 cm,
2009

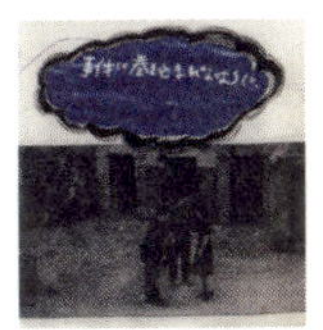

DON'T GET INVOLVED IN
WARS OR ACCIDENTS
collage on printed image
26 x 20 cm, 2010

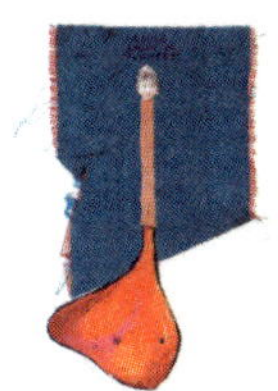

NEVER SHOUT AT
FLOWERS
collage on fabric
39 x 22 cm, 2010

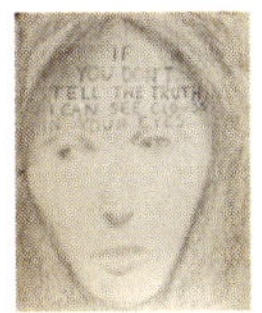

IF YOU DON'T TELL
THE TRUTH I CAN SEE
CLOUDS IN YOUR EYES
pencil on paper
33.5 x 26.5 cm, 2009

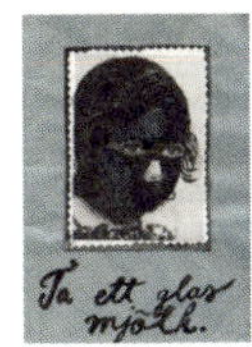

TA ETT GLAS MJÖLK
collage on paper
21 x 15 cm, 2012

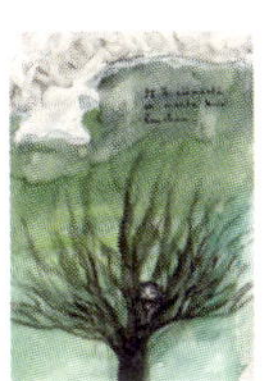

98% ELÄMÄSTÄ ON
MUUTA KUIN HAUSKAA
watercolour, acrylic and
collage on paper
27 x 21 cm, 2013

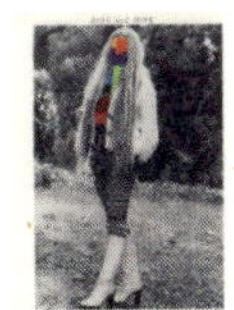

RISE AND SHINE
collage on printed image
26.5 x 21.5 cm, 2010
original image from
"Fellini's Faces"
Verlag Volk und Welt,
1986

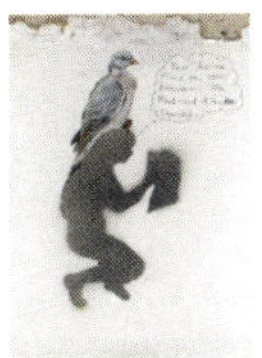

FASS KEINE TIERE AN
SONST BEKOMMST DU
MAUL-UND-KLAUEN-
SEUCHE
collage on book cover
24 x 17 cm, 2009

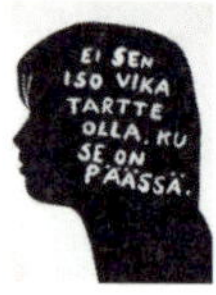

EI SEN ISO VIKA TARTTE
OLLA KU SE ON PÄÄSSÄ
collage on paper
42 x 29.5 cm, 2009
silhouette by Tellervo
Kalleinen

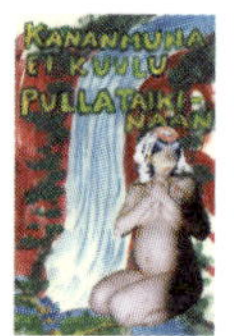

KANANMUNA EI KUULU
PULLATAIKINAAN
collage on paper
21 x 13 cm, 2010
original photograph by
Pavel Bogdanovic

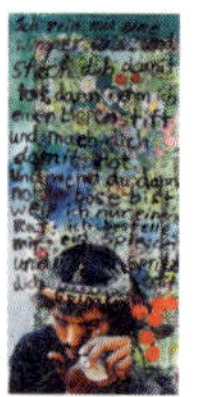

ICH REISS DIR EINE
WIMPER AUS...
collage and acrylic on
fabric, 67 x 29 cm, 2009

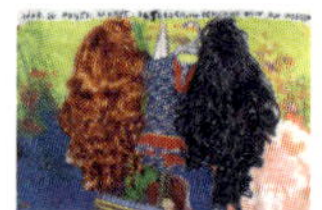

WAS DU HEUTE
KANNST BESORGEN DAS
VERSCHIEBE NICHT AUF
MORGEN
collage & acrylic on paper
21 x 30 cm, 2010

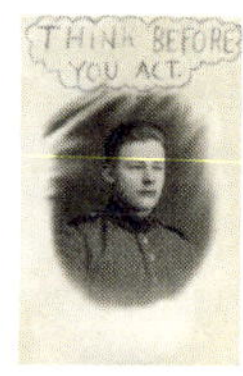

THINK BEFORE YOU ACT
pencil on photograph
13 x 8.5 cm, 2011

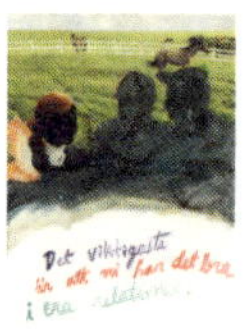

DET VIKTIGASTE ÄR ATT
NI HAR DET BRA I ERA
RELATIONER
collage and watercolour
on paper
29.5 x 20.5 cm, 2012

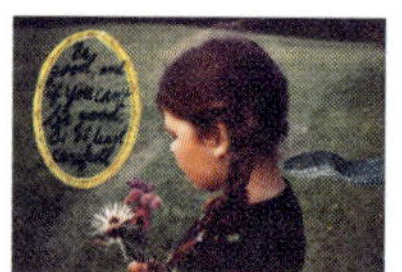

BE GOOD AND IF YOU
CAN'T BE GOOD BE AT
LEAST CAREFUL
collage on photograph
12.5 x 17.5 cm, 2010

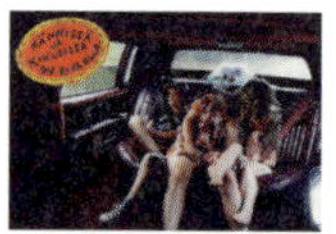

KÄNNISSÄ JA KIHLOISSA
ON KIVA OLLA
collage on photograph
20 x 27 cm, 2010
original photograph by
Ulu Braun

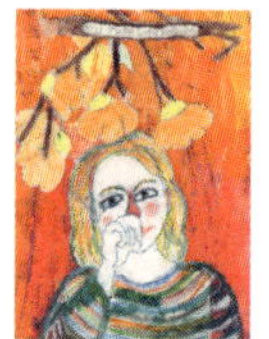

KILL THEM WITH
KINDNESS
collage and acrylic on
paper
30 x 21 cm, 2010

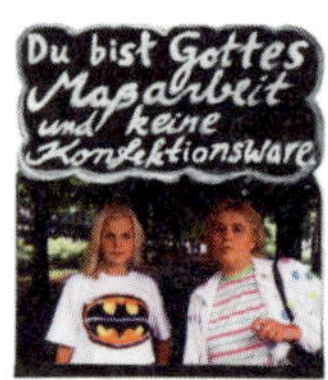

DU BIST GOTTES
MASSARBEIT UND KEINE
KONFEKTIONSWARE
collage on paper
33 x 29 cm, 2009

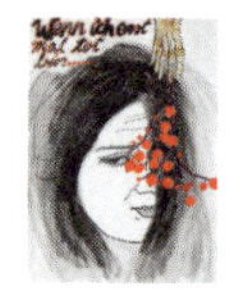

WENN ICH ERST MAL
TOT BIN
ink and collage on paper
60 x 43 cm, 2010

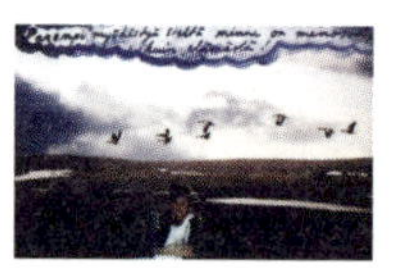

PAREMPI MYÖHÄSTYÄ
SIELTÄ MINNE ON
MENOSSA KUIN
ELÄMÄSTÄ
collage on photograph
17.5 x 26.5 cm, 2011

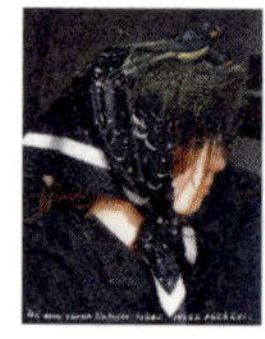

ÄLÄ ANNA SURUN
LINTUJEN TEHDÄ PESÄÄ
PÄÄHÄSI
collage on photograph
20.5 x 27 cm, 2010
Finnish State Art
Collection

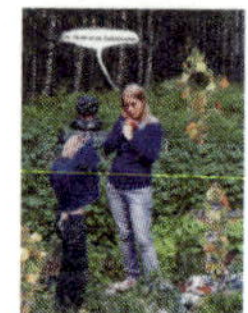

DER TEUFEL IST EIN
EICHHÖRNCHEN
collage on photograph
30 x 20 cm, 2009
original photograph by
Maija Blåfield, sculpture
by Teuri Haarla

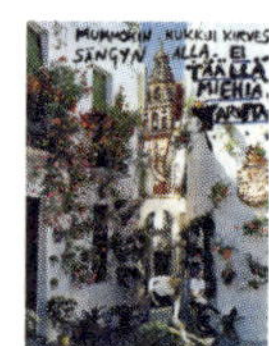

MUMMOKIN NUKKUI
KIRVES SÄNGYN ALLA. EI
TÄÄLLÄ MIEHIÄ TARVITA
collage on printed image
18.5 x 20 cm, 2011

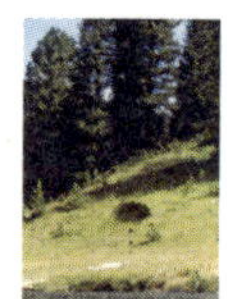

ONE TURNS AROUND IN
HIS GRAVE
ink on photograph and
paper
18.5 x 12.5 cm, 2012

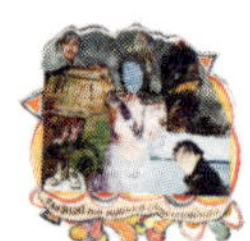

FANTASIAT OVAT
MANSIKOITA ELÄMÄN
KERMAKAKUSSA
collage on paper
36 x 34 cm, 2012

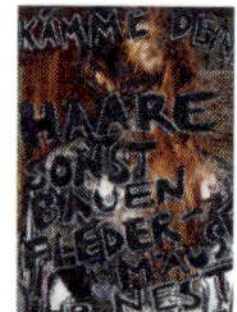

KÄMME DEINE
HAARE SONST BAUEN
FLEDERMÄUSE IHR NEST
DARINNEN
acrylic on photograph
30 x 20 cm, 2010

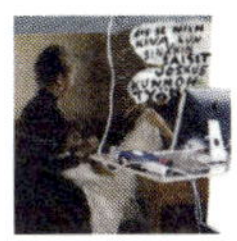

OIS SE NIIN KIVA KUN
SINÄKIN SAISIT JOSKUS
KUNNON TYÖN
collage on printed image
20.5 x 19 cm, 2010
original painting by
Albert Edelfelt, „Sewing
Women", 1887

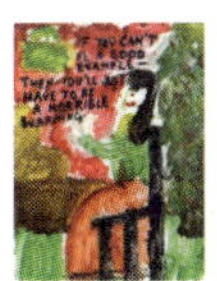

IF YOU CAN'T BE A GOOD
EXAMPLE THEN YOU'LL
JUST HAVE TO BE A
HORRIBLE WARNING
gouache on paper
37.5 x 24.5 cm, 2009

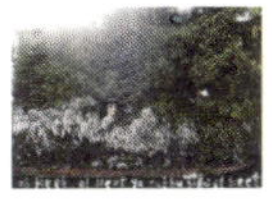

AL HEET AL HEET YA
RABBU WASILNI EL BEET
collage and acrylic on
photograph
27 x 20 cm, 2010
private collection

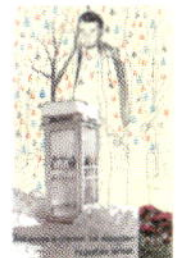

ÄLÄ ANNA IHMISTEN
TAI ASIOIDEN NUJERTAA
SINUA
collage on paper
21 x 13.5 cm, 2012
original drawing in the
collage by Mirka Raito

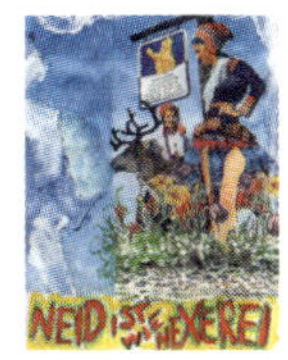

NEID IST WIE HEXEREI
collage on paper
29.5 x 21.5 cm, 2011

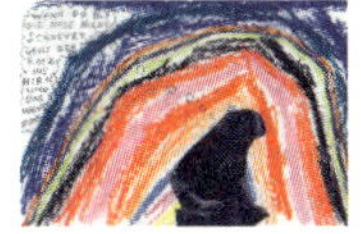

WENN DU DIE NASE
NICHT SCHNEUZT, GEHT
DER ROTZ INS HIRN UND
DAS MACHT DUMM
crayon and collage on
paper, 14.5 x 21 cm, 2009

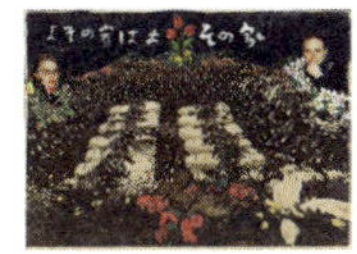

THAT'S THEM, THIS IS US
collage on printed image
14.5 x 19.5 cm, 2011

ET PAS DE BÊTISES
acrylic on a record cover
30.5 x 50 cm, 2010
original record, Freeman
2', Love Records

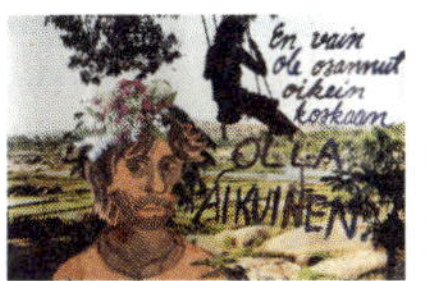

EN VAIN OLE OSANNUT
OIKEIN KOSKAAN OLLA
AIKUINEN
collage on photograph
50 x 74 cm, 2010

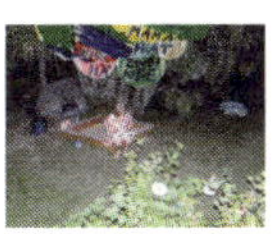

MAMA HAT NUR ZWEI
HÄNDE
collage on photograph
19.5 x 27 cm, 2010
original photograph by
Ulu Braun
private collection

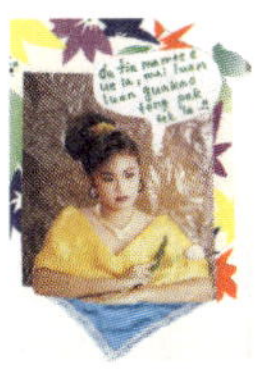

DU TIA MAMEE E UE LA
MAI LUAN LUAN GUAKAO
TENG PAK TEK LA
collage on printed image
24 x 16 cm, 2009

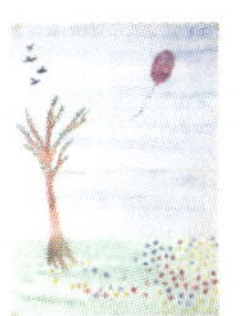

LEV OCH LÅT ALLA
ANDRA LEVA
watercolour on paper
59 x 41.5 cm, 2010

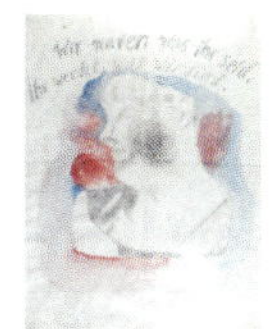

WIR WAREN WAS IHR
SEID IHR WERDET WAS
WIR SIND
watercolour and pencil
on paper
71.5 x 52 cm, 2010

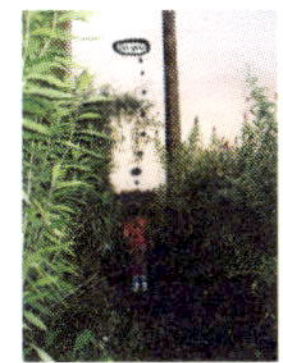

GO GIRLS
collage on photograph
19.5. x 14.5 cm, 2009
private collection

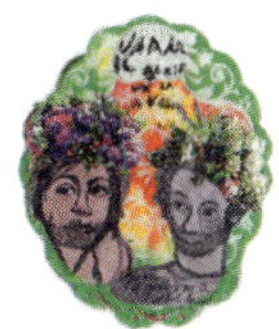

JAAR IL-QARIIB WA-LA
AKH IL-BAᶜEED
collage on fabric
73 x 59 cm, 2010

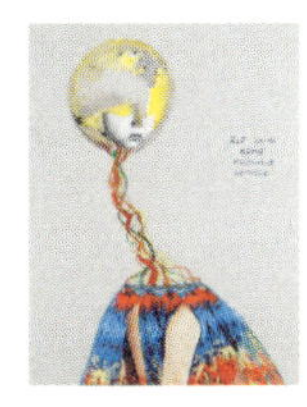

ÄLÄ LAITA KÄTTÄ
KUUMALLE LEVYLLE
collage on paper
37.5 x 28 cm, 2011

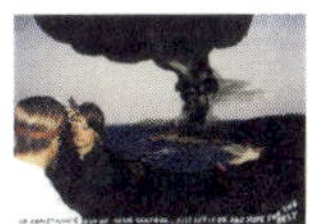

IF SOMETHING'S OUT OF
YOUR CONTROL, JUST
LET IT BE AND HOPE FOR
THE BEST
ink and collage on
photograph
12.5 x 17 cm, 2011

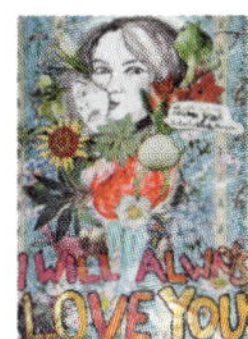

ICH WERDE NOCH
AUF DEINEM GRAB
SCHUHPLATTLER
TANZEN / I WILL ALWAYS
LOVE YOU
collage on wrapping
paper
69 x 49.5 cm, 2009

IMPRINT

CONCEPT & COLLAGES
Niina Lehtonen Braun

EDITORS
Niina Lehtonen Braun
Christina Kral

DESIGN
Christina Kral

TEXT
Sonja Commentz

TRANSLATIONS
Catriona Shaw, Nathan Moore, Maaria Laurila

PROOFREADING
Catriona Shaw

My heartfelt thanks go to all those who contributed their mother's and grandmother's sayings for this project.

Warmest thanks for all the support during the realisation of this book:
Ulu Braun, Christina Kral, Fouad Asfour, Patrick Beier, Emma Aulanko, Teemu Tuonela, John-Patrick Morarescu

Heartfelt thanks for their words:
Maijaleena Mattila, Wiltrud Braun, Elli Lehtonen, Kirsti Mattila

Special thanks go to Milan & Stella Braun

This publication was supported by: FRAME (Finnish Fund for Art Exchange) and the Arts Council of Finland

The Deutsche Nationalbibliothek lists this publication in the Deutsche Nationalbibliografie; detailed bibliographic data is available on the Internet at HTTP://DNB.D-NB.DE

PRINTED AND PUBLISHED BY

KERBER VERLAG, BIELEFELD
Windelsbleicher Str. 166–170
33659 Bielefeld
Germany
Tel. +49 (0) 5 21/9 50 08-10
Fax +49 (0) 5 21/9 50 08-88
INFO@KERBERVERLAG.COM
WWW.KERBERVERLAG.COM

KERBER, US DISTRIBUTION
D.A.P., DISTRIBUTED ART PUBLISHERS, INC.

155 Sixth Avenue, 2nd Floor
New York, NY 10013
TEL. +1 (212) 627-1999
FAX +1 (212) 627-9484

KERBER publications are available in selected bookstores and museum shops worldwide (distributed in Europe, Asia, South and North America).

ISBN 978-3-86678-846-6
WWW.KERBERVERLAG.COM

PRINTED IN GERMANY